George Herbert Mead

ON SOCIAL PSYCHOLOGY

THE HERITAGE OF SOCIOLOGY

A Series Edited by **Morris Janowitz**

George Herbert Mead

ON SOCIAL

PSYCHOLOGY

Selected Papers

Edited and with an Introduction by

ANSELM STRAUSS

THE UNIVERSITY OF CHICAGO PRESS

CHICAGO AND LONDON

First Edition published 1956 under the title
The Social Psychology of George Herbert Mead

The University of Chicago Press, Chicago 60637
The University of Chicago Press, Ltd., London

© *1934, 1936, 1938, 1956, 1964, and 1977 by*
The University of Chicago. All rights reserved
Revised Edition 1964. Fifth impression, with revised
Introduction, 1977. Printed in the United States of
America

03 02 01 00 99 98 97   11 12 13 14

ISBN: 0-226-51665-2 (paperbound)
LCN: 77-73619

♾ The paper used in this publication meets the minimum
requirements of the American National Standard for
Information Sciences—Permanence of Paper for Printed
Library Materials, ANSI Z39.48–1984.

Contents

Introduction

When George Herbert Mead died in 1931 at the age of sixty-eight, he had not published a single book. Indeed, he had published few major papers for someone who would gain recognition posthumously as one of the most brilliantly original of American pragmatists. During the decade before his death, sociologists at the University of Chicago, where Mead taught philosophy, discovered what original contributions Mead was making to that branch of their field known as "social psychology." Graduate students in sociology flocked to his classes and later were instrumental in introducing his writings on social psychology into the standard sociological literature. His concepts became common property among sociologists; his lines were quoted freely in textbooks, and his pages were reproduced in readers designed for mass student audiences. Through the sociologists, social psychologists who were trained in psychology departments also discovered Mead. While his point of view can hardly be said to be a dominant influence on American sociology and social psychology since World War II, his impact continues to be felt. Moreover, he remains an oft-quoted elder statesman in both fields.

Since the 1960's additional of his writings on philosophy, education, and social reform have been reprinted, and there has been an increased recognition that he is one of America's major thinkers. Only some aspects of his thought, however, have been incorporated into contemporary social science. Part of my purpose in writing this introduction to selected pages of his work is to suggest certain misapprehensions of Mead's intellectual position as well as to focus attention on its strikingly original character. Unquestionably Mead can still stimulate new research and theoretical enterprise.

This introduction was revised by Anselm Strauss in 1977.

American sociology from the 1890's until World War II was dominated by the work of men at the University of Chicago. Although Sumner was at Yale, Ross at Wisconsin, Cooley at Michigan, Giddings at Columbia, and Sorokin later at Minnesota and Harvard, the massed graduate faculty at Chicago, along with its former students, was the major influence upon prewar sociology. The Chicago department and its organ, the *American Journal of Sociology*, were organized approximately when the University of Chicago itself began. That university was, from its outset, to be a graduate institution, for President Harper had deliberately raided competitive scholarly establishments with the express aim of creating the country's most influential graduate departments. Sociology during its earliest years there included at least two outstanding scholars, Albion Small and W. I. Thomas; and in neighboring departments were men like Dewey and Tufts. Within the decade, a star-studded faculty had firmly established Chicago as a dazzling intellectual center.

Mead came in 1894, at John Dewey's invitation, to the Department of Philosophy, remaining until his death. His influence upon the field of sociology must be attributed—especially in light of his scant writings—to the evolution of sociology at Chicago itself. But the nature of his influence is also linked with his own intellectual career. It is to the latter consideration that I turn first.

A striking perspective of Mead's career and influence can be got by comparing him, however briefly, with Dewey. Dewey was born in 1859, Mead in 1863. Dewey published his first book in 1886, when he was twenty-seven years of age, his second in 1888, two more in 1894; and at forty-three, he was acclaimed for his great volume on experimental logic. His continued regular and voluminous publication on an enormous range of scholarly and public subjects is brought home to us by the posthumous book-length bibliographical itemization of his writing. Mead's output was much more restricted in range, being devoted almost entirely to philosophical and psychological issues, and including a relatively few articles on education, particularly as it related to science and social reform. He was forty before his first major paper appeared (he had published only two previously, on education). Whereas Dewey became known to the general public for his educational views during the nineties and the following decade, Mead was listed in *Who's Who in America* only in 1910 (about seven years after Dewey) because of his full professorship at Chicago. He never came to general notice, except on the local-reform scene. He did not become, and probably had no wish to become, the national spokesman for liberal causes that made Dewey such a deservedly conspicuous figure. As for recognition by philosophers themselves: as late as 1912 Ralph Perry, who later edited William James's letters, failed to mention Mead in his *Present Philosophical Tendencies*; and in James Pratt's review of pragmatism (1909), Mead's early contributions to that movement were also overlooked.[1] Mead finally had his books published for him, as it were, by his students, who either pulled together their collected notes (as in *Mind, Self, and Society*) or made available his own notes and unpublished writings to the intellectual community.

One of the intriguing biographical questions about Mead, then, is his reluctance to publish a major volume—and in a field where books are a staple commodity. Dewey sheds some light on this matter in remarks delivered at his friend's funeral and later published in Mead's *Philosophy of the Present*. (Dewey's daughter, Jane, later noted, "The Meads remained the closest friends of the Deweys even after the removal of the Deweys to New York, until their death.")[2] Dewey commented that while "Mead was an original thinker, he had no sense of being original. Or if he had such a feeling he kept it under." He also noted Mead's characteristic "great originality and unusual deference to others...." Yet Mead's *Philosophy of the Present* betrays a rather clear consciousness that he was pushing pragmatism in previously unexplored directions, and a number of passages in his last work, published in *The Philosophy of the Act*, show him in a critical posture even toward some of Dewey's positions. In his social psychology, de-

[1]   (New York: Longmans); *What is Pragmatism?* (New York: Macmillan Co.).

[2]   Jane M. Dewey, "Biography of John Dewey," in Paul A. Schillp (ed.), *The Philosophy of John Dewey* (Evanston, Ill.: Northwestern University, 1939), pp. 25-26.

veloped fully during the 1920's, he certainly must have recognized his own originality. Dewey knew it and undoubtedly conveyed some of this knowledge to Mead. Again I quote Dewey's daughter: "Since Mead published so little during his lifetime, his influence on Dewey was the product of conversations carried on over a period of years and its extent has been underestimated." Indeed, Dewey directly took over Mead's special development of social psychological ideas and "made them a part of his subsequent philosophy, so that, from the nineties on, the influence of Mead ranked with that of James." We should not be astonished to learn that James was also Mead's teacher, along with Royce. Probably more important than Mead's humility and belated recognition of his own genius was his slight interest in immediate fame, combined with continuous—and possibly laborious—refining and extending of his ideas.[3] Whatever the explanation for Mead's scant publication during his lifetime, it meant delayed recognition by philosophers.

Mead's impact on sociology and social psychology came early. One reason, already alluded to, was that Chicago sociologists carried his ideas from the classroom into their working lives (and as Charles Morris has suggested, into their personal lives also). Mead influenced students like Charles Ellwod and L. L. Bernard, but it was not until the 1920's that he had perhaps his major impact on the burgeoning discipline of sociology. Curiously enough, W. I. Thomas and Robert Park, the chief influences in Chicago sociology during the years just before World War I and in the following decade, seem not particularly to have drawn on Mead's thinking, although Park was certainly influenced earlier by Dewey's writing

[3]   Jane Dewey implied this when she wrote that he "was continuously reworking his ideas so that most of his work was published only after his death." Helen S. Perry, the biographer of Harry S. Sullivan, has remarked to me that she is struck by the similarity between Mead and Sullivan insofar as neither published much while alive and both seemed constantly to be working over their ideas, possibly too intensively or rapidly to pause for publication. Both men were fortunate in having devoted students who got those ideas into print posthumously. Sullivan, incidentally, knew of Mead's work through Sapir, an anthropologist linguist at the University of Chicago.

on communication. But the link in the twenties and thirties between the sociologists and Mead was perhaps Ellsworth Faris, who introduced students directly to the writings of Dewey and Mead. (Dewey had come to the sociologists' attention, not only through early writing on communication and education, but through his 1922 lectures on social psychology.)[4] Certainly not all of these students read or heard Mead, since there were several streams of faculty influence in the department. An autobiographical note will illustrate that last point. Before I went to Chicago as a graduate student in 1939, I had been directed to the writings of Dewey, Thomas, and Park by Floyd House, who had been a student of Park in the early twenties. House never mentioned Mead, that I can recollect. But within a week after my arrival at Chicago, I was studying Mead's *Mind, Self, and Society*, directed to it by Herbert Blumer, who as a young instructor had taught Mead's class after Mead's unexpected death.

By 1939, Mead's writing was already getting a fairly wide reading from sociologists, and so he began to enter into the mainstream of sociological thought elsewhere. He began to become *the* social psychologist for sociologists—as evidenced, for instance, by his later appearance in the standard chapters on social psychology and personality included in sociological textbooks. Why the sociologists found his writing so useful is exactly the question posed some pages ago. A partial answer to that question, perhaps, is that in the thought of leading sociologists a focus upon psychological aspects of society had long been central. But that answer, I would contend, is only partly satisfying. We must take into account that only certain features of Mead's thought were incorporated into sociology, and we must ask why.

Almost exclusively, sociologists lit upon Mead's ideas about socialization, notably his concepts of "generalized other" and his rather strikingly socialized "self." These ideas appealed in the twenties and thirties because sociologists found them handy ammunition against biological explanations of behavior. Later they found Mead's notion of self not only an effective counter to Freudianism and to individualistic psychologies but also a useful way to think

[4] *Human Nature and Conduct* (New York: Holt, 1922).

about the socialization of group members. By a curious irony of history, Dewey had earlier helped to fill those functions for sociologists; but since, in fact, he had never worked out Mead's kind of detailed discussion about socialization, his writing today does not appeal much to sociologists.

In general, I would argue that what sociologists—including such widely read functionalist theorists as Parsons, Davis, and Merton—selected from Mead's writing was very restricted and pertained mainly to how culture and norms got "internalized" into the person, that is, how self-control was a reflection of social control. Mead's treatment of the self as a process was transformed into something much more static, in accordance with the sociological view of internalized social control. The "generalized other" became just another way of talking about reference group affiliation, and Mead's notion of role tended to be reinterpreted to fit with the structural concept of status and its associated role-playing. It is even possible to maintain that sociologists, who tend principally to be social determinists, read Mead as if he too were a social determinist, although his reiteration of the potential influence of individuals upon society should have warned against any such interpretation.

Whether the main drift of Mead's thought was reinterpreted is perhaps debatable, but the selective attention given it is not. Quotations from Mead are almost always taken from the "self" section of *Mind, Self, and Society*—mind and society getting short shrift! Mead's remarkable treatment of time—hardly touched upon in that volume but treated extensively in *Philosophy of the Present* and in *The Philosophy of the Act*—has not yet been mined for its relevance to sociological concerns. His concept of perspectives, again worked out in much detail in those volumes, has not penetrated sociological thinking much nor has its implication for social change been understood. His strikingly processual view of social organization has yet to receive that elaboration which would freshen, and perhaps transform, more traditional views. His philosophic handling of the relations between permanence and change—that is, the problem of continuity—surely will eventually have its proper impact on sociological thought.

What can be said about Mead's use by and impact on social psychologists and sociologists in the period since 1965? To begin with, the ritualistic quoting of or mere referring to Mead continues steadily, in textbooks and in serious writing alike. By ritualistic, I mean that it is not especially clear that Mead has affected the basic stance or work of the author. There is also an occasional germane effort to relate one's research to specific ideas or suggestions by Mead.

However, the constant and probably increasing influence of Mead is linked with the complicated intellectual history of the 1960's. Telescoping that history severely, one can say that functionalism lost much of its attractiveness for younger American sociologists. Its competitors have included phenomenology, ethnomethodology, neo-Marxism, and the continuing tradition of interactionism. None of those constitutes a homogeneous school, regardless of outsiders' perceptions, but all have paid some attention to Mead, whether approvingly or disapprovingly, whether agreeing with elements of Mead's thought or qualifying it.

Thus Cicourel, an ethnomethodologist: "To the Meadian dialectic of the 'I' and the 'me' is added the . . . notion that participants in social exchanges must assume that their use of verbal and nonverbal signs or symbols are the 'same' or this 'sameness' (in an ideal sense) must at least be assumed to hold." More generally, Cicourel believes that a scholar like Schutz has "made more explicit the ingredients of social interaction also discussed by James, Mead. . ."[5] Similarly, a collection of essays entitled *Phenomenological Sociology*[6] contains enough references to Mead to make one suspect that he is at least part of the intellectual apparatus of those who think of themselves as phenomenologists, albeit alternative intellectual idols yield them more stimulation or inspiration.

On the other hand, to most neo-Marxists, Mead doubtless seems irrelevant or misleading, since he, like Dewey, represents a classic specimen of American liberalism: muddle-headed meliorist, idealis-

[5] Aaron Cicourel, "Basic and Normative Rules in the Negotiation of Status and Role," in Hans Dreitzel (ed.), *Recent Sociology, no. 2* (New York: MacMillan, 1970), pp. 4–45; quotation from pp. 24 and 32.

[6] George Psathas (ed.), *Phenomenological Sociology* (New York: Wiley Interscience, 1973).

tic—star gazer at his best, and misguided, if perhaps implicit, supporter of capitalism at his worst. A frontal attack by a young sociologist on the entire interactionist tradition, including Mead, finds it "structureless"—focusing on microscopic interaction and virtually ignoring the larger social structures which determine interaction.

Yet particular younger sociologists seem ready to attempt a reconciliation of Marx and Mead. To some the Marx represented by the long unavailable *Grundrisse* seems to hold views not entirely at swords point with the pragmatists who followed some years later, all unaware of this aspect of Marx. (See, for example, Rogers' attempt at reconciliation of neo-Marxism and Mead, albeit he seems more bent on reconciliation *with* Mead.)[7]

Mead, however, has always had his most extensive audience in sociology among the interactionists. Among the younger sociologists, the social and political events of the late 1960's led to a resurgence of interest in interactionism, for it represents a more voluntaristic view of social life than social structuralism and a more direct contact with people "in the field" than questionnaire research. The older interactionists—Blumer, Lindesmith, Becker, Klapp, Stone, Shibutani—continue to draw for general stance or specific ideas upon Mead. The younger interactionists, influenced of course by their teachers, who at the very least introduced them to Mead, also draw visibly from Mead's writings. (Perhaps some of the seemingly ritualistic offerings to Mead really represent a nonspecific but very genuine debt to the man?)

Also, with the diffusion of interactionist thought and of phenomenological sociology across the Atlantic, Mead has come to the attention of Europeans. A friend of mine at the Centre de Sociologie Europeén volunteered that Mead was a remarkable man, albeit another able French scholar, equally influenced by interactionism, does not once mention Mead in his book on American sociology.[8] In Germany, where phenomenology is relatively strong and sometimes

7   Richard Ropers, "Mead, Marx and Sociology," *Catalyst* 7 (1973), 42-61.

8   Nicholas Herpin, *Les Sociologues Americains et Le Siecle* (Paris: Presses Universitaires de France, 1973).

combined with interactionism (partly via the influence of Berger's and Luckmann's *Construction of Social Reality* and by their actual teaching in Germany), Mead is increasingly noted and quoted.[9] By contrast, the English have discovered Mead largely through the footnotes of American interactionists. In general, among Europeans the influence of Mead seems also to have generated a general stance toward issues of identity and interaction: "general" because it is difficult to assess accurately how Mead does speak to his overseas readers, who after all do operate in somewhat different intellectual climates than our own.

The richness of Mead's writing for sociological enterprise can only be suggested in this brief introduction. Perhaps a few examples will suffice. Let us take the matter of "time," in which there has been some renewed sociological interest.[10] In general, much of the sociological writing on organizations leaves their temporal features unanalyzed. When handled explicitly, the focus is upon such matters as deadlines, scheduling, rates, pacing, turnover, and concepts of time which may vary differentially by organizational position. The principal weakness of such analyses stems from an unexamined assumption that the temporal properties worth studying pertain to the work of organizations and their members. For instance, the work-time of personnel must be properly articulated— hence deadlines and schedules. Breakdowns in this temporal articulation occur not only through accident and poor planning but through differential valuation of time by various echelons, personnel, and clientele. But a close reading of Mead suggests that the temporal order of the organization be analyzed in terms of a much

9   Peter Berger and Thomas Luckmann, *The Social Construction of Reality* (Garden City, N.Y.: Doubleday, 1966). See also, Richard Grathoff, *The Structure of Social Inconsistencies* (The Hague: Martinus Nijhoff, 1970).

10   Cf. Wilbert Moore, *Man, Time, and Society* (New York: Wiley, 1963); also Barney Glaser and Anselm Strauss, *Time for Dying* (Chicago: Aldine, 1968) and *Status Passage* (Chicago: Aldine, 1971). My own discussion of time owes much to collaboration with Barney Glaser and to earlier work with Rue Bucher, Leonard Schatzman, and Melvin Sabshin.

wider range of temporal dimensions; for, as stated by Mead, perspectives imply temporality.

One way of translating Mead's conception is to take seriously the idea that people bring to any organization their own temporal concerns and that their actions on the organizational site are profoundly affected by these concerns. Thus, in a hospital, one should study not only the organization of work-time (schedules, deadlines, timing of work shifts) but many other considerations deriving from more subtle temporal concerns. For instance, we might scrutinize the previous hospital experiences of patients and personnel (their hospital careers), their experiences with various types of illness (their illness careers), their personal careers, and the highly personalized conceptions of time evidenced, for instance, by dying patients. The family's temporal concerns are also of great relevance.

This discussion leads me to remark upon Mead's rather implicit treatment of social organization and society. He sometimes referred to these matters in rather structured terms, but most often a processual view dominated his writing. He pictured social structures as somewhat less organized than do most sociologists and anthropologists. The implication is that organizations are something like Melville Dalton's description of industrial establishments; they somehow work, although they have no single goal, no wholly agreed upon consensus; but they service the diverse aims of their personnel and clientele through bargaining, deals, agreements, and negotiation plus the more institutionalized mechanisms.[11] Something like a concept of "negotiated order" seems implied by Mead's views.[12] When one sees this, it is a simple matter to link it with the preceding discussion of temporality; for the various temporal considerations brought to groups and organizations must receive some articulation

11   *Men Who Manage* (New York: Wiley, 1959).

12   Cf. A. L. Strauss *et al.*, "The Hospital and Its Negotiated Order," in E. Freidson (ed.), *The Hospital in Modern Society* (New York: Free Press of Glencoe, 1963); see also Herbert Blumer's discussion of articulated lines of action in his "Society as Symbolic Interaction," in A. Rose (ed.), *Human Behavior and Social Processes* (Boston: Houghton Mifflin, 1962), pp. 179–92; A. L. Strauss, *Varieties of Negotiated Order* (San Francisco: Jossey-Bass, forthcoming).

—although precise details must be empirically discovered through research. In general, however, there are organizational mechanisms which contribute toward that temporal articulation, but there are also non-institutional mechanisms, including continual negotiation and certain less self-conscious forming of agreements. Temporal order refers to this total, delicate, and continuously changing articulation of temporal considerations.

Such a conception of temporal order fits very well with Mead's continual emphasis upon emergence in social relations. He and Dewey are, in fact, our great American spokesmen among the philosophers of what was once referred to as "emergent evolution." For contemporary sociology and social psychology, this concept might mean that persons are somewhat freer agents than is allowed in the more usual sociological view: freer not only to find ways to circumvent norms and rules, but also freer to help change the social structures within which they find themselves. More than one critic of social or cultural determinism has argued against the model of the individual as mere reflection of the larger social unit, or even as something of an automaton. But that critique need not necessitate an abandonment of the tremendously useful mode of thinking which we call "structural." That analytic mode need only be combined with a systematic search for the particular groups of individuals which are able to institute given changes, or to evade what specific rules, and why; and under what conditions; and with what consequences to the establishment, to themselves, and to others. The supplementary inquiry, of course, is who obeys or attempts to make other people obey those rules and why, how, and with what consequences.[13]

13   Howard S. Becker has attempted something like this in his discussion of the processes whereby deviants get defined and how those definitions are made to stick as well as how deviants attempt to counter those definitions. See his *Outsiders*, rev. ed. (New York: Free Press of Glencoe, 1973). Alfred R. Lindesmith's book on the organization of narcotic traffic and attempts at its control also contains an illuminating historical documentation of how narcotic addiction got defined as a public evil, largely through the efforts of one of the federal agencies. See his, *The Addict and the Law* (Bloomington, Ind.: Indiana University Press, 1965).

Among social scientists in the contemporary period there is a strong reaction against reification of social structures and against reliance on extreme structural explanations, with a revised view of social organization and organizations as more "open" and "fluid." Mead's influence on these intellectual trends, however, seems to have been either incidental or transmitted through the writings of sociologists like E. C. Hughes and Herbert Blumer and their students. I myself believe that Mead's processual perspective on the constructed—and continually reconstructed—world, plus his suggestive analysis of the nature of symbolic transactions, imply a pathway through which we might escape some of the more limiting conceptualizations to which many social scientists adhere. For instance, he directs us, albeit implicitly, to look at modern society as if it were a congeries of social worlds. Alternative models of mass society conceptualize it as composed of anonymous, alienated individuals, as highly bureaucratized and/or rationalized, and so forth. The Meadian vision of society does not necessarily preclude those others, but we can hold them in abeyance while looking at society *qua* social worlds.

In one of his seminal passages, Mead asserts that in "the most highly developed, organized and complicated human social communities" individuals have membership in two kinds of groups. "Some are concrete social classes or subgroups" like political parties, clubs, and corporations. Then Mead points to what are generally termed "aggregates," but which he refers to as "abstract social classes or subgroups, such as the class of debtors and the class of creditors." Mead characteristically conceives of this second type of group in interactional and processual terms. He hazards that an individual's

> membership in several of these abstract social classes or subgroups makes possible his entrance into definite social relations (however indirect) with an almost infinite number of other individuals who also belong to or are included within one or another of these abstract social classes or subgroups cutting across functional lines of demarcation which divide different human social communities from one another, and including members from several (in some cases from all) such communications.

Then he relates this membership to significant symbols and universes of discourse, in short, to the "social process of communication."

This amounts not merely to a recognition that any aggregate has the potential of becoming a functioning group—Louis Wirth used to say that potentially groups can form around anything: antipathy toward Jews, white skin—but that the basic social process of communication permits an enormous, unlimited, and ceaseless proliferation of functioning groups. These can be severely delimited social worlds (such as Harvey Zorbaugh described for Chicago in the 1920's, or as in recent years have been studied for the same city by Morris Janowitz and his students, Gerald Suttles and William Kornblum)[14] or international in scope (the worlds of physicists, chess players, or advocates of birth control). They can be rooted in or transcend space. They can be tiny or enormous in membership. They can have relatively discernable, "tight" boundaries or permeable, "fluid" boundaries. The activities and the communications of members can focus primarily on matters intellectual, occupational, professional, political, religious, sexual, or recreational. Social worlds are characteristic of any substantive area.

Furthermore, some organizations can be viewed as embedded within a social world (the American Medical Association in the world of medicine, the Daughters of Bilitis in the homosexual world), so that they cannot be understood merely by focusing only on them but require an examination of their relations to other organizations embedded either in the same or in related worlds. Some—possibly most—organizations can also be viewed as arenas wherein members from various sub-worlds or other worlds stake differential claims, seek differential ends, engage in contests, and make necessary alliances in order to do the things they wish to do. The Meadian emergent-evolution-via-communication view also implies that social worlds inevitably splinter or fragment, but that

14   Harvey Zorbaugh, *The Gold Coast and the Slum* (Chicago: University of Chicago Press, 1929); Morris Janowitz, *The Community Press in an Urban Setting* (Chicago: University of Chicago Press, 1962; rev. ed., 1967); Gerald Suttles, *The Social Order of the Slum* (Chicago: University of Chicago Press, 1968); William Kornblum, *Blue Collar Community* (Chicago: University of Chicago Press, 1974).

conversely the members of different sub-worlds are always joining forces so that there is alliancing, merging, coalescing, which processes may lead sub-worlds to dissolve, disappear, or at least pull out from the original world.

The Meadian view also implies that social movements are not merely features of political or religious arenas (most literature on social movements is restricted to those arenas) but of all social worlds and sub-worlds. There are movements in painting, poetry, literary criticism, and certainly in the academic disciplines and sub-specialties. Some of these movements spill over to more than one other world. Generally, they result in organizations or affect extant ones.

Other phenomena can be usefully reconceptualized in terms of social worlds. Thus fashion is not limited to clothing styles; fashions flourish in every world. Also, careers are not in character simply organizational or occupational: they are pursued within and can only be understood fully by taking into account the context of specified social worlds. Moreover, notions of "*the* mass media" ought to be corrected. There are multiple media (magazines) in many worlds, most of which never reach the news stands or come to the attention of social scientists. Also, public opinion is not simply a matter of legislation and government but arises in every social world, and segments of it, around issues perceived of importance by its members. Also, nations probably should not be conceived as organized around a common value system, or as consisting of a core and a periphery—with people on the periphery (workers in nineteenth-century France) as essentially "out" of "society." A nation is perhaps better conceived as a territory within which various social worlds exist (local, regional, national, also international) with a variety of relationships among them. Likewise, the members of certain worlds have much more control over the governmental apparatus, including the "power" to manipulate and coerce the members of other social worlds—not excluding those who, like the members of some religious sects, do not really conceive of themselves merely as members of the nation, or others (members of nationality groups) who may only be "part" of the nation by virtue of force or coercive negotiation.

Mead might not have accepted such deductions from his work, so I shall have to accept sole responsibility for asserting them. However, another admirer of Mead unquestionably has drawn some of the same conclusions, for some years ago Tomatsu Shibutani[15] astutely formulated his version of a central issue of Mead:

> Each social world is a universe of regularized mutual response, an arena in which there is some kind of organization that facilitates anticipating the behavior of others. Each social world, then, is a culture area, the boundaries of which are set neither by territory nor formal membership, but by the limits of effective communication.

The limits of effective communication! That suggests both the difficulty and the challenge of following through on Mead's message—or at least on some of his message.

The major dimensions of Mead's thinking are perhaps best grasped in relation to several intellectual antecedents, for these flit in and out of his pages in the guise of protagonists or allies. From his predecessors Mead took his basic problems, some of his terms, and parts of his suggested solutions.

By the outset of the nineteenth century, natural science had had a shattering effect upon earlier conceptions of the universe and man. Scientists now worked with notions of a world of matter in motion: this could not but have an effect upon philosophic and political thought. Individualistic doctrines developed which regarded the individual knower as a passive receiver of the physical world impinging upon his sense organs. Individual freedom, individual autonomy, the doctrine of natural rights, contract, the rule of reason, atomistic theories of group life: all these reflected the impact of seventeenth- and eighteenth-century science.

These brands of individualistic and rationalistic philosophy were countered early in the century by idealistic philosophers, notably by the influential German Romantics. Intuition and faith displace reason as the cornerstone of knowledge and action; the passive individual in an impinging physical world is supplanted by a world

15   "Reference Groups and Social Control," in A. Rose (ed.), *Human Behavior and Social Processes* (Boston: Houghton Mifflin, 1962), pp. 238-47; quotation from pp. 136-37.

which has existence only in relation to an active agent; group, folk, spirit, and collectivity take precedence over the autonomous individual; and the later Darwinian revolution is ushered in with mystical and historical conceptions of change, evolution, and development. Other pre-Darwinian philosophers, like the Frenchman Auguste Comte, exalt the role of reason in the form of science but, like the Romantics, conceive of individual action within societal contexts.

The Romantic writers had a profound influence upon Mead, as upon Dewey, insofar as they stressed social evolution and made the environment in some subtle sense dependent upon the acting organism. But, since Mead lived after Darwin, the Romantic treatment becomes in Mead's hands divested of its mysticism and is given biological and scientific twists. Most important, the role of reason again is raised in high service to human action, where rationalists and political liberals had placed it, rather than made subordinate to faith and intuition. Likewise the Comtean rejection of metaphysical thought and adulation of scientific method are taken over almost wholly; but the specific interpretation of the method—along with that of Comte's rationalistic contemporary, J. S. Mill—is rejected in favor of an evolutionary and highly social interpretation. Mead also, in ways reminiscent of the French sociologist Durkheim, finds in Comte ammunition against individualistic psychological theories.

But it is to Darwin and his successors that Mead is most indebted: he regarded Darwin as having provided the empirical underpinning for the revolutionary but inadequate Romantic notions of evolution. The corpus of biological writing allows the pragmatist to challenge mechanical conceptions of action and the world and to restate problems of autonomy, freedom, and innovation in evolutionary and social rather than mechanistic and individualistic terms. Mead's pragmatic devotion to reason prevents him from going the way of certain descendants of Darwin—Freud, Macdougall, Veblen, and Le Bon among others—who stressed irrational and non-rational determinants of human behavior. Darwin's work itself, insofar as it deals with man's psychology, is given an elaborate recasting by Mead. Darwin's treatment of expressive gestures is revised in the light of human communication; and biological evolution emerges in the topmost species as something new and different—a true emergent.

Among Mead's important predecessors were those psychologists who pursued genetic interests. The study of child development, itself receiving great impetus from evolutionary writing, became focused upon the rise of speech, thought, and self, in contrast to a later concern with emotional and personality development. Mead owes some of the focus of his work to Tarde and to his contemporaries, Baldwin and Cooley. Later he took issue with the Watsonian brand of behaviorism; it excluded covert aspects of human acts as metaphysical or mental, whereas Mead wished to include mental activities within the orbit of the social act itself. To indicate the extent of his agreement and divergence, he titled his own approach "social behaviorism."

The outlines of Mead's philosophical system are sketched in those selections comprising Part I of this volume. In "Evolution Becomes a General Idea" and "The Problem of Society," Mead, the philosopher of evolution, is asserting the primacy of the evolutionary process. This process flows not only through species but through societal organizations, the human included. As species disappear and evolve, so do institutions and societies. In man, evolution can be directed through intelligent action—itself made possible by the purely human capacity for symbolization. Science is the finest instance of intelligence at work and represents the hope of mankind for the solution of problematic social situations. Because of human intelligence, with its associated self-reflexiveness, social institutions can indefinitely take new forms. Like Dewey, Mead is saying that the Darwinian revolution has forever unfettered us from static conceptions of social organization.

This initial line of reasoning introduces us, in large scope, to three of Mead's central preoccupations: (1) science as the instrument, par excellence, for the intelligent control of environment, physical and social; (2) the rise and function of socially reflexive behavior; and (3) the problem of maintaining order in a continuously changing social organization—that is, the problem of intelligent social control. Mead's social psychology is dominated by the second preoccupation; his social philosophy by the third; while his more technical philosophical concerns are focused around the method of science and particularly its implications for control over and contact with the environment.

When Mead writes about scientific method, he does so in accordance with the basic pragmatic position on intelligence. "Intelligence" is really a verb, not a noun: it is an *activity* which arises whenever an organism encounters ambiguity in its world. But what is ambiguous or problematic is always in relation to what is known or taken for granted. This is true for all organisms, including the scientist himself. In the essay entitled "The Nature of Scientific Knowledge," Mead is particularly interested in relating the scientist's act to the larger communal context.

It is the particular scientist who recognizes and is disturbed enough by ambiguity to wish to fashion an appropriate scientific solution. What appears ambiguous to him does so because he is a member of a particular society at a given time and place. While the problem arises within the individual thinker's experience, he must eventually bring his solution to the community for validation. In doing so, he makes a contribution, however minute, toward changing his community. He contributes toward change, not merely because he has answered a vital question, but because his answer may challenge some portion of that which was taken for granted in order to raise and answer the question in the first place. Mead has here affirmed that the scientist—indeed, any human—affects his social world just because he is a sentient, acting being. Scientific method is merely the most effective way to incorporate continuously arising problematic experiences into an ongoing social order.

Mead is interested in the relationship of the scientist to the physical world as well as to the social. He contends that the scientist is interested not in trying to grasp the structure of the world but in going after the solution of a problem "in a world which is there." Like the German Romantics, Mead makes the environment relational to the person; but he anchors the relationship firmly within community action. Through the thinker's problem-solving act, the world gets revised and "enlarged." Intelligent activity does not seek to know the world but "undertakes to tell us what we may expect to happen when we act in such and such a fashion."

In the selection titled "Mind Approached through Behavior," Mead suggests how the pragmatists, especially James and Dewey, met the challenge of the newer currents of science by discarding a structural psychology and moving toward a behavioristic science. The pragmatists, Mead included, emphasize the active role that men play in shaping their environments and destinies—a recurrent theme in Mead's writing.

In "The Process of Mind in Nature," a general philosophical treatment with social-psychological implications is given to relationships existing between the subject and the physical world. Romantic philosophy had failed because it denied the presence of a physical world that lay outside and preceded the organism; however, Mead retains the romantic idea that the organism is an active agent rather than a passive recipient of external stimuli. His central thesis is that action ("the act") determines the relation between the individual and the environment. Stimuli are encountered during the act and affect its course, and their function is misconstrued if we state otherwise their relation to the active organism. Identical stimuli are different for different organisms and for the same organism during different acts. Perception is selective and occurs during action.

In addition, Mead makes action toward the self an integral facet of the act. One takes himself into account while acting toward the non-self. This self-reflexivity is dependent upon language and arises during childhood as a result of participation in groups. Mead is thus making of human perception an exceedingly complicated activity, in which stimuli are responded to selectively during the course of acts and are interpreted symbolically and with reference to self. Since acts may have considerable duration, and perception "functions in the act and all along the act," the perceived environment is different by the end of the act from that at the beginning: some objects of perception have been redefined, others have dropped out as functionally unimportant, and new ones have arisen. These new objects and redefinitions are funneled back to the groups and communities to which the individual belongs, for the individual's act, and is incorporated perceiving, is itself but a segment of the larger communal action.

In the selections taken from *Mind, Self, and Society* we see

Mead's elaboration of the basic positions already sketched. Nothing new is added except detail, but to the social psychologist this detail is essential. Here Mead offers us a set of concepts directly pertaining to crucial matters such as complex mental activities, self, self-control, audience, role-playing, social interaction, motivation, group membership, and group functioning.

We left Mead relating perception to act; he develops this relationship further. Stimuli arise during the act and affect its course. The stimuli may arise in the form of the actions of others, whose action in turn may be a response to ours. In all species, except man, where the process is more complex, the gestures of each animal set off immediate answering gestures (barks, growls, movements) in the other. The entire course of the interaction Mead terms "the conversation of gestures." This conversation can be co-operative, as among a hive of bees, or antagonistic, as in a dogfight. No self-consciousness need be attributed to the responding animals.

Among humans the conversation is much more complex, for we typically indicate to ourselves the meanings of our own gestures. This assigned meaning is in terms of the perspective of some other person—often the person toward whom we are directly acting. But others who are absent may be implicated in our gestures; we may be acting toward them, too, and in answer to their gestures. When our gestural meanings take on identical meanings to ourselves and to others, we have the "significant gesture" or "significant symbol." Mead hypothesizes that only through the verbal gesture (sounds) could man have become self-conscious about his gestures, but this seems not to be a necessary point in his argument. The important point is that typically human meaning arises during co-operative group action. In simpler terms, we may say that every group develops its own system of significant symbols which are held in common by its members and around which group activities are organized. Insofar as the members act toward and with reference to each other, they take each other's perspectives toward their own actions and thus interpret and assess that activity in communal terms. Group membership is thus a symbolic, not a physical, matter, and the symbols which arise during the life of the group are, in turn, internalized by the members and affect their individual acts.

The symbolic conversation of gestures need not take place between actual persons but may occur "inside" a single person. Here we have thought or mental activity. The person imaginatively acts and, with the positions of significant other individuals in mind, looks back at his proposed action. Mead underlines the fact that this internalized conversation allows men to bring the future into the act, as opposed to language-less animals who must respond rather immediately and directly to present stimuli. Human thought involves the pointing-out of meanings to one's self and thus requires a self-conscious actor—one who can delay overt action while he surveys the meanings and consequences of proposed acts in terms of others' probable responses. In the end, the person can put a number of responses together in unique combination—a very complex act indeed. This is Mead's elaboration of the much simpler notion of the act-with-duration discussed in earlier selections.

The organization of responses requires an actor who also acts toward himself: one must be simultaneously his own subject and object. Mead asks how this is possible, and he again answers by looking at the communicative process. What is necessary to become an object to self is that the individual step outside himself, so to speak, and look back at himself. Mead, following numerous genetic psychologists, notes that the infant cannot do this. He suggests some general steps in learning to take others' roles toward self. The most important is when the child learns not only to assume multiple position via-à-vis himself but to organize these positions into a system. Childhood games, Mead suggests, are among the situations in which the child acquires the ability to do this. This generalized system of attitudes is termed the "generalized other" (Mead's best-known term).

The generalized other is society's representative in the individual. In the absence of others, the individual can yet organize his behavior with regard to his conception of their related attitudes. Hence the generalized other is closely linked, in Mead's discussion, both with self-control and with social control.

Mead says this in yet another way by setting the "me" against the "I" as two responding sides of the self. The "me" is the controlling, limiting, societal side of the person. The "I" is the impulsive side of behavior, upon which the "me" makes a judgment after the person acts—immediately after, or long after, or many times after. The "I" is never completely predictable; one may surprise one's self. Hence it is the "I" which introduces novelty and creativeness into the situation. Action which surprises self can be exciting as well as disturbing. Like the scientist's new solution, it can change what formerly was taken for granted. Consistently, Mead asserts that this novel behavior, and its assessment, occurs within large social contexts and reacts back upon those contexts. Everyone makes some contribution toward changing his community.

This socialized individualism is pursued further by Mead. Insofar as each individual participates in different groups, or participates in identical groups in different ways, it follows that no man's "me's" are identical with any other man's. This gives ample leeway for an emphasis upon individuality within worlds of common symbolization. In the sections dealing more specifically with society, the relationships between individual and ideal communality are further discussed.

In Part VIII, some of Mead's views of Comte, Cooley, and Bergson can be read. We find him noting with approval, for instance, Comte's conviction that "we must advance from the study of society to the individual rather than from the individual to society." But Mead also criticizes the earlier positivistic conceptions of scientific method held by Comte and his contemporary Mills, because of their misunderstanding of perception and the possibilities of novelty raised by perception. Mead appreciates the work of his own contemporary, Cooley, on the nature of the self, but believes that Cooley never quite freed himself from a dependence upon biological explanation: his conception of self was not sufficiently social. Bergson's emphasis upon novelty and the exciting possibilities of life are lauded by Mead, but his own emphasis upon science and rationality leads him to point a critical finger at Bergson's reliance upon irrationality.

In "History and the Experimental Method," Mead suggests that the past—historical or otherwise—is significant not in itself but in relation to present and future action. There is no single past to be recaptured in its pure essence, only a past reconstructed from within a current frame of reference. There are thus as many pasts as there are perspectives. This statement of the noble office of the historian is another version of the hypothesis that remembering is an active process, reconstructive and highly selective. Other psychologists have investigated memory from this same viewpoint. What Mead adds is that remembering is always part of larger acts; from this follows his discussion of social movements and their reconstruction —even construction of their own pasts.

Finally, in the excerpts on "time" from *Philosophy of the Present*, we see Mead thinking with great originality and expressing himself with unusual felicity and brilliance. With characteristic emphasis upon emergence, he argues that reality is always in the present, that the past refers to "that conditioning phase of the passing present which enables us to determine conduct with reference to the future which is also arising in the present," and that "the novelty of every future demands a novel past." Mead links particular presents with particular social acts in which one is engaged; so that what he terms "functional presents," rather than "specious presents," are the important phenomena, linked as they are with the social enterprises in which individuals are engaged. Mead's most brilliant elaboration of temporality as genuine possibility is found, perhaps, in the selection titled "The Objective Reality of Perspectives." Here he reviews and criticizes Whitehead's notion of an organization of perspectives, carrying Whitehead's one step further by relating that organization to social organization itself, via conceptions already encountered by the reader in excerpts from *Mind, Self, and Society*. Mead's elaboration of his ideas about temporality was abruptly ended by his unexpected death. Since those ideas are among his best, they ought to be more widely known. [16]

The mounting interest in Mead's writing today, combined with

[16] In this edition of Mead's writings, occasional minor changes have been made for clarity. Much of the original publication drew upon students' notes or unpublished papers, whose punctuation and grammar left something to be desired. The changes in this edition consist mainly of repunctuation or additional punctuation, of occasional correction of grammar, and of infrequent rephrasing or pinpointing of referent. Readers who wish to quote Mead in the original must, therefore, check with the original.

his complexity as a thinker, has brought about different interpretations of what he "really meant." Debates about various of his views
have been carried on in the sociology journals,[17] and recently two
philosophers have differed about whether Mead retained essentially
the same position over the years or whether his *Philosophy of the
Present* represents his most mature perspective. Another philosopher speaks of Mead's work as a "major unfinished system of
thought"[18] but Berenice Fisher,[19] a sociologist-historian, agrees
with an earlier judgment of Charles Morris that "Mead was not a
systematic thinker but used his lectures to work out a series of
constantly developing ideas. This, indeed, seems to be one whole
aspect of Mead's thinking—his lecture style of moving into a
problem at various angles, his addresses to different audiences
groping with different aspects of the social world, his discussions
about the problems of time and perspective."

We can certainly expect this continuing reinterpretation of
Mead's thought to continue, but as Fisher perceptively remarks:

> Without the still unwritten biography of Mead, these various images
> of him as a man of knowledge—his role as teacher and colleague, his
> involvement with social reform, his working out philosophic prob-
> lems, his fate in the hands of his successors—must have a certain
> ambiguity.

And, in

> the mid-thirties ... Morris wondered whether Mead's democratic
> idealism could survive the growing political forces on the right and

17   Cf. Herbert Blumer, "Sociological Implications of the Thought
of George Herbert Mead," *American Journal of Sociology* 71 (1966),
535–44, and "Reply," *ibid.*, pp. 547–48; Robert Bales, "Comment on
Herbert Blumer's Paper," *ibid.*, pp. 547–97; Joan Huber, "Symbolic
Interaction as a Pragmatic Perspective", *American Sociological Review*
38 (1973), 274–84; G. Stone, D. Maines, H. Farberman, and N. Denzin,
"On Methodology and Craftsmanship in the Criticism of Sociological
Perspectives," *ibid.*, 39 (1974), 456–62.

18   Andrew Reck (ed.), *Mead* (Indianapolis: Library of Liberal Arts,
Bobbs-Merrill, 1964).

19   "Mead as a Man of Knowledge," *History of Education Quarterly*
(Winter 1969), pp. 497–504; quotations from pp. 499 and 504.

the left. Morris seemed to feel that Mead's contribution to social psychology could endure separate from this broader social commitment. But that is doubtful. Rather, the reconstruction of his thought would have to include both, and the survival of the basic insight would be contingent upon the kind of man who could understand it.

In short, Mead seems due for increasing reconstruction, rediscovery, reassessment, rephasing, redeciphering, and no doubt continuing re-translation. Since his thought is so rich, the reworking will doubtless reflect his complexity.

Part I

1

EVOLUTION BECOMES

A GENERAL IDEA

PASSING as we have from Kant to the Romantic idealists, we proceed from a conception of static forms which are originally given, and which serve as the whole basis of Kant's transcendental philosophy, to an idea of the development of the forms through a process, an evolutionary process. Kant conceived of the basic forms of the world as being given in the character of the mind itself. The forms of space and time—given in the sensibility; the forms of the understanding—given in the categories; and the forms of the reason, are all there in advance of experience. If the object, as such, arises under Kant's doctrine, it is because of certain contents of the sensibility passing into these forms. That is what makes it an object. It is not an object for our cognitive experience unless it has these forms that give it its reality. Sensuous experience itself, unless it takes on some form, has no meaning, no reality; it cannot be known except insofar as the experiences have some form. And in the Kantian doctrine, the form is given in advance. This is what Kant expressed in terms of the "transcendental logic," the term "transcendental" meaning

First published in *Movements of Thought in the Nineteenth Century*, ed. Merritt H. Moore (Chicago: University of Chicago Press, 1936), pp. 153–68.

the logical pre-existence of the form to the object. This concept, you see, belongs to pre-evolutionary days. The logical pre-existence of the form to the object cannot be stated in terms of process; therefore it falls outside of evolutionary ideas. In order that there might be an object there, Kant, as over against the empiricists, said that the form must be there originally, in advance. The latter undertook to show how an object might arise out of the mere association of different states of consciousness. Kant insisted that, in order for there to be an object, the form must be there first.

But the Romantic idealists changed all that. For them, the forms arose in the very process of experience, in the process of overcoming antinomies, overcoming obstacles. We are responsible for the forms. In other words, we have, in experience, not a pouring of the characters of our sensibility—colors, sounds, tastes, odors—into certain fixed forms, but a process of experience in which these very forms arise. Logic, as the romanticists conceived of it, was a dynamic, not a static, affair—not a simple mapping-out of judgments which we can make because of the forms which the mind possesses, but a process in which these very forms themselves arise.

The process of experience, according to these idealists, creates its own forms. Now this has a very abstruse sound, of course; but what I want to call your attention to is that it is nothing but an abstract statement of the principle of evolution. These Romantic idealists were undertaking in the field of philosophical speculation what Darwin and Lamarck were undertaking in the field of organic phenomena at the same period. What the Romantic idealists, and Hegel in particular, were saying, was that the world evolves, that reality itself is in a process of evolution.

This was a different point of view from that which characterized the Renaissance science of which I have previously spoken. This Renaissance science started off with just as simple elements as it could. It started with mass and motion. And Newton defined "mass" first as a quantity of matter; but, as that involved a conception of density and there was no way of telling just how dense your matter was, he had to get another definition. And he found it in terms of inertia, that is, the response which a body offers to a change of state in either its rest or its motion. If you want to measure the mass of a body, you measure its inertia. You see how much force is necessary to set it going, and so forth. And in that way you measure its mass, so that mass is really measured in terms of accelerations, that is, accelerations that you add to motions of a body. We come back to these simple conceptions of mass and motion; but we really define our mass in terms of certain sorts of motion, that is, velocities and accelerations. With these very simple conceptions the physicist undertook to build up a theory of the world. Newton gave the simple laws of mass and motion, and then, on the basis of mathematics, worked out an entire mechanics, which up to within a very short time has been the classical theory of the physical world. On the basis of this physical theory, there is just so much motion; there is just so much mass; there is just so much energy in the universe. When the system was more fully worked out, as it was in the nineteenth century, the principles of the conservation of energy were added to those of Newton, although they were implied in his system anyway.

Now, such a world as this is made up simply of physical particles in ceaseless motion. That is all there is to it. We speak of the different objects about us—trees, houses, rivers, mountains—all varied, all part of the infinite variety of nature—but what this science does is to break them up into ultimate physical particles, molecules, atoms, electrons, and protons. The object is nothing but a congeries of these; and, as already stated, the relationship between the particles in one object and in another object are just as real and just as important as the relations found between the particles within any single object itself. For you, the tree is something that exists by itself. When it has been cut down, it is so much lumber. The stump continues to exist as a thing by itself. And yet, from the point of view of mechanical science, the relationship between atoms and electrons in the stump of the tree with those in the star Sirius is just as real as the relations existing between the electrons in the trunk of the tree. The trunk is not an object there because of the physical definition that you give to it.

Every field of force that surrounds every electron is related to every other field of force in the whole universe. We cut our objects out of this world. The mechanical world reduces to a mass of physical particles in ceaseless motion. So far as such a world can be said to have any process of its own, it is that which is represented in the term "entropy."

With the appearance of steam engines, people tried to work out the theory of them. And a Frenchman, Sadi Carnot, had the happy idea of thinking of the heat which was responsible for the formation of steam as flowing downhill through different degrees of temperature. When the steam was hot, its expansive power was great; and then, as it lost heat, it lost its power to expand. As it flowed down the hill of temperature, it lost its power. Of course, energy is not lost in the universe. It is just dispatched into surrounding objects. Thus, Carnot was able to work out a theory of steam engines which hinged upon this knowledge of energy flowing down a temperature hill. You put your piston rod into this stream, and it will work the engine; but when it is at the bottom of the hill, it can do no more work. The mill cannot be turned by water that has passed. Well, now, this presented a picture of the whole universe as just a congeries of atoms in the sort of motion that was called heat. When you set any sort of motion going, you know that you use up energy by friction in some way or other and that you produce heat. The whole universe seems to be running down toward a condition in which this motion will be evenly distributed through the entire universe. All manifestations of energy are due to the fact that they are on high levels, so to speak; but, given time enough, in the course of millions of years, everything will get evened out and all the particles will be in a fairly quiescent condition, with a slight, even motion of a Brownian sort distributed throughout the whole universe. That is the conception of entropy. That is the goal of the universe, if it has one, in which there will be some kind of energy evenly distributed throughout. We can be very thankful that we do not exist at that time. Of course, we could not exist then in any meaningful sense. That mechanical conception which science presents has no future —or a very dark one, at best. Not dark in the sense of catastrophies, for those are always exciting; but dark in the very monotony of the picture. The conception of entropy is anything but exciting. Such a universe would answer only to an infinite sense of ennui.

The scientific conception, the mechanical conception, of the world did not seem to be one that gave any explanation to the form of things. As I have said, science does not justify us in taking a tree, a plant, an animal, or a house as separate objects by themselves. As we know, from the scientific standpoint there is no difference between life and death—simply a shifting of energies. From the scientific standpoint, the forms of things have no real significance. Of course, if you start off with a certain thing, given a certain form, you can use scientific technique to analyze it; but your abstract mechanical science, that to which Newton gave form, does not account for any object, does not account for the acceptance of one object rather than another.

It was Kant who took the first step toward a theory of the heavenly bodies. He was very devoted to the mechanical science of his period; but his imagination carried him a step farther, and he tried to conceive how the present form of the heavens might have arisen out of earlier forms. His statement was one that really got its scientific formulation in Laplace's conception of the solar system as a great nebula, intensely hot to begin with and which gradually cooled down. Kant had to assume a whirling nebula which cooled down and resulted in a series of rings moving about the center as it condensed, gradually developing into a system of bodies of unspecific form. The velocity of the bodies on the outside of the system would keep them from moving in toward the center, and out of these rings the planets would arise. That is the suggestion which Laplace took from Kant and made into an explanation of the way in which the solar system arose. This was the first step toward a theory of the evolution of the heavens.

But what I now want to present is something different from this picture which mechanical science gives of the universe. It is an attempt to state an object in a certain form and to show how that form might arise. When you think of it, that is the title of Darwin's book, *The Origin of Species,* "species" being nothing but the Latin word for form. What is the origin of these forms of things? Mechanical science does not offer any explanation of them. Anyway, from the point of view of mechanical science, the form has no meaning. All that this science says about a particular form is that in referring to a certain object you are isolating a certain group of physical particles, taking them off by themselves. Really, they are related to all physical particles. But the universe that we know is more than particles. It is a world of forms. Now, the question is: Where do these forms come from? Certain of the principal forms, Kant said, come from the very structure of our own minds. The theology of the period said the forms of animals and plants go back to a creative fiat of God. He gave the earth its form and all the stellar bodies their forms and their motions, as well as those of the plants and animals. And that, of course, was the point from which the descriptive sciences of the time—biology, botany, and zoölogy—started. They assumed species of plants and animals which had been created by God when he made the earth.

What Darwin undertook to show was that some of these forms must conceivably have arisen through natural processes. But how could the forms as such have arisen? Mechanical science could not explain them, because, from the point of view of mechanical science, form does not exist. There are only two objects—one the world as a whole and the other the ultimate physical particles out of which it is made. All the other so-called objects are objects that our perception cuts out. That is, we distinguish the chair from the table and ignore the relations between them because we want to move them about, we want to sit on the one and write on the other. For our purposes, then, we distinguish them as separate objects. Actually, they attract each other as physical particles, parts of a single, all-inclusive electromagnetic field. The forms are not explained by the mechanical science of the period. The biological and other sciences—such as cosmology, astronomy— all explained certain forms which they found, insofar as they did account for them, by saying that they were there to begin with. And even Kant assumes that the forms of the mind are there to begin with.

Now the movement to which I am referring, under the term "theory of evolution," is one which undertakes to explain how the forms of things may arise. Mechanical science cannot explain that. It can break up forms, analyze them into physical particles; but it cannot do more than that. Biological science and astronomical science both start with certain forms as given. For example, Laplace's conception is of rapidly revolving, hot nebular bodies which were present to start with. Biological science started with certain living forms; geology, with definite types and forms of rocks. These sciences classify things in accordance with the forms that are found. But they do not generally undertake to show how the forms arise. There is, of course, the science of the growing form, embryology. But this is a recent science. It accounts for the way in which the adult arises out of the embryo. The older theory of biology assumed the form already there; it even conceived of a complete man as given in the very cells from which the form of the embryo developed. The assumption was that the form was there as a precondition of what one finds. This is Aristotelian science. It is also essentially Kantian. We have seen how we conceived of the forms of the mind as given as the precondition of our experience.

Now, Lamarckian and Darwinian evolution undertook to show how, by a certain process, forms themselves might come into being, might arise. Starting with the relatively formless, how could one account for the appearance of forms? Lamarck started with the hypothesis that every activity of the form altered the form itself, and the form then handed on the change to the next generation. As a picturesque example, assume that the progenitors of the giraffe wanted, or had, to feed off the leaves of trees, and so stretched their necks. They handed this stretched neck on to their longer-necked offspring. The inheritance of so-called "acquired characteristics" was Lamarck's suggestion to account for the appearance of forms. He assumed, as did Darwin, that you start with relatively formless protoplasm, and went on to show the process by means of which forms might arise from that which was relatively formless.

We were discussing Romantic idealism, and we pointed out

that it was a development or an expression of the spirit of evolution, of the definite entrance of the idea of evolution into Western thought. Indeed, we spoke of Hegel's philosophy as a "philosophy of evolution." This highly abstruse, speculative movement is simply a part of this general movement toward the discovery of the way in which the forms of things arise, of origins. As a scientific undertaking, it was not aided by the physical science of the time. It had to make its own way, and this it did to an amazing extent. In later generations it became a guiding idea in practically all investigations.

I mentioned earlier the distinction between the conception of evolution that belonged to the older, ancient thought which got its classical expression in the Aristotelian doctrine and the evolutionary theory of this period. The Aristotelian evolution was the development of the so-called form, the nature of the thing which was already present. It presupposed the existence of the form as something that was there. In this conception, a metaphysical entity was thought of which existed in and directed the development of the form. The species—which is the Latin word for the Greek term "form"—was actually conceived of as a certain nature that supervised the development of the seed of the embryo into the normal adult form. Under the conception of Christian theology this form was thought of as existing first in the mind of God, then as appearing in the plants and animals and various other objects that he created, and finally as arising in our minds as concepts. The form, however, was not thought of exactly in the Aristotelian sense as existing in advance, as being an entelechy, the nature of the object existing in advance of the actual animal or plant.

The difference between that conception of evolution and the modern conception is given, as I have already pointed out, in the very title of Darwin's book, *The Origin of Species,* that is, the origin of forms. It is an evolution of the form, of the nature, and not an evolution of the particular animal or plant. What this theory is interested in is the evolution of the nature of the object, of the form, in a metaphysical sense. It is this which distinguishes the later theory of evolution from the former, namely, that the actual character of the object, the form or the nature itself, should arise instead of being given.

As you may remember, Darwin got the suggestion for his hypothesis from Malthus' doctrine of population. This was an attempt to show the relationship which exists between population and the food supply, and what effect this relationship may have on the future of the race. Of course, Malthus' statement was greatly disturbed by the introduction of machine production; this upset many of his calculations, if not the theory as a whole. Yet, it is interesting as an attempt to state in definite ways what the experience of the race will be in the light of a single factor in its environment, that is, the food supply.

Darwin became very much interested in this problem, and it led him to undertake to explain certain variations which take place in forms as being due to the pressure of population. In nature there are always more forms born into the world, more plants and animals, than can possibly survive. There is a constant pressure which would lead to the selection of those variants which are better adapted to the conditions under which they must live. This process of the culling-out of these better adapted forms would, in time, lead to the appearance of new forms. What lies back of this conception is the idea of a process, a life-process, that may take now one, and now another, form. The thing of importance is that there is a distinction made between this life-process and the form that it takes. This was not true of the earlier conception. In it, the life-process was thought of as expressed in the form; the form had to be there in order that there might be life.

The idea of which I have just spoken I have referred to as Darwinian. The same idea lies back of the conception of Lamarck. He assumes a life-process which may appear in one form or another, but which is the same process whatever form it takes on. The particular form which it does assume depends upon the conditions within which this life-process is run. Thus we find the same fundamental life-process in plants and in animals—in the amoeba, in man, and in every form between. It is a process that starts in the separation of carbon and oxygen. These two, in the form of carbon dioxide, exhaled by animals as a by-product of the assimilation of food, are found in water solution in plants as carbonic acid. Through the mediation of the action of chlorophyl and light this eventually becomes food, in the form of various sugars and starches. These starches are then carried to tissues that expend energy, that burn up and set free energy in the life of plant or animal, get rid of waste produucts, set up the means of reproduction, and so pass on from one plant or animal to another, from one generation to another. The essentials of that life-process are the same in all living forms. We find it in unicellular forms, in multicellular forms. The only difference is that in the case of the latter we find a differentiation of tissues to carry out various functions; we find different groups of cells that take up one of the phases of the life-process and specialize in that—the lungs take in air, oxygen; another group of cells becomes the means of the circulation of the blood; others take over the functions of ingestion, of locomotion, of secreting fluids that make digestion and reproduction possible. In other words, separate groups of cells carry on different parts of the life-process. The whole process, however, is the same as that which goes on in unicellular forms. That, you see, is involved in this conception of evolution—a life-process that flows through different forms, taking on now this form, now that. The cell, as a single entity in the whole, remains fundamentally what it was in the unicellular form. All living cells bathe in some fluid medium; those cells on the outside of us are dead. Living cells are those which are bathed in the fluids of the body, such as the blood or lymph. They are the only ones which are alive, and they carry over into the body some of the original sea from which our original unicellular existence migrated. These cells went from the surface to the bottom, and there multicellular forms arose. From the bottom of the sea to man, they had to bring this precious fluid in which alone cells can live. This was first found in plants. And animals then came and lived upon the plants; but the life-process has flowed through all and remains the same life-process.

Given such a conception as this, it is possible to conceive of the form of the plant or the animal as arising in the existence of the life-process itself. It is very important that we should get the conception of evolution that is involved in it and distinguish it from the earlier conception, especially if we are to understand the appearance of this conception in its philosophic form. We are concerned with a theory which involves a process as its fundamental fact, and then with this process as appearing in different forms.

Now, the Romantic idealists, who first developed a philosophy of evolution, came back, of course, to our experience of ourselves—that reflexive experience in which the individual realizes himself insofar as, in some sense, he sees himself and hears himself. He looks in the glass and sees himself; he speaks and hears himself. It is the sort of situation in which the individual is both subject and object. But in order to be both subject and object, he has to pass from one phase to another. The self involves a process that is going on, that takes on now one form and now another—a subject-object relationship which is dynamic, not static, a subject-object relationship which has a process behind it, one which can appear now in this phase, now in that.

To get the feeling for this Romantic idealism, one must be able to put himself in the position of the process as determining the form. And it is for this reason that I have said what I have in regard to evolution. That does not get us as deep into our experience as the subject-object relationship does. Logically, it is of the same character, namely, a process in this case, a life-process, going on that takes now one form and now another. The process can be distinguished from the form; yet it takes place within the different forms. The same apparatus for digestion has to be there; the same apparatus for expiration, for circulation, and for the expenditure of energy have to be there for the life-process to go on; and yet this life-process may appear now with this particular apparatus and now with that. In your thought you can distinguish the process from the form. And yet you can see that there must be forms if the process is to take place. We have spoken of the unicellular animal as having no form in that sense. That statement is not entirely correct. We know that there is a high degree of organization of molecular structure in the cell itself. We can follow it out in a vague sort of way. You cannot have a process without some sort of a structure; and yet the structure is simply something that expresses this process as it takes place now in one animal and now in another, or in plants as against animals. That life-process that starts off with carbon dioxide, with water and carbonic gas, goes on through plant and animal life and ends up as carbon dioxide, in the carbonic acid gas and water that we breathe out. That process is something we can isolate from the different organs in which it takes place, and yet it could not take place without some sort of organ. We can separate the process from particular organs by recognizing them in one or another animal, in one or another plant. But we could not have the process if there were not some structure given, some particular form in which it expresses itself.

If, then, one is to make a philosophy out of this evolutionary movement, one must recognize some sort of process within which the particular form arises. In the biological world this process is a life-process, and it can be definitely isolated as the same process in all living forms, because in the scientific development of physics and chemistry, as well as of physiology, we are able to find out what this life-process is, to think of the life-process apart from the particular form in which it goes on—to separate, in other words, such a function as the digestive process from the digestive tract itself; to be able to realize that the ferments essential to digestion, the breakdown of starches and proteins and the organization, the synthesis, of these into organic products which the animal can assimilate, goes on in the amoeba, which has no digestive tract at all. The importance of the digestive tract is dependent upon the life of the particular group of cells that go to make up an animal. The problem presented to the animal form is the conversion of edible protoplasm, which is found in plants, into an assimilable form. The plant had to protect its fluid with cellulose. In order to get at the fluid, the animal has to be able to digest away the cellulose. Such an animal as the ox has to have a very complicated apparatus within itself; it sets up a whole series of bacteriological laboratories and brings into them microorganisms that ferment the cellulose that surrounds the edible protoplasm. The digestive tract of the animal is, then, an adaptation to the sort of food which these living cells feed upon. The animal has to have a structure which will enable it to get at the edible protoplasm itself. On the other hand, the tiger, which lives on the ox, has a rather simple assimilative problem on his hands. The ox has done the work, and the tiger can feed on his flesh. Of course, we are in the position of the tiger, except that we take the ox from the stockyards! The point is that our digestive system, like that of the tiger, can be much more simple than the ox's. Our whole life-process is not devoted to digesting away cellulose that surrounds food.

This indicates the way in which the form arises, so to speak, within the life-process itself. The form is dependent upon the conditions under which the life-process goes on. It is the same process, but it meets all sorts of difficulties. It has to have a particular apparatus in order that it may meet each of these difficulties. Such a life-process as this, which is the same in all these forms, was entirely unknown to the ancient physiologist. He could look at the animal only from the outside. He could see what were the function of the mouth and the feet, of the various limbs and external organs; but he could not get inside the animal and discover this process that was flowing on, that was taking on these different outer forms as the plant or animal needed a certain apparatus to enable it to live under certain conditions. It is essential to science and to the philosophy of evolution that it should recognize as basic to all a certain process that takes place, and then that it should undertake to show the way in which the forms of things arise in the operation of this process.

The question as to whether a Darwinian or Lamarckian hypothesis is to be accepted is not really of such great importance. The important thing about the doctrine of evolution is the recognition that the process takes now one form and now another, according to the conditions under which it is going on. That is the essential thing. One must be able to distinguish the process from the structure of the particular form, to regard the latter as being simply the organ within which a certain function takes place. If the conditions call for a certain type of organ, that organ must arise if the form is to survive. If conditions call for an organ of another sort, that other sort of organ must arise. That is what is involved in the evolutionary doctrine. The acceptance of the Darwinian hypothesis is simply the acceptance of Darwin's view that selection under the struggle for existence would pick out the organ which is necessary for survival. The heart of the problem of evolution is the recognition that the process will determine the form according to the conditions. If you look at the life-process as something which is essential in all forms, you can see that the outer structure which it takes on will depend upon the conditions under which this life-process runs on.

Now, if you generalize this, make a philosophic doctrine out of it, you come back to some central process which takes place under different conditions; and the Romantic idealists undertook to identify this process, first of all, with the self—not-self process in experience, and then to identify this self—not-self process with the subject-object process. They undertook to make these one and the same. The subject-object relationship is, from the philosophical standpoint, and especially from the epistemological standpoint, the more fundamental one. But the self looms up very importantly here, as you can see, for it is a self that is a subject. As I pointed out above, the object was in some sense explained by the empiricist. If you are to put the object into the subject-object process, you have to find a subject that is involved in the presence of the object. The old doctrine assumed that the world was there and that human beings later came into it. In other words, according to this view, the object was there before the subject. The appearance of the subject seems to have been purely accidental, incidental. The object might just as well be there without the subject being there. But, what the Romantic idealists insisted upon is that you cannot have an object without a subject. You can see very well that you cannot have a subject without an object, that you cannot have a consciousness of things unless there are things there of which to be conscious. You cannot have bare consciousness which is not consciousness of something. Our experience of the self is one which is an experience of a world, of an object. The subject does involve the object in order that we may have consciousness. But we do not as inevitably recognize that the subject is essential to there being an object present. According to our scientific conception, the world has arisen through millions of years, only in the last moments of which have there been any living forms; and only in the last second of these moments have there been any human forms. The world was there long before the subjects appeared. What the Romantic idealist does is to assume that for these objects to be present there must be a subject. In one sense this might be said to be reflecting the philosophical dogma that the world could not be present unless created by a conscious being. But this problem is something more profound than a philosophical dogma. It is the assumption that the very existence of an object, as such, involves the existence of a subject to which it is an object.

Well, if we are to find an instance of that in which the object involves a subject, as well as the subject involving an object, we can come back to the self. The self can exist as a self only insofar as it is a subject. And significant objects can exist only as objects for a subject. We can see that the self-process of the Romantic idealists—this fusion of the two phases of experience, the self-experience on the one hand and the subject-object experience on the other hand—was one which enabled them to insist, not only that the subject involved an object, but also that the object involved a subject. This, then, was the central process for them: the self, the not-self, are expressions of a single process, and in this also is found the subject-object relationship in which both terms are always mutually involved. Just as there can be no self without a not-self, so there can be no subject without an object and vice versa.

One more word about evolution. We have a statement of the human animal as having reached a situation in which he gets control over his environment. Now, it is not the human animal as an individual that reaches any such climax as that; it is society. This point is cogently insisted upon by Hegel, the last of the Romantic idealists. The human animal as an individual could never have attained control over the environment. It is a control which has arisen through social organization. The very speech he uses, the very mechanism of thought which is given, are social products. His own self is attained only through his taking the attitude of the social group to which he belongs. He must become socialized to become himself. So when you speak of this evolution, of its having reached a certain climax in human form, you must realize that it reaches that point only insofar as the human form is recognized as an organic part of the social whole. Now, there is nothing so social as science, nothing so universal. Nothing so rigorously oversteps the points that separate man from man and groups from groups as does science. There cannot be any narrow provincialism or patriotism in science. Scientific method makes that impossible. Science is inevitably a universal discipline which takes in all who think. It speaks with the voice of all rational beings. It must be true everywhere; otherwise it is not scientific. But science is evolutionary. Here, too, there is a continuous process which is taking on successively different forms. It is this evolutionary aspect of science which is important in the philosophy of the contemporary French philosopher, Henri Bergson, whose work we will consider later.

2

THE PROBLEM OF SOCIETY—

HOW WE BECOME SELVES

WHAT I have wanted to make evident is that science itself has been advancing at a great rate and has become conscious of its experimental method, which seemingly has been the source of its advance. It has been natural that philosophy should take these phases of the scientific advance as a basis for its interpretation of life, for science, as we know, is not a thing which exists by itself, even though it uses abstruse mathematical methods. It is an instrument by means of which mankind, the community, gets control over its environment. It is, in one sense, the successor to the early magic that undertook to control its environment by magical methods. It is a means of control. Science is something that enters into all the minutiae of life. We cannot brush our teeth without it. We cannot eat or drink without science coming in to tell us what should be eaten, what vitamins in the upper part of the alphabet ought to be used, how they can be obtained in the orange juice and the spinach that are on the menu. It tells us how to blow our noses and indicates with whom we may shake hands and whom we should avoid. There is hardly a point in life at which science does not tell something about the conduct that is an essential part

First published in *Movements of Thought in the Nineteenth Century*, ed. Merritt H. Moore (Chicago: University of Chicago Press, 1936), 360–85.

of our living. It is, in a way, independent of the community, of the community life. It goes on in separate institutions, in universities that cloister themselves from the community, under separate foundations that demand that this work shall be entirely free so that the scientist may entertain whatever view he cares to hold, use whatever methods he has worked out. The scientist demands a freedom in his operations which is greater than that which anyone else in the community can demand. He seems to stand outside the community; and yet, as I have said, his statements, the directions which he gives, enter into the whole minutiae of social life. Society is feeling its dependence upon scientific method more and more, and will continue to do so if it is to go ahead intelligently. The control over community life in the past has been a control of situations. The control, as such, has been almost inevitably conservative. It has preserved orders which have established themselves as social habits that we call "institutions." A conscious social control has taken on this form: The law must be obeyed; the constitution must be honored; the various institutions such as the family, school, courts, must be recognized and obeyed; the order which has come down to us is an order which is to be preserved. And, whenever the community is disturbed, we always find this return to the fixed order which is there and which we do not want to have shaken. It is entirely natural and, in a certain sense, entirely justifiable. We have to have an order of society; and, when what is taking place shakes that order, we have no evidence that we will get another order to take the place of the present one. We cannot afford to let that order go to pieces. We must have it as a basis for our conduct.

The first step consciously taken in advance of this position is that which grew out of the French Revolution, that which in a certain sense incorporated the principle of revolution into institutions. That is, when you set up a constitution and one of the articles in it is that the constitution may be changed, then you have, in a certain sense, incorporated the very process of revolution into the order of society. Only now it is to be an ordered, a constitutional revolution by such and such steps. But, in any case, now you can change the order of things as it is going on.

That is the problem of society, is it not? How can you present order and structure in society and yet bring about the changes that need to take place, are taking place? How can you bring those changes about in orderly fashion and yet preserve order? To bring about change is seemingly to destroy the given order, and yet society does and must change. That is the problem, to incorporate the methods of change into the order of society itself. I do not mean to say that society has not always recognized that change could take place, but it did not undertake to find a process by means of which this should go on. It simply assumed that change was going to take place toward some fixed goal. If you are going to have a society in which everyone is going to recognize the interests of everybody else—in which the golden rule is to be the rule of conduct, that is, a society in which everyone is to make the interests of others his own interest, while actually each person seems to be pursuing his own interest—how can that goal be reached? It was assumed, of course, that this was to be done through a religious current, through a change in the heart of the individual. But in the last analysis that goal was to be reached in the world to come, not in this one. That was the religious solution. The order we find is one given by God for this world and must be preserved. The final perfect society was to be a New Jerusalem that belonged to another world. The religious goal was one of otherworldliness. We have other conceptions, councils of perfection set up, such as that of a society in which you should bring liberty in the sense of everyone's respecting the rights of everyone else, one's liberty being in that sense only circumscribed by intrenching on others' liberty. That is more or less an abstraction. To take a practical illustration, how are you to determine where the liberty of a man in the control of his property is to be restricted? He needs controlling. We will say that he, or rather a group of men, own shares in a railroad, and that they choose to deal with rates in a fashion which will serve their own interest. Well now, if they are to have complete control over their property, and then the community comes in and says that theirs is property of a different sort, that their acts must have the approval of the community, how are we to determine where the restriction in the control of the property is to take place?

How is society to find a method for changing its own institutions and still preserve the security of those institutions? That is the problem that presents itself in its most universal form. You want a society that is going ahead, not a fixed order, as the religious solution would have it. You want a society that is progressing. Progress has become essential to intelligent life. Now, how are we to get ahead and change those situations that need changing and yet preserve the security of them? You see this is an advance in which we cannot state the goal toward which we are going. We do not know what the goal is. We are on the way, but we do not know where. And yet we have to get some method of charting our progress. We do not know where the progress is supposed to terminate, where it is going. This is a seemingly insoluble problem.

Science does, in a sense, present the method for its solution. That is, it recognizes that progress is of the nature of the solution of a problem. What these problems present are inhibitions, the checking of conduct. And the solution of the problem stops this checking process, sets it free so that we can go on. The scientist is not looking ahead toward a goal and charting his movement toward that goal. That is not the function of the scientist. He is finding out why his system does not work, what difficulty in it is. And the test of his solution of the difficulty is that his system starts working again, goes on. Science is occupied with finding what the problems are that exist in the social process. It finds what the problems are, what processes have been definitely checked. Then it asks: How can things be so reconstructed that those processes which have been checked can be set going again? The illustration which I have given from the field of hygiene is as good as any, but you can find similar illustrations elsewhere.

Take, as another example, the social problem of recreation, with all the dangers that gather about its various forms, particularly about commercialized recreation. Shall we recognize the legitimacy of the expression of the play instinct, the freedom for the play one wants, when at the same time we recognize that dangers go along with it? You do not set up an ideal form of recreation. You find out what the dangers are, just what it is that finds expression in play, what the freedom is that is demanded there; and you see how you can combine the control or avoidance of danger with the freedom of expression. That is the sort of problem we are meeting. We have to let freedom of activity go on, and yet dangers must be avoided. And what science does is to give a method for studying such situations. Again, on the social side, or on the biological side in dealing with questions of disease, we have the question of how we shall deal with these problems. As a further instance, take the question of crime. What are the conditions out of which crime itself springs? How, on the one hand, can you protect society against the criminal and yet, on the other hand, recognize those conditions which are responsible for the criminal himself? What procedure can you set up by means of which you can guard society against the criminal and at the same time protect the individual against unfair conditions under which he has been living? Here we have a series of clashing problems, and what we have to do is to get a way which will recognize that what we feel is essential in each, so that the problems can be adjusted and the essential processes of life can go on. When we get such a method, we have the means for the solution of our problems. Let me illustrate this further in the problem of juvenile crime, so-called. There we have a situation in which certain definite habits embodied in our institution of the court prove unsatisfactory. The child is brought before the court by the police. The social habit left simply to itself would condemn the child to the penitentiary and thus make a confirmed criminal out of him. But it is possible to modify those habits by what we call the "scientific method."

What I wish to point out is that the scientific method is, after all, only the evolutionary process grown self-conscious. We look back over the history of plant and animal life on the face of the globe and see how forms have developed slowly by the trial-and-error method. There are slight variations that take place in the individual forms and occasional, more pronounced variations that we call "mutations." Out of these, different forms gradually arise.

But the solution of the particular problem of an animal—the food problem, we will say—is one which may take thousands of years to solve in the gradual development of a certain form. A form which passes, for example, from the eating of meat to the eating of vegetables develops a type of stomach capable of handling this latter kind of food. Here we have a problem which is met gradually by the appearance of some form that does commence to develop an adjustment to the problem, and we can assume that from its progeny those particular forms will be selected which are adapted to such digestion. It is a problem which has to be met if there is to be development, and the development takes place by the seemingly incidental appearance of those forms which happen to be better able than others to meet the peculiar demands set up. If we put ourselves in the same place, there is the same problem. The food problem faces us as it does all other animal forms. We have to get our food from both the vegetable and the animal kingdoms. But if it is a question of our being able to get the food that is shut up inside a cellulose covering, we do not wait through long periods until we develop stomachs which will be able to digest this substance. We work out a milling process by means of which we set free that which is digestible. That is, we solve the problem directly by what we call the "scientific method." Food which we need is shut off from us by a cellulose covering. We work out a mechanism to get rid of this covering. There is an evolutionary problem made self-conscious. The problem is stated in a definite form; this, in turn, excites the imagination to the formation of a possible hypothesis which will serve as the solution of it; and then we set out to test the solution.

The same process is found in social development, in the formation of great societies among both invertebrates and vertebrates, through a principle of organization. Societies develop, just as animal forms develop, by adjusting themselves to the problems that they find before them. They have food problems, problems of climate, just as individual animals do; but they meet them in a social fashion. When we reach the human form with its capacity for indicating what is important in a situation, through the process of analysis; when we get to the position in which a mind can arise in the individual form, that is, where the individual can come back upon himself and stimulate himself just as he stimulates others; where the individual can call out in himself the attitude of the whole group; where he can acquire the knowledge that belongs to the whole community; where he can respond as the whole community responds under certain conditions when they direct this organized intelligence toward particular ends; we have this process which provides solutions for problems working in a self-conscious way. In it we have the evolution of the human mind which makes use directly of the sort of intelligence which has been developed in the whole process of evolution. It makes use of it by the direct method that we call "mental." If one goes back to a primitive society, one finds the beginnings of the evolution of what we call "institutions." Now these institutions are, after all, the habits of individuals in their interrelation with each other, the type of habit that is handed down from one generation to another. And we can study the growth of these habits as we can study the growth and behavior of an animal.

That is where science comes in to aid society in getting a method of progress. It understands the background of these problems, the processes out of which they have developed; and it has a method of attacking them. It states the problem in terms of checked processes; and then it has a test of the suggested solution by seeing whether those processes can continue or not. That is just as valuable—in a certain sense more valuable—a contribution of science as any of its immediate results that we can gather together. This sort of method enables us to keep the order of society and yet to change that order within the process itself. It is a recognition that intelligence expresses itself in the solution of problems. That is the way in which evolution is taking place in the appearance of problems in life. Living forms have found themselves up against problematic situations: their food gone, the climate changed, new enemies coming in. The method which nature has followed, if we may speak so anthropomorphically, has been the production of variations until finally some one variation has arisen which has survived. Well, what science is doing is making this method of trial and error a conscious method.

Up to this period the so-called social sciences have been gathered about the more or less dogmatic theory of certain institutions. It was assumed that each institution stood upon certain rational doctrines, whether those of the family, the state, the church, the school, or the court. The early theory was that these institutions were established directly by God. The divine right of kings was simply the assertion that the state had as divine an origin as the church; and it was assumed that God was also responsible for the ordering of the family and the other institutions. They all came back to a direct structure which was given to them. If the theories did not place this structure in divine ordinance, they brought it back to certain natures in the institutions themselves. And it was assumed that you could work out the theory which would determine what the institutions ought to be. The development of evolutionary doctrine had as great an effect in this field as any it had in biology. Spencer, and others following immediately in his path, carried over the evolutionary theory into the development of human institutions. People went back to primitive societies, which at first were regarded as much more primitive than they were, and then undertook to show how, out of the life of these people, different institutions arose through a process of evolution.

I pointed out earlier that a certain part of the stimulus which directed this thought came from the Hegelian movement. The Hegelian doctrine was in one sense an evolutionary one. At least it was particularly interested in the development of what we term "self-consciousness," in the process of thinking where that arose. And it was the Hegelian thinkers who turned to the study of human institutions, but they did so on the economic and the political side. On the economic side, we have the Marxian doctrine of the human institution in the economic process. On the political side, we have the development of the state, especially the city-state. Hegel's son Karl was quite a notable author in the early study of the city-state, particularly of the way in which it developed. The whole study of so complex a dogmatic structure as the Roman law, for example, was brought back to an evolutionary consideration. Later, attention was directed toward social forms as social forms, apart from any dogmatic structure that lay behind them.

Take, again, the attitude of the community toward crime. On the evolutionary side, you go back to a situation, we will say, of blood vengeance. A man from one clan kills a man from another. Immediately there arises within the injured clan a man who is determined to revenge the death by killing someone from the other clan, and the next of kin sets out to kill the slayer. When he accomplishes this, he sets up at once the need of vengeance on the part of the first group. Again, the next of kin goes out to slay in his turn. And this process goes on until, we will say, the clans are nearly exterminated. Well now, when clans were brought together in a tribe in order to defend themselves against other tribes, such a decimation of fighting members of the group became a serious matter, and the tribe came to consider how this problem could be met. A court was worked out in which vengeance took the form of paying a fine. And some sort of a court had to be constituted which should pass upon obligations. In this way a means was gradually built up of getting rid of blood vengeance. There you have an evolutionary process in which the court arises.

When it is carried through and it becomes necessary to organize society more exactly and fit the penalty more definitely to what is felt to be the character of the crime, there arise all the penalties which belong to a court of law. And we get the institution of criminal law which still carries over some of this sense of vengeance which is to be enacted. There must be some suffering on the part of the man who has gone against the interests of the community, who has trespassed on the rights of others. In the older, medieval state the community was called together to witness the suffering of the individual who was being punished. The community thus got satisfaction out of the vengeance, particularly any specific individuals who were themselves injured by the so-called criminal. That element of vengeance demands that where some particularly outrageous crime has been committed, the community feels the need for somebody to suffer. And under such circumstances it is difficult to get impartial justice. It becomes more important to the community that someone should suffer than that the specific individual should suffer. So in our criminal law we have this motive of exacting suffering, and we have a partially worked-out theory which states that where a person has committed a crime he should pay by a certain amount of suffering for the wrong he has done. If the wrong is great, he must suffer more than if it is a lesser wrong. So we inflict punishment by putting him in prison. If the sin is heinous, he is put in for ten or twenty years; if lighter, for perhaps only a few weeks or months. We fit the punishment to the crime.

But we know that that process does not work at all. We have no such exactly measured sets of sufferings as to be able to put them accurately over against wrongs. When the sense of vengeance has died down, we are not sure whether we want the other person to suffer at all. We want to get rid of crime. And so we change our theory from wanting the person to suffer for a wrong he has done to seeing that we keep him from doing the same wrong again. So we have retribution, not in the sense of vengeance but as repression of crime itself. But you know how difficult it is to work those two motives together, trying to find out just how much repression of crime does take place through the action of the law. And when we come to juvenile offenses, we feel the situation should be approached from an entirely different standpoint. So we put aside criminal law, and we have the judge sitting with the boy or girl; we get members of the family, perhaps some person interested in social service, possibly the school teacher, and they all talk it over and try to find out just why what happened did happen, and they attempt to discover some situation whereby the criminal can be put back into a social position and be kept from doing the sort of thing he has done in the past. Thus we try to get rid of crime by a social process. That parole system has been carried over from the juvenile court into the adult court. Very good results have been obtained where politics has not come in to corrupt the process. There we have the development of an institution from both ends. You can see how, out of the attitude of vengeance, the court itself has arisen, and then how, out of the operation of an institution of that sort, one having conflicting motives in it, such as repression of crime on the one hand and a demand for vengeance on the other, that institution can be approached from the standpoint of reinstating the individual in society. There is a social problem here, the problem of an individual who has abused the rights of somebody else but whom we want to put back in the social situation so that he will not do it again. There we have the development of a social process by a real scientific method.

We try to state the problem as carefully as we can. Here is a boy who has allied himself with a gang and has been carried away with the sense of adventure and has committed a burglary which could send him to the penitentiary for years. But that would be absurd. It would make a criminal out of him, and no good would be accomplished at all. It is very questionable whether it would even keep other boys from doing the same thing, for the sense of adventure makes the attitude of the criminal something attractive in itself. It is astonishing how, when we are somewhat relaxed by an attack of grippe or disease, we turn to criminal tales for our relief! If you go through the hospitals you will find such tales being read in great quantities. The creation of crime taken in itself can be looked at from the point of view of adventure, especially for the adolescent. If you approach things scientifically, you can see what the attitude is. You can see that the boy has approached it from this attitude of adventure, does not realize its import; and if he is made to realize it, you can make a very good citizen indeed out of him. What you want to do, then, is to state your social situation in such a fashion that you can reconstitute the boy as a normal citizen, give him opportunities for play in which he can express his demand for adventure with a recognition of what the rights are that make a possibility of citizenship. That has to be brought home to him. He wants to be a citizen in the community, and he has to see that he must have the same respect for the rights of others that he claims for himself. And at the same time you must have a situation where the boy can lead a normal life. Work out specific hypotheses, and by means of them you may get the boy back into society again.

Take any institution as such and look at it from the standpoint of evolution, the way in which that is determined in society, and then you can see the development in society itself of a technique which we call the "scientific technique," but it is a technique which is simply doing consciously what takes place naturally in the evolution of forms. I have been pointing out that the process of evolution is one that meets such a problem as that of blood vengeance, where members of the tribe are at work killing each other as fast as they can. And the community works out there—in a somewhat bungling fashion, if you like—a court which undertakes to meet this situation. It becomes established, acquires a dogmatic structure, holds on to motives which belonged to the earlier situation. But finally we see the situation as one in which we try to do with self-consciousness what took place by a process of evolution. That is, we try to state the problem with reference to a particular child; we want to see what can be done toward bringing together what was a healthful expression of adventure on the part of the boy with rights which he himself claims. So the juvenile court represents a self-conscious application of the very process of evolution out of which the courts themselves arose.

What I am trying to do is to connect this entire evolutionary process with social organization in its most complex expression, and as that within which arise the very individuals through whose life-process it works, giving birth to just such elements as are involved in the development of selves. And, as I have said, the life-process itself is brought to consciousness in the conduct of the individual form, in his so-called self-consciousness. He gets a much more effective control over his environment than the ox can get over its. The process is one in which, in a certain sense, control is within his own grasp. If you think of it, the human being as a social form actually has relatively complete control over his environment. The animal gets a certain slight kind of control over its environment; but the human form, in societies, can determine what vegetation shall grow, what animals shall exist besides itself; it can control its own climate, erect its own buildings. It has, in a biological sense, complete control over its own environment. That is, it has attained to a remarkable degree an end which is implied in the whole living process—the control by the form of the environment within which it lives. To a degree human society has reached that goal.

It has often been pointed out, of course, that evolution does not reach any goal. The concept means simply the adaptation of a form to a certain environment. But adaptation is not simply the fitting of the form into the environment, it carries with it some degree of control over that environment. And in the case of the human form, of human society, we have that adaptation expressing itself in a very high degree of control. Of course, we cannot change the chemical and physical structure of things, but we can make them over into those forms that we ourselves need and which are of value to us. That is possible for us; and, as I have said with reference to the question of food and to the question of climatic influences, we can in a very large degree determine that control. So there is, within limits, a development toward complete adaptation where that adaptation expresses itself in control over the environment. And in that sense I think we can fairly say that human organization, as a social organization, does exercise control and has reached a certain goal of development.

Well now, this social process I have been sketching in these broad strokes has become of increasing interest to reflective thought throughout this whole period. Of course, to some extent it has always been of essential interest to man in the social situation in which he lives. What I am referring to specifically is the character of the social organism—its organization, its history, and the conditions under which it can be controlled. The statement of the functions of the different parts of the social organism is that study which we have in a so-called "social science," and more particularly in sociology. This had its inception in the thought of Comte, and then was enriched by the idea of evolution as brought in by Spencer. From that time on, the attempt to understand human society as an organization has been of increasing interest to the Western world. Men have been trying to see the habits out of which society has arisen, to find out under what conditions it operates, and how problems that arise in it can be definitely controlled. This involves looking at human institutions from the standpoint I have suggested, that is, as social habits.

While during the century there has been this increased interest in the study of the social organization, there has been a corresponding interest in the experience of the individual. Part of this is due to our scientific attitude. As we have seen, it is the unique experience of the scientist that presents the problem, and it is in the mind of the scientist that the hypothesis arises. It is not only in the scientist as such that this uniqueness of the experience has been recognized as of importance. After all, the scientist is simply making a technique out of human intelligence. His method is the same as that of all intelligent beings, even though it involves a simple rendering in self-consciousness of the whole process of evolution. That in the experience of all individuals which is peculiar to the individual, that which is unique in his experience, is of importance, and what the last century increasingly recognized was the importance of these unique individual experiences.

The emotional side of these experiences, as we know, registers itself in the folk poetry, in the lyric expression of the self—a registration of values from the point of view of the individual. There have always been some neat ways of scientific observation, although accurate presentation of it belongs really to the Modern world, that world which has grown up since the period of the Renaissance. But what I am particularly calling attention to is the interest we have in that which is peculiar to the individual as it is revealed in our literature, in our journals, and in our newspapers. The curious thing about the newspaper is that it records happenings to individual persons; and it assumes that it is of interest to us to know that a certain individual at a certain time was run over by an automobile or that a certain person fell down, hurt himself in such and such a way, and that John or Jane has had such and such an experience in such a place. It is curious to note the interest that centers about individuals, and the assumption that the world at large will be interested in these happenings.

Well now, what I want to connect with this journalese interest in happenings to particular individuals is the character of our literature, not simply in its lyric poetry, where the emotion of the individual is presented so that it can be handed on to others, but particularly in our novels and the drama. In these we have this interest in the experience of the individual presented as it has been during the last century because it does answer some very profound interest on the part of all the individuals who take up their morning and evening papers, who read all sorts of stories and novels, go to movies, listen to the radio, get those experiences of other individuals which, as I say, have an interest for us which is rather astonishing when one just stands off and looks at the situation. They seem to be so unrelated. We seem to be interested in just a particular occurrence. We speak of it as sensational and perhaps are apt to regard it as an attitude not entirely helpful on our part when we are interested in this fashion.

What is the import of this interest? I wanted to bring this up in sharp contrast to what I am going to develop later, that is, that the human self arises through its ability to take the attitude of the group to which he belongs—because he can talk to himself in terms of the community to which he belongs and lay upon himself the responsibilities that belong to the community; because he can recognize his own duties as against others—that is what constitutes the self as such. And there you see what we have emphasized, as peculiar to others, that which is both individual and which is habitual. The structure of society lies in these social habits, and only insofar as we can take these social habits into ourselves can we become selves.

We speak of this interest on the emotional side as "sympathy" —passing into the attitude of the other, taking the role of the other, feeling the other's joys and sorrows. That is the effective side of it. What we call the "intellectual side," the "rational side," is the recognition of common stimuli, of common emotions which call out responses in every member of the group. And insofar as one indicates this common character to others, he indicates it to himself. In this way, of course, by taking the attitude of the others in the group in their co-operative, highly complex activity, the individual is able to enter into their experiences. The engineer is able to direct vast groups of individuals in a highly complex process. But in every direction he gives, he takes the attitude of the person whom he is directing. It has the same meaning to him that it has to others. We enter thus into the attitudes of others, and so make our very complex societies possible. This development of a form that is able so to communicate with others that it takes on attitudes of those in the group, that it talks to itself as it talks to others, that imports into its own life this conversation and sets up an inner forum in which it works out the process that it is going to carry on, and so brings it to public consideration with the advantage of that previous rehearsing, is all important. Sometimes we find that we can best think out an argument by supposing that we are talking to somebody who takes one particular side. We have an argument to present, and we think how we will present it to that individual. And as soon as we present it, we know that he would reply in a certain way. Then we reply in a certain fashion to him. Sometimes it is easier to carry out such a conversation by picking out a particular protagonist we know. In that way in the night hours we are apt to go through distressing conversations we have to carry out the next day. That is the process of thought. It is taking the attitude of others, talking to other people, and then replying in their language. That is what constitutes thinking.

Of course, conditions are different in a human society from simpler situations. I was pointing out the difference between a human society and a society of invertebrates. The principle of organization is not that of physiological plasticity, not that of holding the form itself physiologically to its particular function; it is rather the principle of organization as found in the form of human intercommunication and participation. It is what the human individual puts into the form of significant symbols through the use of gestures. He is then able to place himself in the attitude of others, particularly into just such attitudes as those I have spoken of as human institutions. If institutions are social habits, they represent certain definite attitudes that people assume under certain given social conditions. So that the individual, insofar as he does take the role of others, can take the habitual attitude of the community against such social situations as these.

As I have pointed out, he does this in the process of indicating to others the important elements in a situation, pointing out those elements which are of importance in the social process, in a situation that represents one of these social habits, such as the family situation—one that involves the rights of different individuals in the community, such as a political situation. What the individual does is to indicate what the important characters in a co-operative process are. He indicates this to other members of the community; but as we shall see, especially in the case of vocal gestures, he indicates it to himself as to others; and just insofar as he does indicate it to himself as to others, he tends to call out in himself the same attitude as in others. There is a common attitude, that is, one which all assume under certain habitual situations. Through the use of language, through the use of the significant symbol, then, the individual does take the attitude of others, especially these common attitudes, so that he finds himself taking the same attitude toward himself that the community takes. This is what gives the principle of social control, not simply the social control that results from blind habit, but a social control that comes from the individual assuming the same attitude toward himself that the community assumes toward him. In a habitual situation everyone takes a certain attitude insofar as the habit is one which all have taken, that is, insofar as you have "institutions." If, now, the individual calls out this attitude in others by a gesture, by a word which affects himself just as it affects others, then he will call out the same attitude in himself that he calls out in others. In this way he will be acting toward himself as others act toward him. He will admonish himself as others would. That is, he will recognize what are his duties as well as what are his rights. He takes the attitude of the community toward himself. This gives the principal method of organization which, as I have said, we can study from the standpoint of a behavioristic psychology, a method which belongs to human society and distinguishes it from social organizations which one finds among ants and bees and termites. There one finds societies that run up into the millions; and we find these as finely organized as human societies are, and so organized that individuals' lives are largely determined by the life-process of the whole. We get far more complex and intricate organization, of course, in human society than among the invertebrates. This principle to which I have referred—organization through communication and participation—makes an almost indefinite organization possible. Now the study of the way in which this organization takes place, the history of it, the evolution of it, is what has been opened up to the human mind in the last century. We now see the way in which out of a primitive group there can gradually arise the very highly organized societies of the present day. We can study that process in the evolution of institutions, and we can see how that process is modified or may be modified in the presence of problematic situations.

This evolution also takes place in human society, but here it takes place not through physiological plasticity, not through the development of peculiar physiological functions on the part of the separate individuals. It takes place through the development of what has been referred to on the logical side as a universe of discourse. That is, it takes place through communication and participation on the part of the different individuals in common activities. It takes place through the development of significant symbols. It is accomplished almost entirely through the development of vocal gestures, through the capacity of the individual to indicate by means of his own gestures to other forms and also to himself, those elements which are of importance in co-operative activity. So far as we can see, the stimuli that keep the invertebrates occupied are those of odor and contact. But we find no evidence of any language among them. It is through physiological development and plasticity that their very complex communities operate. But the human form, subject to no such development as this, can be interwoven into a community activity through its ability to respond to the gestures of other forms that indicate to it the stimuli to which it is to respond. We point things out. This pointing-out process may be with the finger, by an attitude of body, by direction of head and eyes; but as a rule it is by means of the vocal gesture, that is, a certain vocal symbol that indicates something to another individual and to which he responds. Such indication as this sets up a certain definite process of pointing out to other individuals in the group what is of importance in this co-operative activity.

The peculiar importance of the vocal gesture is that it affects the individual who makes it just as much as it affects the individual to whom it is directed. We hear what we say; if we are talking with our fingers we see what we are saying; if with attitudes of the body, we feel what we are saying. The effect of the attitude which we produce in others comes back on ourselves. It is in this way that participation arises out of communication. When we indicate something to another form, we are calling out in that other individual a certain response. The very gesture we make calls out a certain sort of response in him. If that gesture affects us as it affects him, it has a tendency to call out some response in ourselves. The gesture that affects another, when it is a vocal gesture, is one which may have the tendency to influence the speaker as it influences others. The common expression of this is that a man knows what he is saying when the meaning of what he is saying comes to him as really as it goes to another. He is affected just as the other is. If the meaning of what he says affects the other, it affects himself in the same way. The result of this is that the individual who speaks, in some sense takes the attitude of the other whom he addresses. We are familiar with this in giving directions to another person to do something. We find ourselves affected by the same direction. We are ready to do the thing and perhaps become irritated by the awkwardness of the other and insist on doing it ourselves. We have called out in ourselves the same response we have asked for in another person. We are taking his attitude. It is through this sort of participation, this taking the attitudes of other individuals, that the peculiar character of human intelligence is constituted. We say something that means something to a certain group. But it not only means that to the group, it also means that to us. It has the same meaning for both.

There is a certain, what we would call "unconscious direction" that takes place in lower vertebrate forms. A group of animals is said to set up a sentinel. Some one form is more sensitive than others to stimuli of danger. Now the action on the part of this one which is more sensitive than the rest, the action of running from danger, for example, does cause the other forms to run also. But the first one is not giving a signal in the human sense. It is not aware of giving such directions. Its mere running is a stimulus to the other forms to run in the same direction. It works in the same way as if the form knew what its business was, to catch the first evidence of the enemy and give the evidence to the whole group, thus setting them all going. But in the experience of the animal there is no such procedure, no such intent. The animal does not influence himself as he influences others. He does not tell himself of the danger as he tells it to others. He merely runs away.

The outstanding characteristic in human communication is that one is making a declaration, pointing out something that is common in meaning to the whole group and to the individual, so that the individual is taking the attitude of the whole group, so far as there is any definite meaning given. When a man calls out "Fire!" he is not only exciting other people but himself in the same fashion. He knows what he is about. That, you see, constitutes biologically what we refer to as a "universe of discourse." It is a common meaning which is communicated to everyone and at the same time is communicated to the self. The individual is directing other people how to act, and he is taking the attitude of the other people whom he is directing. If in this attitude of the other person he makes an objection, he is doing what the other person would do, and he is also carrying on the process which we call "thought." That is, you indicate to somebody else that he is to do something, and he objects to it. Well now, the person might in his attitude of the other make the same objection himself. You reply to the other person, trying to point out his mistake or admitting your own. In the same way, if you make some objection, you reply to your own objection or admit your mistake to yourself. Thinking is a process of conversation with one's self when the individual takes the attitude of the other, especially when he takes the common attitude of the whole group, when the symbol that he uses is a common symbol, so that it has a meaning common to the entire group, to everyone who is in it and anyone who might be in it. It is a process of communication with participation in the experience of other people.

The mechanism that we use for this process is words, vocal gestures. And we need, of course, only a very few of these as compared with those we need when talking to others. A single symbol is enough to call out necessary responses. But it is just as real a conversation in terms of the significant symbols of language as if the whole process were expressed. We sometimes do our thinking out loud, in fully organized sentences; and one's thought can always presumably be developed into a complete grammatical unit. That is what constitutes thinking.

Now, it is this inner thought, this inner flow of speech and what it means—words with their meanings—that call out intelligent response; it is this that constitutes the mind, insofar as that lies in the experience of the form. But this is only a part of the whole social process, for the self has arisen in that social process; it has its being there. Of course, you could carry such a self as that over to a Robinson Crusoe island and leave him by himself, and he could carry that social process on by himself and extend it to his pets. He carries that on by himself, but it is only because he has grown up in society, because he can take attitudes and roles of others, that he can accomplish this.

This mental process, then, is one which has evolved in the social process of which it is a part. And it belongs to the different organisms that lie inside of this larger social process. We can approach it from the standpoint of evolution; and we can approach it more particularly from the standpoint of behavioristic psychology, where we can get back to what expresses itself in the mind. We also can get somewhat underneath the experience that goes on in the self in what we term "pathological psychology," a psychology that enables us to get hold of the various processes that are not themselves evidenced in this stream of inner conversation to which I have referred. The term "pathological" simply means that this type of psychology has been pursued largely in dealing with pathological cases. It is a study, for example, of the way in which our special world arises in our experience through our distance senses and our contact experiences—through the collation of the elements which we reach through vision and with the elements which we reach through the tactual sense—the process by which we have built up an implemental world by the use of our hands; for example, the process by which, for purposes of food, we reach with the hand for a distant object. Man comes into that process and gives to the organism a physical thing which is not the food, not the consummation, whatever it may be, but a physical thing. Our world is made up out of physical things. We deal with things as if we could handle them. We think of things as being "pulver-ized," broken up into parts so we can get hold of them. A physical thing is a unit into which we break up our environment. The proc-ess by which we build our world of physical things is a process, too, of which we are not immediately conscious. The child, the infant that is uncertainly groping toward a ball, is gradually build-ing up a world of such physical things; but the process takes place underneath the level of our own consciousness. We cannot get at it in its immediate inception, only indirectly by this type of psy-chology, a psychology that does enable us to get into the workings of the individual process as it lies inside of the whole social proc-ess to which it belongs.

And this is what constitutes the self as such. A self which is so evidently a social individual that it can exist only in a group of social individuals is as much a result of the process of evolution as other biological forms. A form that can co-operate with others through the use of significant symbols, set up attitudes of others and respond to them, is possible through the development of great tracts in the central nervous system that are connected with our processes of articulation, with the ear, and so with the various movements that can go on in the human form. But they are not circumscribed within the conduct of a single form. They belong to the group. And the process is just as much an evolution as is the queen bee or the fighter among the ants. In those instances we get a certain particular evolution that is taking place, belonging to a certain particular society, one which could exist only in such a society. The same is true of the self. That is, an individual who affects himself as he affects another; who takes the attitude of the other insofar as he affects the other, insofar as he is using what we term "intelligible speech"; who knows what he himself is say-ing, insofar as he is directing his indications by these significant symbols to others with the recognition that they have the same meaning for them as for him; such an individual is, of course, a phase of the development of the social form. This is a branch of what we term "behavioristic psychology," one in which we can see how the self as such has developed.

What I want to make evident is that the development, the evo-lution, of mind as well as of institutions is a social evolution. As I have just stated, society in its organization is a form, a specie that has developed; and it has many forms developing within it. You see, for example, at the present time in reference to the question of food that the problem is one which is met by very intricate social organizations. Where the individual himself responds simply to the odor or sight of food, we recognize it as a biological process. When the whole community responds to the need of food by the organization of its industries, of agriculture, of milling, of transportation, of cooking and preparation, we have the same process, only now, not by separate individuals, but by a social organization; and that organization is just as really an evolution as the stomach of the ox. That stomach is very complicated. The evolution of a social mechanism by which grain is sowed and reaped in South America and North America, is carried to great milling establishments and there converted into flour, and then carried and distributed by dealers so that the individual groups can get it and prepare it in such fashion that it can be readily assimilated—that is just as much evolution as the development of bacteriological laboratories in the digestive tract of an ox. It is a process, however, which takes place much more rapidly than it is taking place in the case of the ox. There we have something that answers to a physiological plasticity in the case of invertebrates— the adjustment of different organs within the body to accomplish what we accomplish by mechanical means. It is this ability to control our environment that gives us what we term "mind."

What we attach to the term "mind" particularly is its privacy. It belongs to the individual. And what takes place there takes place, we say, in the experience of the individual. He may make it accessible to others by telling about it. He may talk out loud. He may publish. He may indicate even by his uncontrolled gestures what his frame of mind is. But there is that which goes on inside of a man's mind that never gets published, something that takes place within the experience of the individual. Part of it, of course, is that which answers to what is going on in the physiological mechanism there, the suffering that belongs to one's teeth, the pleasure one gets in the palate. These are experiences which he has for himself because they are taking place within his own organism. But, though they are taking place within his own organism, and no one else can experience the same thing, the organism does not experience it as its own—it does not realize that the experience is its own—until a self has arisen. We have no reason to assume, for example, that in lower animals there are such entities as selves; and if no such entities, then that which takes place within the organism cannot be identified with such a self. There is pain; there is pleasure; there are feelings which are not exactly painful or pleasurable, such as heat or cold. These various feelings belong to the organism, the tensions of the various muscles, the movements of the joints, so essential in our intelligent social conduct. These belong to the organism in a certain sense. But the individual animal does not associate them with a self because it has no self; it is not a self.

A self can arise only where there is a social process within which this self has had its initiation. It arises within that process. For that process, the communication and participation to which I have referred is essential. That is the way in which selves have arisen. That is where the individual is in a social process in which he is a part, where he does influence himself as he does others. There the self arises. And there he turns back upon himslf, directs himself. He takes over those experiences which belong to his own organism. He identifies them with himself. What constitutes the particular structure of his experience is what we call his "thought." It is the conversation which goes on within the self. This is what constitutes his mind. For it is through this so-called "thought," of course, that he interprets his experiences. Now that thought, as I have already indicated, is only the importation of outer conversation, conversation of gestures with others, into the self in which the individual takes the role of others as well as his own role. He talks to himself. This talking is significant. He is indicating what is of importance in the situation. He is indicating those elements that call out the necessary responses. When there are conflicts, the problem gives rise to the hypotheses that form in his mind; he indicates them to himself and to others. It is this process of talking over a problematic situation with one's self, just as one might talk with another, that is exactly what we term "mental." And it goes on within the organism.

Part II

3

THE NATURE OF SCIENTIFIC

KNOWLEDGE

WE HAVE reached certain points in the implications of the method of experimental science which may be summarily restated. In the first place, the scientist's knowing is a search for the unknown, a discovery, but it is a search for what has disappeared in the conflicts of conduct, that is, for objects which will remove the antagonism—it is a search for the solution of a problem. This dissipates the Platonic puzzle of how we can seek to know what is unknown. Plato's solution of the puzzle is found in the form of ignorance as a problem, that of recollecting what has been forgotten. Unfortunately this theory could not apply to the discovery of new types of objects which were foreign to the world of past experience.

In the second place, experimental science implies a real world uninfected by the problem, which can be used to test the discoveries which science makes. If knowledge is discovery of the unknown, this world is not known—it is simply there.

In the third place, as the world that is there is not known and may not therefore as non-known have ascribed to it the logical necessity that does obtain in the logical structure of hypotheses,

---

Reprinted from *The Philosophy of the Act*, ed. Charles W. Morris (Chicago: University of Chicago Press, 1938), pp. 45–62.

experimental science finds nothing contradictory in the later appearance of a problem which has been used to test the solution of a former problem. That a contradiction should appear in the hypothesis is proof of its faulty and, in that sense, unreal character, but that the sun ceases to be an object revolving about the earth in no way invalidates the world by which we test the hypothesis of the revolution of the earth on its axis by the shifting of the path of the pendulum's swing. Logical necessity obtains in the field of reflective thinking. To transfer it to the world that is there, and within which thought is occupied in the solution of problems, would be to dismiss experimental science as a meaningless and pernicious discipline and to return to the science of dogma.

In the fourth place, in observation and in experiment, science finds a field that belongs both to the world that is there and to the reflective thought of discovery, that is, of knowledge. The problem does not exist *in vacuo*. It is in the world that is there, but a certain portion of the world that is there has disappeared. The disease that is conveyed by contact disappears in the evidence of sporadic cases, notwithstanding its epidemic character. But the scourge is all the more tragically there. The instances of the disease are now observed and recorded by physicians and health officers who are seeking to discover the mechanism of the spread of the infection. These data embodied in various hypotheses exist in the minds of the investigators. As the observations of competent investigators of the actual epidemic, they are there as parts of the experiences of these individuals and the records of them are parts of their biographies. The test case of the heroic scientist, who has remained immune to the fever after wearing the clothes of those who were sick and sleeping in their beds and who succumbs to it when stung by the mosquito, begins in the field of scientific data and personal biographies and ends in the impersonal world to which belongs the two-chaptered history of the yellow-fever parasite. Insofar as these data are imbedded in the lives of these individuals, they are personal but hard facts. So long as they are tentatively suggestive of objects that would harmonize conflicting ways of cataloguing and treating the disease, they are in the minds of men as part of the structure of their ideas.

We must distinguish here between what belongs to the experience of the individual *qua* individual and what is in his mind and may be termed "subjective." In the former sense the observation may be called private because the investigator alone observes it. Indeed it may be such an instance that he alone can observe it, if, for example, it is his own ache or pain, or if no one else has seen it, and it is an instance that is not repeated. This circumstance does not abstract it from the world that is there, since these men are there in that world together with the events that take place in their lives. But, insofar as the experience suggests what is known of the relation of the mosquito to malaria and a possible parasitic organism that may be the cause of yellow fever, we are in the presence of an idea and of what we will call "subjective." Such an object is not as yet there and may never be there. It is an ideal object. Such objects have the same locus as erroneous objects after the error has been detected and are not to be confused, because they are placed in individuals' minds, with individuals' experiences, which are peculiar to them, but are objects in the world that is there. I am not ignoring the problems involved in this distinction. I am merely insisting that experimental science never take the position so common in philosophy, which confuses the two. To the experimental scientist the data of observation and experiment never lose the actuality of the unquestioned world because they can happen only in the lives of particular individuals or because they are fitted to serve in the mental processes of discovery. They are solid realities that can bridge the gaps between discredited theories and the discoveries of science.

It is the position of the positivist that what is observed is as a fact of experience, there in a sense in which it never can be false. He recognizes that there may be false inferences drawn from the observation or the experiment, but as a fact of immediate experience it simply is and therefore is not open to possible question. This assumption does not answer to the procedure of science, for whatever may be the theory of sensation, the scientist's observation always carries a content or character in what is observed that may conceivably be shown under other conditions to be erroneous, though the probability of this be very slight. In psychological terms, an observation is never a mere determination of a sensation (if there is any such thing in adult experience) but is a perception, and, whether all perceptions involve judgments or not, they are frequently illusory as in the perceptions of mirrored objects, and can never be free from the possibility of analogous errors.

What gives to the observation or experiment its validity is its position in the world that is there, that is not questioned. It is indeed carefully isolated from what has fallen into question, and this meticulous cleansing from all implications of the abandoned doctrine, and all as yet hypothetical interpretations, creates the impression of an experience which may not be subjected to any further question; but, as we know, there is no part or portion of the world that may not conceivably be the field of a scientific problem.

In the so-called exact sciences we seem to approach an object which is nearly free from all possibility of contingency—the physical particles. These particles are approximations to that which is unextended in space and time, but they carry a character—that of mass or of electrical energy—which does not approach zero, however minute it may become, and it is a character which is reached from numberless observations and not a little speculative theory. Furthermore, the procedures in our laboratories and observatories by which these characters are reached involve perceptual objects of the most complex nature, subject under other conditions to all sorts of conceivable questions. In other words, while the methods of mathematical analysis and extensive abstraction constitute a body of doctrines which in themselves are necessary, as long as the terms carry the same references, their applications are dependent upon their functioning within the problematic situations which arise in research science and appeal for their validity in practice to the court of observation and experiment.

The scientist's attitude is that of a man in a going concern which requires at various points readjustments and reconstructions. The success of the readjustments and reconstructions is found in the triumph over the difficulty, as evidenced by the fact that the concern continues to operate. He finds his tests in the parts of the whole which still operate. This does not imply that readjustments cannot be called for later at these very points to which he now appeals for confirmation of the success of his solutions of the immediate problems before him. Surrounding the most profound analysis of the structure of matter, and the widest survey of the galaxies of the heavens, lies the field of things within which experiment and observation take place without question, and which gives its validity to cosmologies and electronic theories of matter. It may seem a misnomer to speak of the world within which lie the observation and experiment as surrounding such hypothetical constructions as the electrical theory of matter or the galactic form of the universe, since these hypothetical constructions so far transcend, in the subatomic world or in the indefinite stretches of the heavens, all the world of objects which includes our observations and experiments. We seem rather to be islanded in a very minute region occupied by perceptual objects that are in their constitution vague, indeterminate, and incurably contingent, surrounded from within and from without by a universe, that is occupied by objects that approximate exactness of definition and necessity in their forms and changes. And yet the scientist, when he times microscopic oil drops as they move toward or away from charged plates, or when he measures the distances of photographed stars from one another before and during an eclipse, has not at all the attitude of a man perched insecurely upon obscure and adventitious data. The world that is there has taken up into itself all the order, definition, and necessity of earlier scientific advance. It is not there as hypothesis, insofar as the hypotheses have justified themselves in experiment, nor is it there as analyzed relations, events, and particles. These characters have passed into things, and for the time being at any rate, they are there unanalyzed, with the same authority as that of the so-called sensible experience. It is only necessary to emphasize again the distinction of the data as parts of the mental process of anticipating hypothetical objects, and as imbedded in the world of unquestioned reality in the experience of the individuals to whom the problem has come and who are trying to solve it, as well as in the impersonal world within which these individuals exist.

What renders such a statement of the world (not as known but as there) somewhat bizarre is that we enter the world of the scientist by the process of learning. In schools and institutions of higher learning we are taught the doctrines of modern science. Most of us take no part in the work of discovering what is there found out, but we acquire it by a process of learning, in which we may retrace some of the steps which research has followed, while in the main we accept it largely on faith in the men and their methods, especially faith in the checking-up of the results of certain individuals by all the others in the field. Scientific journalism as well as the daily press keeps us informed of the latest advances, and, having learned these facts, we say that we now know them. The world that stretches so far beyond our experience seems in this sense a world of knowledge.

It is true that all acquirement of information, insofar as it is more than a mere parrot-like facility in repeating what is read or heard, is a reflective process in which a problematic situation is met with discovery, though the hypotheses and their tests are those of others. Our own hypotheses and tests have to do largely with the competence of the sources upon which we draw. Admitting, however, all the criticism that the layman can bring to his education, this world of knowledge is evidently of quite a different character from the world that is there, the world that is seen and felt, whose reality is the touchstone of our discoveries and inventions and very different from the discoveries and inventions themselves, which are the knowledge par excellence of research science.

It is in the acquirement of information that the copy theory finds its explanation. There, what is known must answer feature for feature to its prototype. This field of so-called knowledge is that of the assimilation of the experience of others to one's own experience. There may be involved in it the discovery of these other experiences by the individual, and it is insofar knowledge, but the content of that which is said to be learned is not discovered in the sense in which the other has discovered it.

In its simplest form what takes place here is the indication to one individual by another of an object which is of moment in their co-operative activity. This gesture becomes symbolic when it arouses in the individuals the attitudes which reaction to the objects involves, together, generally, with some imagery of the result of that action. It becomes communication when the individual indicating the object takes also the attitude of the individual to whom he is indicating it plus that of his response, while the individual to whom the object is indicated takes the attitude of him who is indicating it. We call this taking of one another's attitudes consciousness of what we are doing and of what the other is doing, and we incorrectly apply the term "knowledge" to this. The mechanism and import of this social procedure will be discussed later. What I wish to point out is that this process in itself does not involve discovery, any more than does that of perception. When doubt and discrepancies arise in the process of communication, the necessity of establishing agreement between the symbols mutually used, and that which they symbolize and the results of the conduct they imply, calls for a one-to-one correspondence between the symbols and those things and characters symbolized in the experiences of the different individuals, and this gives rise to the theory of knowledge as an agreement between the state of mind and that which is known. Such a determination of mutual agreement in co-operative conduct is indeed essential, not only to this conduct, but to what is called "thinking" in the individual, but it is not a discovery of that which needs to be known. It is at most a part of the technique by which the discovery is made. When the discrepancy arises, we must discover what the import of the symbols is, and here real knowledge takes place. We find out what the other person is referring to—in common parlance, what he means—but the process can go on without discrepancies. The other indicates to us what is there, and our so-called consciousness of this need not introduce any reflective attitude in our conduct. To call the correspondence between the attitudes involved in pointing out a savage dog and the conduct which takes place "knowledge," whether one points it out to one's self or to another, is to give to "knowledge" an entirely different value from that involved in discovery.

In any education that is worthy of the name, what is acquired does go toward the solution of the problems that we all carry with us, and is the subject of reflection, and leads to the fashioning of new hypotheses and the appearance of new objects; but this takes place after the communication which is the mutual indication of objects and characters by the use of gestures which are common symbols, that is, symbols with identical references. The correspondence theory of knowledge has grown up around the recognition of the relation between that which the symbol refers to in the object and the attitudes of response in others and in ourselves. There is here a one-to-one correspondence, but the relation of these objects and their characters to what we can infer from them in the discovery of the novel element which meets our problematic situations is of an entirely different sort.

In this "meeting of minds" which takes place in conversation, learning, reading, and thinking, there are generally present problematic situations and discovery, though this is by no means always the case. If someone informs us that an expected acquaintance has arrived, there is no more of a problem, or discovery in the sense of a solution, than would be involved in the friend's appearing around the corner. The varied landscape and hurry of events that sweep us along in books of travel and adventure embrace no more of reflection than the travel and adventure in which we are involved. A great deal of learning is a direct following of indications, or a gradual taking-over of the form and technique of others that goes on without inference. A good deal of thinking even, notably much of reverie and also straight-away ordering of conduct in an unquestioned situation, may be free from dubitation and ratiocination. A field of concentrated inferential thought does include the common reference of symbols in conversation, writing, and thinking—that part of logic which has to do with the technique of communication either with others or with one's self—together with the epistemologies and metaphysics which have sprung from this and obscured it with their tangled and forest growth. Here lie the problems of successful reference to identical objects and characters through identical symbols mutually employed by different selves, and these problems are of peculiar interest and importance to those involved in the exact and mathematical sciences. These problems demand theories of definition and implication, insofar as this does not depend upon the concrete content of that to which reference is made.

The environment of living organisms is constantly changing, is constantly invaded with other and different things. The assimilation of what occurs and that which recurs with what is elapsing and what has elapsed is called "experience." Without anticipating a later discussion of the social nature of the self and of thinking, I shall claim that the analysis of experimental science, including experimental psychology, never operates in a mind or an experience that is not social, and by the term "social" I imply that in the thought of the scientist the supposition of his mind and his self always involves other minds and selves as presuppositions and as standing upon the same level of existence and evidence. It may be that the scientist, in a self-centered moment, might think away all else but his self and its thinking, but even if in imagination he succeeded in annihilating all save the dot on the *i*, its having any thoughts at all would depend entirely upon its preserving its previous habits of conversing with others and so with himself; and, as this precious hoard of past experience wore away under incessant use and decay, the dot would follow the *i* into nonentity. The dividend that I wish to see declared on this social nature of mind and the self is the equal immediacy that may attach to the assimilation of others' experience with that of our own. We so inevitably utilize the attitude of the other, which is involved in addressing ourselves and in attending to him, that we give the same logical validity to what he relates of his experience as that which we give to what we relate to ourselves of our own past experience, unless on other grounds we are occupying the seat of the critic. It has, of course, only the validity that attaches to a relation, and is one remove from the assurance that attaches to the so-called memory image. But this validity at this remove is all that we can claim for most of our memory. Memory images constitute but a minute part of the past that stretches out behind us. For most of it we depend upon records, which come back to one form or another of language, and we refresh our memory as surely in inquiring of a companion what took place on a certain occasion as in questioning ourselves. His testimony may not be as trustworthy as our own because of difference of interest and possible prejudice, but on other occasions for the same reason his testimony may outrank our own in reliability. While the actual image of the event has an evidential character that is peculiar, not infrequently it may be shown by the testimony of others to have been the product of imagination or to have been shifted from its proper place in the record. But still more fundamentally, the building-up of a memory record involves, in the first place, a social world as definitely as the physical world, within which the events took place, and involves, in the second place, experience which was actually or potentially social in its nature to the extent that whatever happens or has happened to us has its character over against actual or possible audiences or observers whose selves are essential to the existence of our own selves, the mechanism of whose conversation is not only as immediate as our replies but, when imported into the inner forum, constitutes the mechanism of our own thought.

I am anticipating the detailed presentation of this doctrine of mind to make clear my distinction between information and knowledge as discovery through inference. Information is the experience arising from the direction of attention through the gestures of others to objects and their characters, and cannot be called "knowledge" if that term is denied to perception as immediate experience under the direction of the attention springing from the organic interest of the individual. Perception is not itself to be distinguished from information, insofar as one uses a social mechanism in pointing out objects and characters to himself as another. The perceptions of a self may be already in the form of information. Logically stated they exist in a universe of discourse. Knowledge, on the other hand, deliberately fashions hypothetical objects whose reality it tests by observation and experiment. The justification for this is found in the actual disappearance of objects and their characters in the problems that arise in conduct.

Actually so much both of perception and of information is

shot through with reflective construction and reconstruction that it is difficult to disentangle them. It is, however, a part of scientific technique to accomplish this disentanglement. Observations and experiments are always in the form of information, even while they are being made, but they are scrupulously teased out from the web of inference and hypothesis. From this purity depart in varying degrees our perceptions as well as our information. It is a commonplace that one may be very well informed and do very little thinking, indeed be quite helpless over against a situation in which the information must be used to suggest or test hypotheses. The reliability itself of the observation or information, however, does call for a certain sort of verification, that of its repetition, either in the experience of the individual or in the mouths of other witnesses, and here, as above remarked, we find the source of the copy or correspondence theories of knowledge. Indeed, if information is knowledge, the copy theory of knowledge is entirely legitimate.

In presenting the world that is there as in some sense surrounding what is problematic, it was stated that what had in the past been approved by experiment and observation was taken up into this world and resided there as organized objects, things behaving toward one another in expected manners. Over against these unquestioned things lie the elements and relations of the working hypotheses of science. These are in a peculiar degree the objects of our knowledge. They are still lacking in complete verification. They are received only provisionally, and the objects which we constitute by means of them are complex hypotheses anticipating further tests in the use which we make of them. While they work, they pass as objects, but always with a proviso attached, which keeps the scientist's attention alive to possible departures from the result which the hypothesis implies. He is looking for such departures and eager to find them. In such far-reaching speculations as those regarding the structure of matter this field of knowledge is enormously extended, though it does not actually include the world within which the observation and experiment themselves take place, though the analysis which the investigation involves extends into the world of unquestioned things. For the

purposes of our calculations we state the apparatus of our laboratories, for example, in the same terms which we use in our hypothetical constructions and thus seem to bring them within the
scope of the investigation. But the scientist is in no doubt in regard to the distinction between the finding of fact and the hypothetical form in which he has stated things which are there, irre-
spective of the validity of the expressions into which they have
been translated. Such translations may be perhaps called "objects
of knowledge," though with the recognition that the success or
failure of the hypothesis, into the terms of which we have translated these unquestioned things and their processes, does not affect their reality in the observation or experiment. In this sense
there is no limit to the field of knowledge, for we may state the
whole universe in terms of such working hypotheses, if we only
remember the limits of this formulation. But it is also necessary
to recognize that the *raison d'être* for translation is found in the
function of the apparatus of experimental science and not in the
revelation of reality. What reveals this latter fact is the ineradica-
ble difference between the immediate concrete event to which
appeal is made in experiment and observation and any formulation of this in terms of a current working hypothesis. The actual
position of the spectral line, or of the photographic image on the
plate, is the brute fact by which the hypothesis is tested, and
there is no methodological relation between the exactly determined position of these and a resolution of them into, say, electrons. It is conceivable that this should be done, but it would
vastly confuse and delay the attainment of any knowledge from
the measurement and would have no conceivable connection with
getting that knowledge. To call such a translation "knowledge" is
to depart from the significance which the term "knowledge" has
in an experimental science.

The world, then, in which science operates has, at its core and
in a certain sense surrounding its findings and speculations, the
environment of immediate experience. At the point of its problems the immediate things are so analyzed that they may pass into
the formulations of the scientist's hypothesis, while the finding of
observation and experiment remains immediate experience, that

is, located in the surrounding borderland. It is these two aspects of the world of immediate experience that call for especial attention. From the standpoint of the discovery of the new, from the standpoint of research, the world of immediate experience is a core and seems to be reduced to the island of vague, indeterminate, and contingent data that are contrasted with the clear-cut, sharply defined, and necessary elements and events of scientific theory; an apparently incongruous situation, for the acceptance of the clear-cut, sharply defined, and necessary world is dependent upon the findings in the island of vague, indeterminate, and contingent data, the field of observation and experiment. It is an apparent incongruity that has given birth to much philosophic speculation.

That the incongruity is only apparent is fairly evident, since the scientist, out of whose method and its achievements it has arisen, is not aware of it. If it were presented to him in the terms just used, he would presumably reply that one cannot both have his cake and eat it; that, if one is in search of definition and certainty at a point in experience at which they have disappeared, it is but natural that the definition of the problem should exhibit this fact of their disappearance and that the very data which will serve in the verification of a hypothetical order of defined and necessary things must be themselves infected with indeterminateness and contingency; that the home of experimental medicine is in the hospital; that the gospel of science summons not the logically righteous but sinners to repentance. He would likely add, however, that because, before the discovery of the germ of yellow fever, the clinical picture of the disease was indeterminate and its incidence contingent, there would have been no justification in ascribing the same indeterminateness and contingency to the clinical picture of diphtheria—in other words, that the form in which the data appear in any one problem is pertinent to that problem alone.

But while the statement of the problem, together with the observation and experiment that are involved in verification, constitutes a core of immediate experience whose analyzed elements are indeterminate and contingent as compared with defined elements and necessary relations in a hypothetical scientific theory, these data do belong to objects in an immediate world that is a going concern, and as such is unquestioned. Such a world may be said to contain the problem within itself, and so to surround the problem. It has taken up into itself the solutions of past problems successfully solved. There is involved in it also a considerable apparatus of working hypothesis, which is not always distinguished from the world that is there. The distinction lies in the fact that back of the working hypothesis there is always a question mark, and in the back of the scientist's mind in using the working hypothesis lies the problem implied in its being only a working hypothesis. The world that is there is the common world within which the intelligent community lives and moves and has its being. In physical diameter it may be a small world as compared with the scope of physical hypotheses which in a logical sense it surrounds. Its logical compass of the hypothesis is shown in the data of observation and experiment that must be brought to bear upon the hypothesis before it can be established.

This compass of the problem, and the hypothetical solution of it, is logical insofar as the analysis involved in the problem, the inference involved in the formation of the hypothesis, and the sufficiency of evidence involved in observation and experiment all rest upon a world of things that is there, not as known, but as containing conditions of knowledge. But the world that is there includes and surrounds the problem in the sense that the problem is also there within the field of conduct, for, as has been indicated, the problem arises in the conduct of individuals and out of the conflict of acts which inhibit one another because the same object calls out mutually antagonistic responses. When these problems pass into the field of reflection, they are so formulated that they would occur in any experience, that is, they take on a universal form. Such a formulation is essential to the reflective process of their solution. Their actual occurrence, however, in the world that is there awaits the advent of the conflict of responses in the experience of some individual; and the solution as well, inasmuch as it departs from the common or universal habits of the community, must be an individual achievement before it can become the attitude of all and be thus universalized. So located in its historical setting, the problem is evidently as completely surrounded by the world that is there as the hole left by a name that has been forgotten is surrounded by all the other names and things and happenings by which one attempts its recall. But while occurrence of the problem and of its solution must be in the field of conduct of some one individual, the things and events that constitute its border are matters of common and undisputed validity. The problem must happen to an individual, it can have no other locus than in his biography, but the terms in which he defines it and seeks its solution must be universal, that is, have common import.

This location of the problem in the experience of the individual in its historical setting dates not only the problem but also the world within which that problem arises. For a world within which an essential scientific problem has arisen is a different world from that within which this problem does not exist, that is, different from the world that is there when this problem has been solved. The world of Daltonian atoms and electricity (which was considered a form of motion), within which appeared the problem of the ion in electrolysis and the breakup of the atom in radioactive substances, is a different world from that whose ultimate elements are particles of electricity. Such worlds dated by the problems upon whose solutions they have appeared are social in the sense that they belong to the history of the human community, since reflective thought is a social undertaking and since the individual in whose experience both the problem and its solution must arise presupposes the community out of which he springs.

It is the double aspect of these worlds that has been the occasion of so much philosophic speculation. On the one hand, they have provided the tests of reality for experimental science, and, on the other, they have successively lost their validity and have passed away into the realm of ideas. I have already indicated the scientist's rejoinder to this apparent assault upon his method. His method implies not that there has been, is, or will be any one authentic world that constitutes the core and envelope of his problems, but that there always have been, and are, and will be facts, or data, which, stated in terms of these different worlds by the individuals in whose experience they have appeared, can be recognized as identical; and that every world in which problems appear and are attacked by the experimental method is in such a sense a going concern that it can test hypothetical solutions. I have further insisted that as a scientist his goal in the pursuit of knowledge is not a final world but the solution of his problem in the world that is there.

There have existed two different attitudes toward these so-called facts or data. Because it has been assumed that old watchers of the heavens in the valley of Mesopotamia, and of Hipparchus, and of Tycho Brahe, and present astronomers possessed a certain identity, there has arisen a picture of the world made up of that which can be regarded as common to all, a picture made of abstractions. It is a picture through which we can look before and after and determine the date of Thales when he predicted an eclipse, and what eclipses will take place a thousand years hence. If we assign a metaphysical reality to these facts, then we reach a universe which has been the subject matter of popular and technical philosophies. If, on the other hand, we restrict ourselves to the determinations of experimental science, then we have nothing but the common indication of things and characters in a world that is there, an indication that abstracts from all but that which is there when a problematic situation has robbed it of some object and concentrates attention upon those characters and things which are the stimuli to mutually inhibiting responses. As I have already insisted, it is only in the experience of the individual, at some moment in that experience, that such a conflict can take place. Nonproblematic things are there for everyone. But while these observations took place in individual experiences, in the experiences of those individuals for whom these problems arose, it is the assumption of experimental science that a like experience would have arisen for any other individual whose experience had been infected with the same problem and that, insofar as successive problems have involved identical problematic elements, it is possible to identify the same observation in the experience of different individuals.

The Mesopotamian soothsayer who had hit upon the succession of the eclipses and enshrined it in the Great Saros and the Greek astronomer who by a scientific explanation of the eclipses had worked out the same succession, and the modern Copernican astronomer who substitutes the motion of the earth in its orbit for that of the sun about the earth and dates these eclipses still more accurately, were all observing the same phenomenon. For each there was a different world that was there, but in these worlds there were actual or identical observations of individuals which connect these worlds with one another and enable the later thinker to take up into his own the worlds that have preceded his. The common content of these observations, by means of which different worlds are strung together in human history, depends upon the assumption that different individuals have had or would have the same experiences. So far as there is any universality in these contents, it goes back to an actual or implied indication of the same things and characters by different individuals, in the same or like situations, that is, it goes back to implications in regard to social behavior in inferential processes, especially to the social nature of the knowledge or evidential import of observation.

However, the experimental scientist, apart from some philosophic bias, is not a positivist. He has no inclination to build up a universe of such scientific data, which in their abstraction can be identified as parts of many different worlds. The reference of his data is always to the solution of problems in the world that is there about him, the world that tests the validity of his hypothetical reconstructions. Nothing would more completely squeeze the interest out of his world than the resolution of it into the data of observation.

Part III

4

MIND APPROACHED THROUGH

BEHAVIOR—CAN ITS STUDY

BE MADE SCIENTIFIC?

WHEN the scientific method we have been describing was brought into the problems of psychology, it was recognized that association could not be maintained as the fundamental principle in terms of which they might be solved. We speak naturally of certain elements as associated with each other. Why are certain experiences associated rather than an indefinite number of others? When we come back to account for their strong association, we find we come back to attention, to interest. We are interested in certain connections, and these get fixed in our minds. We give our attention to certain elements in experience, and that fixes them in the order in which they occur. But association is itself something that needs to be explained. Why is there selection in experience? Consciousness is selective; we see what we are looking for. There is a character of conduct about experience that determines what the relations are to be, or at least determines between what elements the relations are going to lie. This

First published in *Movements of Thought in the Nineteenth Century,* ed. Merritt H. Moore (Chicago: University of Chicago Press, 1936), pp. 386–404.

recognition of the importance of conduct as determining what the connections shall be within experience itself is the characteristic of the latter psychology. It has gone under various names.

The older psychology was structural. That is, it took experience as we find it to pieces and found certain relations between the various elements of it. These it explained through association. The latter psychology is functional rather than structural. It recognizes certain functions of conduct. We get experiences of distant objects, and their import for us lies in what we are going to do about them. We are hungry, and we set about getting food. We have become stifled with the air in the room, and we get out-of-doors. We are acting, and in our actions we determine what the relations are going to be between the various elements in experience. The structure of the act is the important character of conduct. This psychology also is called motor psychology, as against the older psychology of sensation; voluntary psychology, as against the mere association of ideas with each other. Finally, the development of these different phases got expression in behavioristic psychology, which gives itself to the study of this conduct to which I have referred. It undertakes to approach the mind from the point of view of the action of the individual. As a psychology, behaviorism has turned away, then, from the category of consciousness as such. Accounts of consciousness had been largely static in character. There were certain states of consciousness, certain impressions—the imagery men had in a spiritual substance that was impressed from without by certain experiences. The senses were the organs through which impressions were made on a substantial entity called "consciousness," and they were made in a certain way, in a spatial, temporal order. Consciousness was dealt with as a sort of substance which received impressions. Following upon this came the fruitful statement of Professor James.

For James, consciousness is not to be regarded as a static substance receiving impressions from without. It is rather a stream that flows on. And this stream has various characteristics, those that we express by its substantive and transitive character. It gathers about a certain experience and then passes on from that to another. Another analogy that James used was of the bird that alights on one branch and then flies to another, continually moving from one point to another point. The transitive phases of experience are those answering to relations; the substantives are those that answer to what we call the "things we perceive." If one is speaking, relating something, and says "and" and then stops at that point, we have the feeling of being ready to go on to something else. The feeling is just as definite an experience as that of yellow or red, of hot or cold; it is an experience of "and," one that is transitive, that is moving on. And these experiences are qualitatively different from each other. If, instead of saying "and," the speaker said "but," we should have an entirely different attitude toward what is to follow. In fact, our whole grasp of what we are hearing or reading depends upon the feelings we have for these different relating articles. If we come upon a thought with a "though" in it, we have one attitude toward what is to come; if "also," a different attitude. We are ready for a certain sort of content. We have a definite sort of experience answering to these relations which appear immediately in experience.

There is also another very important phase of experience which Professor James emphasizes, that which is represented by the spotlight of our attention as over against the fringe of the experience. If one gives his attention to something immediately before him, there lies about this experience a fringe which is very important in the recognition, in the value of that to which one gives attention. For example, when we are reading, we often have the experience of a world which is not immediately before us. The eye in moving over the page has caught a word several lines below. We have to hunt for it to find out what it was. It lies there in the fringe of our immediate experience, and we are ready for it when it appears. But still more, these different attitudes which are connected with the different particles, the "and," "but," "though," "also," also represent the fringe. We are immediately considering something, but we are already going on to something else. And the beginnings of that something else to which we are going on are already forming in the realization of our experience. They are taking place, and they represent the fringe of experience which comes in to interpret that to which we are giving attention.

These conceptions of James's which were so fruitful for the psychological consideration of experience do represent definitely a process which gets its whole statement in our conduct. We are going on to something besides that which is before us. And the structure of the experience itself depends on what we are going on to do. If we see something, we have at least aroused in the organism a tendency to meet it, or to avoid it. And it is this experience of what the contact will be that comes in to give the meaning to that which we actually see. We are continually interpreting what we see by the something that is represented by possible future conduct. So, to understand what is appearing in experience, we must take into account not only the immediate stimulus as such but also the response. The response is there partly in the actual tendency toward the object and also in our memory images, the experiences that we have had in the past. And this relationship of the response to the stimulus is one of very great importance in the analysis of our perception.

Professor Dewey brought out that fact in a memorable article on the stimulus-response concept. He pointed out that the very attitude of being acted upon by a stimulus is continually affected by the response. We start to do something, and the process of doing it is continually affecting the very stimulus we have received. A familiar illustration is that of the carpenter who is sawing on a line. The response of the organism to the stimulation of the line is there to determine what he will look for. He will keep his eye on the line because he is continually sawing. The process of listening is a process in which we turn the head in such a way that we will be able to catch what we are hearing— the listening is essential to the hearing. The process of responding is always present, determining the way in which we shall receive our so-called "impressions." That is, the organism is not simply a something that is receiving impressions and then answering to them. It is not a sensitive protoplasm that is simply receiving these stimuli from without and then responding to them. The organism is doing something. It is primarily seeking for certain stimuli. When we are hungry, we are sensitive to the odors of food. When we are looking for a book, we have a memory image of the back of the book. Whatever we are doing determines the sort of a stimulus which will set free certain responses which are there ready for expression, and it is the attitude of action which determines for us what the stimulus will be. Then, in the process of acting we are continually selecting just what elements in the field of stimulation will set the response successfully free. We have to carry out our act so that the response as it goes on is continually acting back upon the organism, selecting for us just those stimuli which will enable us to do what we started to do.

Out of this stimulus-response concept has developed behavioristic psychology. Now, there are two ways of elaborating the general point of view belonging to behaviorism. One is to consider the process itself in an external way, or, as the psychologists would say, in an objective fashion; just consider the act itself and forget about consciousness. Watson is the representative of that type of behaviorism. The behaviorist of this type is interested simply in the act. He is particularly interested in the act as it can be observed from the outside. Watson is representative of the so-called scientific psychologist who is observing that which can be observed by other scientists. It is a type of psychology which was developed first of all in the study of animals. There you are necessarily shut off from any so-called field of consciousness. You cannot deal with the consciousness of the animal; you have to study his actions, his conduct. And these psychologists carried over the method of animal psychology into human psychology. They carried over from the study of animal psychology a new and, what seemed to be, a very fruitful conception, that of the reflex which could be, in their terminology, conditioned—the idea of the conditioned reflex.

This goes back, as most of you know, to Pavlov's dog. Pavlov was an objective psychologist who was studying the conduct of animals and endeavoring to make a complete statement of that conduct without bringing in the element of consciousness, that is, without having to refer to what was called "introspection" to understand the act. He took a dog and, by putting food in its mouth, collected the saliva that was secreted. If a piece of meat was brought within the vision and the sense of odor of the dog, then saliva was secreted. The dog was all ready to eat the meat, and the glands in the mouth were preparing for the process of mastication. Now, taking the dog in that way and bringing the meat, he was able to determine just what the effect of this stimulus was in the production of saliva. Then, when he brought the meat to the dog, he also rang a bell. He kept this up long enough so that the two experiences would be associated. He did not speak of it as the consciousness of the dog but in terms of the process of the nervous system; and then he found that, if he rang the bell without presenting meat, the same effect was produced, that is, the excess of saliva was secreted without actual sight or odor of the meat. This particular reflex, then, the secretion of saliva, was conditioned by the association of the sound of the bell with the smell of meat, so that, when the meat was not presented, the sound of the bell actually acted as a stimulus in place of the smell of the meat itself.

This conception of conditioned reflex is evidently one that can be carried over into all sorts of fields. I will refer to some of them by way of illustration. First, take the cry of a baby who, for example, is shown a white rat with which he has played before without any fear. If the rat was associated with a loud sound, the sound, especially if not seen, was a natural stimulus of fright. If the white rat was presented to the child when this sound was produced, the child became frightened; and afterward, when the rat was brought to the child and the sound not made, the child was still frightened of the rat. That is, this particular reflex of the fright of the child was conditioned by the sight and feel of the white rat. This can be carried over to a whole set of situations. Take another example from our conventions. We expect a person to act in a certain sort of way. We expect him to be dressed in a certain sort of way. This conduct goes along with a certain type of manners, and these manners go along with a certain type of individual. If we meet a person whose manners are not those we expect, we have an attitude toward this person as one who lacks those particular characteristics. We have conditioned our reflexes by these particular conventions, many of them entirely external and having nothing to do with the character of the man. We assume that certain manners represent courtesy. A great many of the manners have nothing to do with courtesy; but they have become so related to it that if we find a man who has rough manners, we perhaps do not expect courtesy of him. We can carry the conditioned reflex over into other fields, such as that of language, where we have a set of arbitrary symbols. Certain experiences call for certain responses. We can associate with each experience a certain arbitrary symbol, a sound, a written word, and we can become so conditioned that when we hear the sound, see the word, we get the attitude which goes with the original experience.

The conditioned reflex, then, was brought in and used by Watson in his attempt to analyze conduct. You see, this makes possible analysis without bringing in consciousness as such. You do not have to deal with introspection; you do not have to go back and ask the person what he thinks, or feels, what imagery arises before him. One studies simply his conduct and sees what the stimuli are that act upon him under certain conditions. And a sort of an analysis can be made of conduct from his standpoint. What is of importance in this method is that this type of analysis goes back to the conduct of the individual, goes back to his behavior, to what he is doing—not to what he is thinking and feeling, but what he is doing.

The other approach is that of Professor Dewey, also from the standpoint of the conduct itself, which carries with it the various values which we had associated with the term "consciousness." There arose at this time the question which James put so bluntly: "Does consciousness exist?" He wrote an article under that caption. Is there any such entity as consciousness in distinction from the world of our experience? Can we say that there is any such thing as consciousness which is a separate entity apart from the character of the world itself? The question, of course, is difficult to answer directly, because the term "consciousness" is an ambiguous one. We use it particularly for experiences which are represented, we will say, by going to sleep and waking up, going under and coming out of the anesthetic, in losing and regaining consciousness. We think of it as something which is a sort of entity, which is there, which has been, under these conditions, submerged and then allowed to appear again. That use of consciousness is not essentially different from the shutting-off of any field of experience through the senses. If one, for example, turns out the lights in the room, he no longer experiences the sight of objects about him. We say he has lost consciousness of those objects. But you would not speak of him as having lost consciousness. He is simply unable to see what is there. If he gets farther and farther away from a sound, or the sound becomes fainter and fainter, he loses consciousness of that sound; but he does not lose consciousness in the other sense. If we closed up his eyes, shut off his nostrils, ears, mouth, shut him off from a whole series of different stimuli, even those coming to him from the surface of the body and from the visceral tract, he would probably lose consciousness, go to sleep. There, you see, the losing of consciousness does not mean the loss of a certain entity but merely the cutting-off of one's relations with experiences. Consciousness in that sense means merely a normal relationship between the organism and the outside objects. And what we refer to as consciousness as such is really the character of the object. That is, the object is a bright object. If now you close the eyes, there is no bright object there any longer. We would say that you have lost consciousness of it, or simply that the bright object is not there. When the eyes are open, you have access to it; when the eyes close, you have access to it no longer. You see, there are two ways of looking at this having consciousness of the object. You may regard consciousness as a something that exists inside of the organism somewhere, upon which the influence of certain stimuli come to play. You may think of consciousness in terms of impressions made upon this spiritual substance in some unexplained fashion in the organism. Or you may think of it simply as a relationship between the organism and the object itself.

James in his answer to, or his attempted answer to, the question, "Does consciousness exist?" lays stress on the relation between the experience which the individual has had, that which has gone before, and that which follows after. He took the illustration of a person going to a house and entering the first room. Now, that room with its furniture is an experience. You can say that it enters his consciousness, if you like; and still you think of the room as something there with its pictures, furniture, whether he came in or not. If now, the house is burned up by a fire, this particular room with its walls and pictures and furniture has disappeared. The experience which the individual has had of the room, however, is not burned up. He remembers it, remembers how the pictures were hung upon the walls. This, says James, is a cross-section of two histories. And the cross-section is identical. The room belongs to the history of the house. It has been there since the house was built. It is in that particular history. When the person comes into the room, that particular room with its furnishings becomes a fact of his history. He had been elsewhere yesterday. He comes into that particular room, and that room is now a part of his experience; he goes out, and it is related to his former experiences. He had been in other houses, seen other furniture. He compares pictures. Each is related, you see, to his history. On the other hand, this room also belongs to the history of the house, of the architect, of the carpenter. Thus this question of consciousness, according to Professor James's statement, is a question in what history this particular entity, so-called consciousness, lies. From this point of view the consciousness a man has of the room is a cross-section of his history, while the room in the house regarded as a physical affair is a cross-section of the history of the house. Here we have a single cross-section answering to both of these series. Or there is a coincidence of cross-sections. In that case what we would say is that consciousness of the man in regard to the room in the house is nothing but a statement of that room as it lies in relationship to the man's own history: taken in its relationship to the history of the house, it is physical; taken in its relationship to the history of the man, it is a conscious event.

These two are not the only implications or meanings of consciousness. That which represents mental activities of one sort or another—of volition, of analytic and synthetic thought, of purpose and intention on the one side, and on the other side certain contents—has been stated in the past in associational psychology as states of consciousness. On the one hand, as we have seen, the active side can be stated in terms of conduct, while that which might be referred to as the passive definition of consciousness can be regarded as belonging to the object itself. So far as such a division of the spoils takes place, consciousness as a private affair seems largely to disappear. There are other phases of it, as I have said, which we will not refer to now; but these two phases, these two conceptions of consciousness, I wanted to bring out. One is an active, the other a passive, statement. And what I have said is that this active phase, that involved in the motor, volitional side, as well as in the process of analysis and discrimination, can at least be stated in terms of conduct, of the act; and this act can be stated in terms of the organism as such. What we refer to as the passive side, the content side, is found to lie in the object. It can be regarded, of course, in its relationship to the individual. It does belong to his history, though not simply to his history but to that of the object as well. When the man is in the room, the room is stated in terms of his experience. It is interpreted in terms of memory, of his own anticipation. But still it is a room. Without attempting to discuss the various philosophic implications of this, I am pointing out that on the one side you may speak of consciousness in its passive sense and at the same time be thinking of the object, the room itself.

In some fashion, if we turn to the active side we have impulse as perhaps the most fundamental phase of activity; and impulse certainly can be given a statement in terms not only of acts but also of the organism. There are various fundamental physiological impulses, that of attack and flight, those which gather about hunger and sex. These are lodged in the organism itself. James's celebrated theory of the emotions comes back to the reaction to the motor attitudes of the organism itself in conditions such as fear, hunger, love, joy. That is, fear represents our response to our tendency to run away; hatred represents our response to our tendency to attack. The emotions as such are responses of the organism itself to its own attitudes under certain conditions. These responses are expressed in more or less violent action.

What is further involved here, that which James did not bring out which Dewey does, is that there is always some inhibition of these actions. If one could actually run away before the terrifying object, if one could keep ahead of it, so to speak, give full expression to the tendency to run, one would not be terrified. If one could actually strike the very moment one had the impulse to strike, he would not be angry. It is the checking of the response that is responsible for the emotion, or is essential at least to the emotion. Even in the case of joy, if there were no hesitancy about the way in which one expressed his happiness, there would not be that emotion.

We can approach the emotion, then, from the point of view of our own responses to the attitudes of the organism. Here the James-Lange theory recognizes the visceral, as well as the motor, responses involved in the act. We spoke of the emotion as our effective experience of these attitudes. The impulse is something that can be stated at least in terms of the response of the organism itself. It is, of course, out of the impulse that desires, intentions, arise. What is added to the impulse and desire is the image of what we intend. And here we seem to find ourselves in what might be regarded in an unassailable field of consciousness as such. By its very definition imagery would be not the object, but some copy of the object; not the past event, but some memory of the past event; not future conduct, but a picture of future conduct. If you ask, now, where this image is, you would be at a loss to locate it. The easiest thing is to say that it is in consciousness, whether you put that consciousness in your head or say that you cannot locate it spatially. In any case, it is a relationship to something in your head. At least, the assumption of our physiological psychology is that an image answers to the excitement of certain nerve elements which have been excited in past experience. A cruder form of physiological psychology assumed that pictures of what had happened, were lodged, so to speak, in nerve cells, and, if the organism pressed a button, these pictures would come out. But further study revealed the fact that the nerve cells were no more than paths and junctions of paths. They should not be regarded as cubbyholes in which memory images or any other images are stored away. Just where the image is, is, I say, questionable. But you cannot say that the image is not in the objective world, for many of them are.

Here again I am not discussing the various philosophical implications of this analysis, but merely referring to the fact that every book you read has on every page of it your own memory images of words you have read before. Your own eye touches a line of print perhaps only twice. You take in only a relatively small portion of the actual printed line on the page, and the rest of it comes from memory images. I have referred to the attitudes represented by particles, adverbs, conjunctions, prepositions, the "ands," "buts," and "thoughs," which put us in certain attitudes of anticipation of a certain sort of word that is expected. The context we have gone over gives us a pretty definite anticipation of what is going to be there, so that our mind fills in from past experience. We have not time enough to read each word by itself. There are people, children particularly, whose eyes are bound to the page. They have to read word by word; and if they cannot be freed from it, they are slow readers and can accomplish little in this medium. What we have to do is to make most of what we read a contribution of our own. We fill out what we see. That, of course, is evident not only at the time. You suddenly find yourself in a snarl. You see something which is not there. The proofreader has trained himself to notice the words and letters and not the sense.

Well, that is true not only of the printed page. The faces of our acquaintances are largely filled in by our memories of them. We notice very little in the outlines of a face with which we are familiar. The rest of it comes from memory images. If we are seeing a person for the first time, we regard the features in detail, look at the whole face; but even then what we see in each case is in some sense a sort of type. You could not tell what the types of the human face are that you recognize. Yet, there is something about every human face that is in some sense typical, and you fill in there. A considerable part of our perceptual world, the world existing "out there," as we say, is made up out of mental images, the same stuff that comes before us in revery, only in that case we are looking at it from the point of view of imagination. These images actually go to make up objects we see and feel.

The imagery cannot all be put into a consciousness that is distinct from the world about us. It goes back, as I say, to James's question as to whether consciousness as such exists. We have again a type of experience which from one point of view belongs to the external world and from another point of view to the history of the particular individual. Without attempting to discuss the question further, I simply want to emphasize the fact that the former is the passive side of our experience, which we ordinarily term "consciousness," but which under various conditions we do not consider as consciousness but as the object. If you should take away the so-called imagery from what you say you immediately see, from that which answers to what falls on the retina, to the sounds you actually hear, you would find that you have bare skeletal elements; most of the flesh and blood, of the content of the world about you, would have been taken out. What you call the meaning of it will go also. The distinction you make between what we call consciousness and what we call the world is really a functional distinction. It is not a static one. You cannot, then, cut off any particular field of content in our ordinary experience of the world and say, "This is my consciousness as such. This is a certain stuff which belongs inside of my head and not to the world." There are times at which it is inaccessible. But the printed page you see you hand to your friend, who reads it also. A large part of what he reads is his mental image, and what you read is your mental image; and yet you say you are reading the same page.

If one approaches the problem of psychology simply from the standpoint of trying to find out what takes place in the experience of the individual as an individual, you get a surer clue if you take the man's action than if you take certain static contents and say these are the consciousness of the man and that these have to be approached by introspection to be reached. If you want to find out what the man is doing, what he is, you will get it a good deal better if you will get into his conduct, into his action. And you come back there to certain of his impulses, those impulses which become desires, plus his mental images, which from one standpoint are his own but from another standpoint represent certain of his past experiences, or part of his future experience. So-called objective or behavioristic psychology undertakes to examine the acts of the man from outside without trying to get them by introspection as such, although introspection, as I shall show, has a certain definite meaning even for behavioristic psychology.

I have already referred to accessibility. There are certain very genuine experiences which belong to physical objects and yet which are accessible only to the individual himself, notably, a toothache. There is an aching tooth, no question about it; and yet, though others can see the tooth and the dentist can tap it, it aches only for the individual in whose head it is located, and much as he would like to, he cannot transfer that ache to somebody else. There are, of course, a whole series of experiences of which that is typical, which are accessible alone to the person having them. What I want to point out is that you have no question about the aching tooth, no question about the members of your body. Your hands have certain definite characteristics for you. They can be seen by others, but you have the only inside approach to them. And that feeling is one which is just as genuinely a feeling of an object as is that of a table. You feel the table, and you feel your hand. Your hand is softer and warmer than the table. Your hand is not as large as the table. All sorts of distinctions can be made. You are feeling your hand as a physical object, but one having a peculiar character, and that character which it has is one which is accessible only to yourself. Nobody else can get that feel of your hand which you have, and yet that does not make you regard it as less genuinely there. You do not put the feel of your hand in your brain. You may assume that that feel is dependent on what is in your brain, but what the hand is involves the actual character that it itself has. Well now, if anybody else comes up and feels the table, he has a sense of the same table;

but this approach to the feeling is peculiar to the individual. The mere fact of the accessibility to the experience you have of parts of your own body does not lodge them, so to speak, in a consciousness which is located in the brain or somewhere else. It simply means certain objects are accessible to you which are not accessible to anybody else.

There are various phases of nature which lie betwixt and between. Take the beauty of a landscape as an instance. From one point of view it is the response of the individual himself and seems to be accessible only to him, but the painter and the poet succeed seemingly in making it accessible to those who enjoy the picture and the poem. This is more or less debatable. All I want to insist on is that mere accessibility is not in itself evidence of something that belongs to a consciousness. It is much safer, even in such fields as these, to come back to the conduct of the individual if you are going to study him than to come back to something he reports to you by means of introspection.

Without discussing the various logical and metaphysical snarls involved, we will say that the space about us is public. We are all living in the same spatial world and have experiences of the same world. When it comes to a question of color, the thing seems to be dubious, for one man does not see certain colors which another man does see. We seem to have a case there where the color is private while the space is public. And yet, you cannot possibly separate the space from the color. And, while you may say that the space which one person perceives has a different degree of brightness from another, we would not hesitate to call those spaces public. But there is also something definitely private. Take a man's intentions, for example. We do not know what he is going to do. He has an advantage over us on that account. This is notable in the case of warfare, or in the case of a man who is making a feint when he is boxing. The intent which the person has is not evident to the other person. He may make a guess at it, but it is only the person who is going to strike who knows definitely what he intends to do. This is also true of intent not simply in such a situation but in all our intercourse with other people. We have a pretty genuine idea, as a rule, of what we are going to say when we are talking; but the person to whom we are talking probably does not. He may guess from past experience; but, as a rule, what a person is going to say would in some sense present a problem to the other person while it would be present in the mind of the one who is going to say it. It is not public property.

That is also true in very large degree of certain types of mental imagery. There is a field, a sort of an inner forum, in which we are the only spectators and the only actors. In that field each one of us confers with himself. We carry on something of a drama. If a person retires to a secluded spot and sits down to think, he talks to himself. He asks and answers questions. He develops his ideas and arranges and organizes those ideas as he might do in conversation with somebody else. He may prefer talking to himself to talking to somebody else. He is a more appreciative audience, perhaps. The process is not essentially different in these two cases, that is, of thinking and of talking to somebody else. It is essentially the same sort of a process. But the activity, such as it is, is not of the same sort. When you do talk to yourself, you do not ordinarily do it out loud. Sometimes you do talk out loud, and somebody else hears you. But, as a rule, when you talk to yourself, you depend on subtle motor and muscular methods of articulation. Supposing that conversation which takes place by such imagery as that is only accessible to the man carrying it on. He takes different roles. He asks questions and meets them; presents arguments and refutes them. He does it himself, and it lies inside of the man himself. It has not yet become public. But it is a part of the act which does become public. We will say he is thinking out what he is going to say in an important situation, an argument which he is going to present in court, a speech in the legislature. That process which goes on inside of him is only the beginning of the process which is finally carried on in an assembly. It is just a part of the whole thing, and the fact that he talks to himself rather than to the assembly is simply an indication of the beginning of a process which is carried on outside.

Well now, that process of talking to one's self—of thinking, as we say—is a process which we speak of as involving discrimination, analysis. Analysis may be a very physical affair. We can smash up an object by means of a hammer and analyze it. We can take it into the laboratory and use more subtle methods of disintegration. But we are analyzing the object either way. We may analyze a thing for somebody else. He wants to find something in it which he cannot see, and we point it out. We point at the particular part of the object he is to take hold of. Now, that pointing is a process of analyzing the object. For him it is the selection of some part of the object to the neglect of other parts, so that he can get hold of it. Indicating by the finger is just as much analysis as breaking up by a hammer or by chemical reagents. There are various ways of pointing at things. There are people among certain native tribes who can point at things by their own features, their lips, eyes, the way in which they turn their head. I have seen people carry on rather elaborate conversations that way. The ordinary way in which we do our pointing is by means of vocal gestures. Pointing of the finger is a physical gesture.

Words are gestures by means of which we indicate things; and, just insofar as we indicate things by means of our gestures, we are analyzing just as really as if we put them into a test tube of acid or as if we took our hammer and smashed the thing up to find out its different elements. It is a process of analyzing some element by means of our conduct. Thinking, as such, can at least be stated. I am finding all sorts of problems which can be brought up. Even the most recondite intellectual processes come back to the things we do; and, of course, for an intelligent human being his thinking is the most important part of what he does and the larger part of that thinking is a process of the analysis of situations, finding out just what it is that ought to be attacked, what has to be avoided. We have to take the situation to pieces, think it out; and that process may be a process of pointing or of vocal gestures which indicate certain elements in it. Those vocal gestures are the indication of the elements which will lead to certain responses. One of the principal differences between a dog and a man is that, as a rule, we cannot point out to a dog what we want him to give attention to. If you can find out what the dog's interests are, you may be able to point something out to him; but if you want to have the dog tell time, you can never get him to look at a watch and notice where the hands of the watch are. Even if a person does not know what a watch is, you can indicate to a human individual the face of the watch and get him to see the meaning of it. That part of our thinking process, the power of analysis by means of gestures, is the most important part; and we can say, if you like, that we carry that on inside of our heads. The sense in which we do that is to use these pointers, these vocal gestures, the words which we utilize, to point out certain features in a situation; but we do that inside of ourselves. Occasionally, people do hear us. We talk out loud. But as a rule they do not hear us, and we reply to the gestures that we make with other gestures; and in that fashion we get our plan of action made for ourselves.

Well, that is the way in which behavioristic psychology, if carried out consistently enough, can cover the field of psychology without bringing in the dubious conception of consciousness. There are matters which are accessible only to the individual, but even these cannot be identified with consciousness as such because we find we are continually utilizing them as making up our world. What you can do is to get at the organism as something that you can study. Now it is true that you cannot tell what a man is thinking about unless he chooses to tell. If he tells, you have access to that as well as he has; and you know what he is going to do, and it can enter into your own conduct. You can get at your own conduct and at the conduct of other people by considering that conduct in an objective sort of fashion. That is what behavioristic psychology is trying to do, trying to avoid the ambiguity of the term "consciousness." And what is of importance about this psychology is that it carries us back, as I have said, to the act as such. It considers the organism as active. It is out of the interest in the act itself and the relationship of thought to the act itself that the last phase of more recent philosophy dealt with above, that is, pragmatism, arises. Out of the type of psychology which you may call "behavioristic" came a large part of the stimulus for a pragmatic philosophy. There were several sources, of course; but that is one of the principal ones.

Part IV

5

THE PROCESS OF MIND

IN NATURE

*Effect of Modern Physical Science
on the Concept of Mind*

THREE logically disparate factors have largely influenced the conception of mind entertained since the period of the Renaissance: the bifurcation of nature, the relation of the object of experience to the experiencing individual, and the location of contents in experience which have no definite place in an abstract physical environment.

The conception of nature which was introduced by Galileo, through his doctrine of dynamics, reduced it to a statement of matter in motion. Matter was conceived of as that which effectively occupies space, that is, resists the tendency of anything else to occupy the place which is occupied by the body in question; possesses inertia, that is, the tendency to remain in the state of rest or motion in which it is found; has mass, that is, has a quantity which can be measured, given equal density with other things with which it is compared, by the amount of space occupied; and has mobility, that is, the ability to pass from one place

---

First published in *The Philosophy of the Act*, ed. Charles W. Morris (Chicago: University of Chicago Press, 1938), pp. 357–420.

to another provided its inertia is overcome. There were, of course, other characters of matter which had to be recognized, notably the characters of chemical substances, heat, and those of electricity. Heat was resolved into motion of the physical particles of which the objects of experience are made up. The electrodynamic theory of matter undertakes to state chemical characters in terms of the changes which result from the structure of so-called chemical substances out of the two sorts of electrical particles, positive and negative, which it assumes are the ultimate constituents of matter. If nature is ultimately made up of positive and negative particles of electricity which possess mass and inertia, the only other character which it has, apart from the aggregations of these particles and their motions, is that of the differences of the positive and negative particles, which can be stated in terms of mass, volume, and motion.

The more or less tacit acceptance of this doctrine that the reality of material nature can be reduced to terms of extended matter in motion carries with it the implication that these characters of nature which are not those of the effective occupation of space, motion, and the results of these, such as momentum, and in general what are called expressions of energy, do not reside in nature. Color, sound, temperature as felt, odor, taste, as well as all the affective characters of things, could not reside in nature in its reality. The simplest treatment of such characters was to place them in mind, as the effects on mind of the action of a nature which was nothing but matter in motion.

The organism that mediates between nature and mind is itself a natural object and must, therefore, on this conception be stated in terms of matter in motion. The study of it in its mediation between nature and mind can show the natural processes which go on within it when these characters of things, which must be regarded as mental, arise. Thus there arose a physiological psychology. It found itself with a further task upon its hands. These so-called secondary qualities of things could not be separated from the primary qualities—those answering to the real characters of natural objects (effective occupation of space, mass, inertia, and motion), at least insofar as our perception of them was concerned. The same sort of a biologic process goes on in our perception of things as extended and inert and moving that goes on in our perception of things as colored and sounding. If color and sound were mental, why should not extension, inertia, mass, and motion be mental? And Berkeley drew the logical conclusion that nature in all its characters is mental. Hume pointed out that, while we might be forced into taking this position by logical procedure from the premises from which we started, we could not preserve this belief the moment we stopped philosophizing; and science continued to pursue its account of nature unperturbed by the difficulties which its generally accepted doctrines had upon the theory of mind.

What I wish to point out is that the theory of mind found itself obliged to make a place for contents which, for immediate experience, belong as definitely to the outer object as those characters which science conceives to be the nature of the things that are entirely independent of mind.

The mechanical theory of nature which has dominated modern science seems bound to state the relations of minds to matter and of matter to minds in terms of mechanical processes which by their nature leave no place for mind and so-called mental processes. As all mechanical processes can be exhaustively stated in terms of matter in motion, there is no place in its equations for the so-called states of consciousness which became necessary to state the contents of the secondary qualities of things—the effects which objects have upon the mind through the medium of the organism, the imagery which could not be stated in terms of matter and motion, together with the affective characters of things. The logical account of such a situation appeared in a parallelism which assumed conscious states accompanying certain material conditions of the nervous system regarded as a part of a mechanical whole. These conscious states could have no place in the mechanical description of nature. The connections between mind and things became simply that of the simultaneous appearance of certain physical particles in motion and certain conscious states, the former being the conditions for the appearance of the latter. One of the results of this conception has been to translate all conscious activity into states of consciousness which merely accompany the nervous phases of motions in the body. In general, the connections between the experiencing individual and the things experienced—conceived in their physical reality—were reduced to a passive conditioning of states of consciousness by a mechanical nature.

Into such a mind was carried, as previously indicated, whatever in nature could not be stated in terms of matter in motion. This included not simply the so-called secondary qualities but also the whole content of imagery which goes so largely into our perceptual objects, and especially all the aesthetic and other emotional and affective characters of things. The result of this was to force upon the mind the presentation of the world of actual experience with all its characters, except, perhaps, the so-called primary characters of things. Mind had, therefore, a representational world that was supposed to answer to the physical world, and the connection between this world and the physical world remained a mystery.

Pragmatic Reactions to a Scientific Inspired Dualism

The unsatisfactory result of this division of nature between mind and the physical universe led to the objective idealistic systems in which nature was taken entirely into mind, not as the representation of an actual or possible reality outside of mind, but as the sum total of reality, the subject-object relation existing not between mind and what lies outside of mind but between different phases of the spiritual process of reality. The undertaking failed, for one reason, because it identified the process of reality with cognition, while experience shows that the reality which cognition seeks lies outside of cognition, was there before cognition arose, and exists independent of cognition after knowledge has been attained.

Two modern trends of thought have appeared seeking to recognize the independence of nature and cognition and, at the same time, to return to nature the content which had been placed in mind. Realism has reduced cognition to an awareness by mind of all the aspects of nature, asserting that all of these—secondary qualities as well as the primary qualities—simply enter into mind and depart from it without being affected by the contact. The other trend, that of pragmatism, regards cognition as simply a phase of conduct, denying any awareness to immediate experience. It is the relation of mind to body from the standpoint of pragmatism that I wish to consider.

Two pragmatic doctrines have definite bearing on the relation of mind and body. These are (*a*) that the so-called percept in immediate experience is the object, there being no mental state of awareness answering to the object, and (*b*) that reflection, including cognition and thought, is a phase of conduct within which conflicts between reactions are met by reorganization of the environment and of the tendencies within the organism to respond to it—the validity of the reorganization, and therefore of the object of reflection, being tested by the success of the reconstruction. It follows from these doctrines that in immediate experience there is no mind, in the sense of reflection, the relation that answers to that between mind and body being that between a social animal and its environment.

This relation will lie between things in the environment (or the environment as a whole of which the things are constituent parts) and the individual as another thing. The dividing line between the environment and the individual in immediate experience is functional. The individual acts, and that upon which and within which he acts is the environment. The hair that he has cut, the tooth that he has pulled, and the foot that he bathes belong to the environment. The organism that effects these processes is the individual. The contents of the things in the environment are their colors, sounds, tactual qualities, odors, and tastes, their beauty or ugliness, their meanings and values, including characters of past and anticipated experience that go to make up the object. The content of the individual in immediate experience seems to shrink to the efforts and strains involved in attention, postures, and movements of the body, with such boundaries as actual or anticipated contacts define. This statement has reference to what are called physical things as distinguished from social things. The social environment is a narrower one than the physical environment. The physical environment also includes the social environment, that is, social things are also physical things. But persons, or selves, are things in our immediate experience, and the individual in that social environment of things is himself a person, or, better, a self. The same distinction between things in the environment and the individual holds here that holds between the physical things and the physical individual in whose environment they lie. This amounts to saying that social objects, or persons, are immediately present in experience, or, in customary psychological language, are perceived. The social individual or self exists in his efforts and tensions in social conduct toward the social individuals that have all the characters that belong to them as neighbors, members of families, or other groups. They have besides these characters those of physical beings. The boundaries of social things and of the individual as a social being are determined by contacts in social conduct. Social conduct presupposes a group of animals whose life-processes are determined in considerable part by the actions and the consequences of these actions on the part of one another. These actions called out by the peculiar characters, postures, and gestures of the different members of the group constitute social conduct. It is important to note that in immediate experience the environment and the things within it extend both spatially and temporally, that things are therefore at distances from one another, that they change qualitatively and move, and that these relations of extension in immediate experience are always with reference to the here and the now of the individual that answers to the particular environment. Things exist immediately at a distance, and they occur immediately before and after one another. Spatiotemporal intervals are judged and criticized in reflective experience, but, in order that they may be judged, they must exist immediately and in the organization centered about the here and now of the individual implied in the experience.

The other characters of things besides those of extension, those in psychological terminology termed sensuous, and the meanings and other values, are subject also to the organization of environment and individual. In immediate experience the import of this determining nature of the relation between environment and the individual appears in the differences in all the foregoing fields which results from the different positions, sensings, and acts of attention of the individual. The individual opens his eyes, changes his position, and directs his attention, so that the characters of things may become different. Furthermore, the meanings and other values of things are relative to the particular act in which in immediate experience the individual exists as an agent. The action of the individual in all the fields of so-called experience is selective. The contents of things in immediate experience are in a considerable degree dependent upon the individual as acting, as an agent. In this sense the environment of the individual is relative to the individual. If an individual sees two objects where there should be one, or the reflection of an object in a mirror, or a circular object as an ellipse, or a straight stick in water as bent, he may turn his head, or move to another position, or move the object so as to see the object as it is; but he feels no inclination to place the double objects, the reflection, the elliptical coin, or the bent stick, in himself, except insofar as the inclination may be logical, owing to a reflective philosophical attitude. In immediate experience these so-called illusory aspects of things are in the environment. In most cases they are adequate stimuli to normal conduct. They are so genuinely in the environment that, when we undertake for doctrinal reasons to place them in a consciousness, we find that they take the whole environment with them. We are not disturbed by having two distinguishable visual images occupy the same place at the same time in inadequately focused binocular vision. The afterimage or aftervision of a bright object may be placed at different places in the environment, and we may thus vary its dimensions. We are in the same domain of perceptual experience when we recognize the content of memory imagery in the object. We see on the printed page words, light from which never reaches the retina. We see the face of an acquaintance, only to discover that a so-called image has filled out the indistinct vision of another person. We see things hard and cold and smooth and succulent, and there are sensuous contents present that bear the same immediate relation to the individual as do those of vision. When we recall the tenuous images of a past vivid experience, these images are out there somewhere in the environment, in no way disturbing the vision of things we say to be actually there. In dreams such images occupy the whole field of immediate experience, and in hallucinations they compete with other experiences for what we call reality.

The Act in Relation to Distance and Contact Experiences

Our primary adjustment to an environment lies in the act which determines the relation between the individual and the environment. An act is an ongoing event that consists of stimulation and response and the results of the response. Back of these lie the attitudes and impulses of the individual which are responsible for his sensitiveness to the particular stimulus and for the adequacy of the response. It is the adequacy of the response which in immediate experience determines the reality of the stimulation. Things are not real as seen or heard or smelled; they are real as actually or potentially experienced through contact.

In immediate experience events are present in a temporal as well as a spatial thickness. The psychological term for this temporal thickness is the specious present, and this involves an actual duration of things in which, to use Whitehead's expression, an event extends over other events that make it up. A reflective analysis of this duration breaks it up into instants without temporal thickness that have no relation except that of succession. A group of such instantaneous events can have no inner durational connection with one another, such as that of whole and parts, since each event has ceased to exist before the next arises. We replace in reflection the actual wholeness of durational experience in two ways: either by a thought-conspectus of the succession of instantaneous events or by the conception of a persistent force which finds expression in the events. The conspectus reveals uniformities of change, which become the scientific content of the concept of force. The reflective judgments that belong to such a scientific procedure are on a different logical level from judgments of perception, though the term "judgment" in immediate experience is probably a misnomer. There is, however, in immediate experience, with its actual durational connection of stimulation and response, a fulfilment of the former by the latter that I take to be the basis for the reflective judgments of reality. The response is functionally the reality of the stimulation; the end of the act the reality of its beginning. The stimulation implies the response. The fundamental expression of this is found in the location of the reality of the distance experience in contact experience. The completion of any act called out by a distant object would, if all its tendencies were carried out, eventuate in contact objects.

The contacts which are the realities of distant experience are, however, the means for further action, either in the completion of fundamental biologic acts, such as that of eating, or in the mediation of more complex acts. Contacts in immediate experience are in themselves never ultimates. If we set them up in a mechanical science as the reality of the world, we must remember that in conduct they always look beyond themselves to further conduct.

Recurring to the values of the different elements in the perceptual object, it is to be noted that distance stimulation has in it the promise of later experience that justifies or validates it. This later actual or imaged experience is of the same nature as that of the contacts which we are immediately experiencing, in which the distance characters disappear. The world of reality that we assume to be existing at any one moment of experience is, then, of a contact character—things that could be handled, or the divisions of these contact objects which science sets up as its hypotheses. Insofar as our judgments of perceptions and those of reflection place these contact contents in the objects, they have necessarily removed their distance characters, for the contact character implies that the distance has been surmounted and that the result of the act has substituted the realities of contact for the beginnings of the act. It is true that we can generally see what we feel, but the sight is only an invitation to manipulation. However, this vision of the object that we at the same time manipulate is of fundamental importance. It is the maximum vision toward which all visions of the object expand as it approaches us or we approach it and is that visual content which does not perceptibly vary in the perceptual field. Even this visual content varies as we permit the eyes to approach or withdraw from the object, but within the field of manipulation the import of these variations disappears because we can always identify the seen thing with the dimensions of the felt thing. Having made this identification, we proceed to use the richer content of visual experience to identify the same object in different positions and the finer discriminations of vision for the higher degrees of exactness in measurement. The processes of so-called exact measurement are indirect and depend upon the probabilities of variation, but back of them lies the assumption of an application in actual or imagined contact experience of some sort of a unit measure. This contact extensional experience remains the same wherever we are, while visual experience varies with every change of position. The uniform space of a measurable world is, therefore, a contact space.

It is further evident that such a uniform space must also be a timeless space, for we assume the completion of all the acts which perception implies, and, if they are all completed, the time which their normal carrying-out would involve must be annihilated. A uniform space can be obtained only by the sacrifice of time. But time does exist. What has been termed "judgment of perception" (the implication that a contact experience does or will validate the distance stimulation) does not in immediate experience remove the distance—say, visual—character of the object from the realm of existence or even substitute the contact character, which validates it, for the distance content. The colored, sounding, odorous world is there. The individual, apart from the effort involved in reaction, seems to be represented by the "here" and the "now" and by the control which he exercises over the contents of the environment through selective attention. This orientation and selective attention are, however, but phases of the act. There is nothing in this nature of the individual which suggests transferring any of these characters of an environment which is there at a distance to the individual. The fact that what is felt is not, as felt, colored or sounding, does not suggest that color and sound are not in the object as it exists at a distance, though the ultimate contact experience is the justification for the action which they call out—for their being, in other words, distant objects. Nor is there any problem in the relation of the distant stimulations to the individual in immediate experience. What is later interpreted as an epistemological problem appears here simply in getting adequate stimulation and in hesitancy to response in the presence of different stimuli. Nor is there any suggestion in the success or failure of the act that what are later termed the logical and affective values of the objects can be transferred to the individual. There is at this stage in conduct no problem of mind and body. So far as the self exists at this stage, it is a part of the environment like the body, or it is the active individual in social responses.

The Function of the Self in Conduct

The essential condition for the appearance of what has been conceived of as mind is that the individual in acting with reference to the environment should, as part of that action, be acting with reference to himself, so that his action would include himself as an object. This does not mean that the individual should simply act with reference to parts of his organism, even when that action is social, but it does mean that the whole action toward the object upon which attention is centered includes as a part of this action a reaction toward the individual himself. If this is attained, the self as an object becomes a part of the acting individual, that is, the individual has attained what is called self-consciousness—a self-consciousness that accompanies his conduct or may accompany a portion of his conduct.

There are two things to point out here: one is the function of making the individual himself an object in his own act; the other is the mechanism of this conduct.

The making of an individual an object to himself is not found in immediate experience. In immediate experience the introduction of one's self into the act is hampering and embarrassing. In conduct within which readjustment must take place before the act is completed, there is at least a place for such an involution as that of making one's self an object in acting with reference to the environment. Given such a situation, in which because of conflict, readjustment must take place, the function of making one's self an object seems to lie entirely in so pointing out to one's self the different characters of things that a readjustment of responses will become possible. Control in intelligent conduct takes place through attentive selection of stimulations. There is no direct control of the response. Control is secured through the finding and emphasizing of the appropriate stimuli in their relation to one another. Selective attention may be given to different features of the objective field, without the individual pointing them out to himself. Under these conditions a readjustment may take place without what we term "reflection." This is the solution of problems by trial and error.

In the trial-and-error solution studied in the experimentation on animals, we find that a number of trials with failure are necessary to inhibit the wrong response, while the intelligent human individual does not simply repeat the response that has failed. In the experience of the lower animal the memory image of the failure does not arise to inhibit the response until repeated failures have taken place. The human individual in indicating himself as carrying out an act provides a suitable content for the attachment of the memory image. This is to be recognized not only in experimentation upon animals but also in our own conduct. There is a considerable field of our conduct where we also proceed by trial and error. This is true in the acquirement of a great deal of our manual skill in games or in the control of such mechanisms as the bicycle or musical instruments. We gain the control after repeated failures which we can correct only gradually. What appears upon analysis of this conduct is that the individual cannot indicate to himself exactly what he is doing, or what is the same thing, exactly to what stimulus he is responding. He does not present himself as responding to a specific stimulus in a definite fashion. The identification of the self with a certain act serves to isolate it and render it definite, so that the results of past experience enter into it to control its further expression. In the situation noted above, in which one acquires manual skill by the trial-and-error process, what is experienced is that one cannot tell what one has done that has been responsible for one's failure. The individual is unable to identify himself with a specific response. He repeats the same inept motions until gradually he finds himself adjusting himself to the field of stimulation, responding to characters that he has not noted, but still without being able to identify himself with a specific response or to determine just what it is to which he responds in his successful acts. But where stimulus and response define each other clearly, as in leaping over a ditch, or in pounding with a hammer, there he can indicate to himself the stimulus, the self to which it is indicated appearing in the tendency to leap or strike. When the tendency is for the moment inhibited, the results of past experience arise and he finds himself noting to himself elements in the object which were present in the earlier experience, at the same time identifying himself with the varied response, or tendency to respond, which these characters call out, saying, "I cannot jump it," or "The hammer is out of my reach." The effect is not simply to leave the individual in an attitude of defeat against a forbidding environment as a whole, but with a specific object (an unjumpable ditch, a hammer out of reach) while the rest of the environment is freed from this atmosphere of defeat and is ready to call out other reactions. There is a further result, namely, that the ongoing process of advance to a distant goal (such as driving the nail) is present as a self that is seeking to advance in some other way than by direct progress, that is seeking to drive the nail by some other method than by an immediate seizing of the hammer.

The general result is that other tendencies to action are freed to sensitize us to additional stimulations. The psychological elements of an object are a definite stimulation answering to a definite response plus the results of past experience of the response. The object is a collapsed act. It is when these results of past experience have attached themselves to the stimulations that we find a field of objects within which we can act intelligently. The conflict, together with its inhibition, breaks up these objects, and it is not until new objects have arisen that intelligent conduct can proceed. What is essential to this reconstruction is such an analysis of a complex that that which has checked the whole act may be

98PART IV

identified with the specific part of the act to which it belongs, for it is only when a definite tendency to respond answers to a stimulation that it becomes a distinct part of the field of perception and can assimilate the memory images of past experience. To isolate a part of a complex act is, then, to expose the field to the independent sensitizing influence of the other tendencies which were so organized that they acted under the conditions set by the whole act. The immediate function of the appearance of the self in experience is that of analyzing the complex response, in the face of conflict, so that a new field of objects may appear together with a reconstructed act. This takes place through the identification of the self with the defeated element of the act, and then with the entire act, deprived of this element, seeking to reorganize itself out of elements freed from the former organization, sensitizing us to characters in the field of stimulation to which we would otherwise not have responded, that is, which would not otherwise have existed as objects for us in the environment.

The further function of the self as an object in the field of action is to be found in the attention to the universal character of the object in the environment, and its abstraction by means of symbols of communication in the form of what is called ideas.

Whatever endures in the midst of the passing of events (whether this be some sensuous content that persists while other characters come and go, or a structure of the thing that admits of change of content, or an aesthetic, logical, or ethical content that persists while other characters shift) is insofar universal, for it is a character of which there are a number of instances and of which there might be an indefinite number. Within the structure of the thing these universals can also disappear while the structure remains, since there may be what are called more inclusive and less inclusive universals. It is these persistent characters which can be indicated to others or to one's self, for only that which persists can be indicated. That which is indicated must last while attention is held upon it and directed toward it. Such an indication of a character by a specific social gesture, generally vocal, with the tendency to respond to the character pointed out, is what is called an idea that answers to the universal content. It is the attitude of response to these universal characters which answers to them in the individual. The responses are universal because they may be called out by any number of different stimuli and so answer to that universal character in the object which calls them out. In the experience of individuals they are the criteria by which we identify the universal characters in things. Whatever one tends to sit down in is a chair. Whatever one places in a scale of colors is a certain blue. We identify the universal contents in things by presenting ourselves as responding to them, and we call these responses aroused by the significant symbols of social gestures, or language, the meanings of things. It is because we can summon ourselves, as organizations of responses, into the field of experience by means of these symbols, that we are able to isolate these meanings and so further the reorganization of our responses in a plan of action.

The mechanism of bringing the self as an object into the field of experience implies two things: first, that the individual indicates things and their characters to others, and second, that the stimulus of which he makes use is one to which he tends to respond in the same fashion as that in which the others respond. Such stimuli are found chiefly among the vocal gestures, which thus become language symbols, significant symbols. Back of this developed process of speech lies that long process in infancy of stimulating one's self by one's own social conduct and attitudes to play the parts which one's conduct and attitudes call out in those about one. It is a process which has passed under the misnomer of imitation. It leads through play to the building-up of these responses in the roles of others into a self or personality. In this part of the self the child indicates to himself what he wants and can discuss with himself things and actions from the varied standpoints which these different responses represent. Thus in the experience of the individual a self has arisen to serve the functions of reflectively attaching to things and their characters the results of past experience and of indicating and isolating the meanings of things.

The Nature of Mental Processes

It is evident that the mental processes are just those phases of conduct into which the self as an object has come to deepen and render significant our analysis and to make possible the rational solution of our problems. So far as the significant symbols which the individual uses are stimuli to his own responses these processes lie in the individual. So far as things, characters, and imagery are indicated, the processes extend beyond the individual. The locus of mind is not in the individual. Mental processes are fragments of the complex conduct of the individual in and on his environment. The objects and contents of the objects are as much in the environment in the reflective processes as in those of immediate experience. What has taken place in the reflective phase of human experience is this: the actual dependence of the environment upon the individual, which is not present in immediate experience but which has always existed in the relations of living forms to their environments, has, through the appearance in experience of the self as an object, passed into the control which the individual exercises over the environment. We have referred to two phases of this control. One of these is the appearance of new objects through the reference of failures in response to the specific stimulations that call out the response. The double reference of past experiences of the act to the objects and to the self puts at the disposal of the individual results of responses in their relation to what called them out but do not, or may not, immediately appear. We express this in the term "recollection," meaning by this that we summon and control memory imagery, both in the analysis of the object and the complex response to the object, through its place in the self extending into the past from the "specious present." The second phase is found in the appearance of responses which had belonged to complex acts, but which in the inhibition of the act can answer to the new objects appearing in the environment. These responses constitute, as we have seen, the meaning of these objects when they have been indicated by the significant symbols of social conduct and are called ideas. It will be seen that, while an indefinite number of instances of objects in nature appear in our immediate experience, new objects arise in reflective experience only through the interaction of the individual and the environment by means of the mediation of the self as an object.

There is another phase of mental processes which has been barely indicated above, but which calls for further reference. This is the unity of the analyzed or diversified field of the environment and of the responses that inhibition has set free from the organization of the earlier act. What is preserved is the wider organization of the life-process within which the inhibited act lay. One way of expressing this is to say that the environment exists for the individual as that within which the more inclusive act must go on, as containing the conditions for any solution of the problem which arises out of the conflict. The unity of the environment is that of organization of the conditions for the solution of the problem. The problem itself exists within the larger inclusive activity which must go on in some different form, under some reorganization of the parts of the act in the presence of the conditions which appear in the environment. This unity appears in experience through and in the self as an object. In an experience within which individual and environment mutually determine each other, the unity of the environment and of its constituent objects as well as that of the individual arises out of the activity of the individual. Insofar as the individual acts with himself as an object, this organization of the environment and its objects in terms of the conditions of the solution of the problem, and the larger act within which the inhibited process lies make the problem itself an object for the individual. In customary phraseology we say the individual knows what he is trying to do and what are the conditions of his doing it.

A further question arises in regard to this reflexive intelligent conduct concerning the fashion in which the self as an object becomes a part of the individual. In the play period of little children this reflexive act has not yet taken place. The child in one role addresses himself naïvely in another role. These roles are not at first organized into a personality, the child simply passing from the one into the other as the conduct in one calls out a response in the other. In more consecutive play, especially of two or more children, the tendency to take other parts comes in to stimulate and control the execution of the part assumed. Thus a child will stop and applaud himself and then resume his performance. If the play becomes a consecutive whole, the tendency to take all the parts at the appropriate moments is present in the attitude of the individual child, controlling his entire conduct. The child becomes a generalized actor-manager, directing, applauding, and criticizing his own roles as well as those of others.

It is the attainment of this degree of personality which marks the passage from the period of play to that of games. The nature of the game is such that every act in the game is determined and qualified by all the other acts. This is expressed by the rules of the game, and implies in each individual a generalized player that is present in every part that is taken. What takes place in this dramatic fashion in children's plays and games evidently goes on in the formation of the child's personality in the life of the family, and of other groups in which the child finds himself. Through assuming the roles of others, to which he has stimulated himself by his own conduct, he is organizing them into generalized attitudes and becomes a member of the family, of the school, and of his set. I have already indicated the capital part which language plays in this process, owing to the fact that in the use of the vocal gesture the individual tends to arouse in himself the same response as that which he calls out in others. In a word, the self as an object becomes a part of the individual through his having assumed the generalized attitude of a member of the group to which that self belongs, a group that widens until it takes in all rational individuals, that is, all individuals who could indicate to one another universal characters and objects in co-operative activity. In being an object to himself in this role of a citizen of the universe of discourse a person indicates to himself both the conditions of the solution of his problem and the various inhibited responses that are seeking reorganization and associates with these responses the results which they have had in past conduct, thus giving rise to the new objects which provide the field for the new act.

When we ask what actually takes place in the experience of an individual during mental activity, that is, in reflection in the presence of a conflict and its consequent problem, we discover the following situation. The individual in the attitude of a member of a rational group indicates the various characters of the new objects that have arisen as the result of the conflict, and the consequent inhibition of the complex response that was going on, by means of significant symbols. These indications are gestures— mainly vocal gestures—which call attention to these characters in things. It is important to note that the reason these characters excite attention is that there are reactions which they call out. The reactions are those which are in some sense set free by the inhibition of the original act within which they were organized. The original form in which these gestures appear is in the adjustment of the individual to the responses which are ready to take place. In social forms these gestures have become valuable stimulations to other members of the group, such as a brood of chickens, and have been preserved. In the human individual that tends to take the part of the other, they have the double significance of directing his own attention and of exciting the attitude of the other. In the attitude of the other, the individual not only tends to respond to the stimulations but to indicate the response which he tends to make by another significant symbol. There are now two roles, at least, involved in this conversation, that of the generalized actor whose attitude represents an adjustment to all the alternative responses which fall within the larger act within which the conflict has arisen and that of the specialized actor who tends to carry out the response to the stimulation upon which the attention is directed. To recur to the illustration already used, the inhibition of the act of continued walking toward the distant goal sets free the possible responses to stimuli to jump the ditch, or to skirt or bridge it. But they all lie within a generalized process of locomotion, and this generalized process in some sense presents conditions for the selection of one alternative rather than another, or for some combination of them. The specialized actor indicates the response, say, of skirting the ditch, but it is indicated to the generalized actor who represents its relation to reaching the goal. Passing from one role to the other, through the use of the significant symbols, the individual relates this specific response as well as others to the including act. Eventually the specific response or set of such responses falls into place within the larger act, and the individual proceeds.

Mechanism and Novelty

In general, we consider the determination of the organism by the environment as causal, while we consider the determination of the environment by the organism as selective and, insofar, as constitutive, that is, the selection of a group of stimuli with reference to our organized activity is responsible for the cutting-out of these elements among physical things and for a certain logical structure as an object. In our consideration of the environment as determining the organism we reduce both environment and organism to common physical elements when we follow out the causal relations. The effects of the environment upon the organism are mass effects of elements in the one upon elements in the other. Our ability to trace and determine these causal connections is dependent upon our ability to reduce the whole situation of environment and organism to a set of physical particles in motion. In this mechanical whole the operative connections are between the physical elements and their fields of force. It is only by a summation of these that we can say that the environment, or its objects, affect the organism as an object. The actual reduction of the environment and the organism to such elements is only attained at a certain point, for example, in the analysis of matter into electrical particles and electrical effects into fields of force; while in most statements we simply imply such an analysis as an ideal which our scientific method demands for full realization. In this statement of causal necessity we are abstracting from everything in both environment and organism except the physical particles and their motions, as resulting from their fields of force.

When we speak of the determination of the environment by the organism, on the other hand, we imply organisms which have a content which is more than the summation of the physical particles and their motions into which a mechanical science analyzes them. Their living processes are real as processes which reach or fail to reach a consummation. And the objects in the environment have contents which are more than the sum of the motions of physical particles. They are food, enemies, obstacles, protections, etc. These contents always involve the carrying-out of the life-processes of the organisms. In other words, they always involve a future, and a future involves an experience within which that which will happen (is happening insofar as that which is happening always has a bit of the future in it) is uncertain. That which will happen is always different in some respect from what has happened, and this different quality is something that cannot be predicted. In a sense we can predict the future, but what we can predict is always something less than that which happens. Theoretically we can predict to the extent that we can make our statement in mechanical terms, and this implies, as we have seen, that we have abstracted from the determining relation of the organism upon the environment. We can predict the debilitating effect of a disease, but we cannot predict the actual weakness that appears in the experience of the sick person. We can predict that a certain light wave will be experienced as blue, but the actual experience of blue that supervenes in the experience has a character which is novel and could not be predicted in its ultimate peculiarity. As we look over the past, these peculiarities of the novel as they occurred have lost their interest, and we are interested only in the mechanical conditions that determined their appearance without, to be sure, determining these peculiarities. So that when we predict a series of future events, such as the eclipses that will take place in the coming year, the statement is not in terms of the future in the sense of experience. Our attitude in predicting the eclipses that will take place in the coming year is the same as that in which we determine those that took place in the year in which Thales is reputed to have predicted the eclipse which brought to a stop the battle between the Lydians and the Medes. As this is the attitude in which we make our mechanical statements of the past, we may perhaps say that all predictions are in an implied past. But the expression is ambiguous. Degrees of probability represent degrees of approach to a conceivable mechanical statement. We can conceive of a completely mechanical, though highly abstract, statement of the life-process. We can say that we have the highest degree of probability of death as the outcome of all life. We can also conceive of a mechanical statement of the whole process of nature, and the question arises whether we can assume that such a conceivable determination of the positions of all physical particles at all times determines in advance what must be the experience of all organisms, even if such a determination does not imply the possible prediction of the actual experiences as they take place.

The question seems to take this form: Is the conception that we form in our scientific research of the mechanical universe as a whole one from which later scientific reconstructions of the universe can be predicted? The answer to this is in the negative. Our conception of the universe as a whole is, of course, never a complete one, but the form that it takes at any one time is one that answers to the view which science holds at that time. This is generalized so far as possible and is made the structure of the universe so far as that exists in experience. If an essential problem arises in that experience, the implication is definite that the generalization already made is inadequate. Now from such a conception of the universe, one in which an essential problem has arisen, it would be impossible to predict the reconstruction which is required to meet the problem. From the standpoint of the reconstruction that does actually take place in research it is always possible to show the logical necessity by which the new view has arisen out of the old, but such a logical necessity does not obtain from the old view to the new reconstruction. Did the logical necessity in the new situation exist in the old? The abstraction which we make in our explanation under the new conception, and by which we show the necessity of the advance to the new together with the explanation of the old in terms of the new, is one that can in thought be pushed back into or under the old situation. We can see how men conceived the sun to be going around the earth from the standpoint of our recognition of the heliocentric nature of our system. It would have been impossible to have shown the necessity of an advance from the Ptolemaic to the Copernican theory from the conception men had of the Ptolemaic world. The nature of this new abstraction can sustain both views, both the Ptolemaic and the Copernican, one as explicable and the other as actual; but the views which we hold of the universe at any one time do not carry in them as deducible propositions the new views which will arise in scientific research, though the abstractions that we make with each advance are more comprehensive as they not only meet the new facts but explain the old doctrines.

We have, then, two different attitudes of assurance in the face of the future. The one is represented by perception and the other by thought. In perception the attitude is that of a reaction ready to take place, and insofar as imagery of past experience is there, anticipatory of a certain type of experience, though the result is bound as a new experience to be different from what has occurred. The adjustment of the response to the sort of experience that is coming expresses this anticipation even when the imagery is but faintly present, or when this imagery is predominantly motor in its character. On the other hand, that which is going to happen must be a constituent part of that which is given and which is relatively unchanging. Novelty and change always appear against a background of that which is old and unchanging. The problem appears in the midst of a world that is itself not problematic. We can present that which is about to happen in terms of what must belong to it if it is to be a part of the world that is. The statement can be only abstract, for what will happen has a content which in some degree is not and cannot be given. In our everyday perceptual experience this abstraction is hardly evident. The pressures we will receive when we place our feet in new places, when our hands grasp things about us, are so slightly different from the actual pressures we are feeling that practically no abstraction is made. As the future grows more distant, or as that which is to occur departs more from the world of experience about us, the abstraction becomes greater. We find that we can give only certain elements of what must take place. If we are to meet a new personage, or one whom we know under entirely new conditions, we find ourselves rehearsing the secure elements of that which is to take place. A certain social structure is given. Certain common standards and interests are involved. A certain common past experience belongs to all concerned. In terms of these given elements we construct a form which the coming interview must take. This structure is an abstraction from the world about us, made in terms of the necessary conditions which the problematic experience ahead must meet. The statement of these conditions is in terms of thought. They have the immediate reality of the given, of the world that is there; and, as the novel experiences that are coming will appear in a world that is relatively unchanged, these conditions determine the form which the new experiences will take. But this form does not determine the content that will arise. The assurance with which we step into the future is that of the adjustment of the life-process to its environment which is found in the organism, as it appears in perception, but it is not a prevision of the unique experience that will appear.

There is still a further question beyond the predictability of the future experience, and that is as to its determined character. As we look back over that which has taken place, we can give, or assume that we could give if we had all the elements of the situation, the reasons that determine what has taken place. The only situation within which such a proposition holds is a mechanical one, which becomes perfect only when the world is reduced to physical particles, their velocities, and accelerations. In such a world there is no determination as to what elements are in motion, motion and its characters of velocity and acceleration being relative. Such a world, or such an abstraction from the world, does not define the reality of a living being, for a living being acts. Its reason for movement lies within itself, and in that action, as we have seen, the living being determines its environment. The living being acts to reach a certain result in the future, the realization of its act. In this action it may be said to select its own time system and the space that this involves. It thus determines the world within which it lives. Its determination, however, is a selection, and a creation only in the sense of a reconstruction. Undoubtedly new species arise, and with the new species come new environments, but the new environment is oriented with reference to the new species. The form in some sense selects them. If their life-process is to be completed, the objects in the environment must be constituted with reference to these forms. New food, new dangers, new refuges and habitats must appear, though there are the same particles and the same forces or fields of force.

The distinction that arises here is between action and abstract motion. Action has reference to a future condition. Motion can be stated with reference to past and present conditions and, in theory, is entirely determined by these. Action carries with it the implication of a certain world of objects within which it can be completed. When it is so completed, it gives us the perceptual assurance of the existence of this world or environment of objects. The acts so completed, or presented as completed, can then be analyzed into motions. Motions are relative changes of position, with varying velocities and accelerations, of physical things, which physical things can be defined or measured with sufficient accuracy so that they can be identified in their different positions. In motion we have abstracted from the here and now of the actor. This determination of the here and now can be made at any point, that is, any point can be regarded as at rest, and the corresponding changes in position that take place can be stated in terms of the motions of the other objects. The actor determines the point of departure, the *terminus a quo*, of his actual or possible motion. He sets up there the Cartesian co-ordinates of space. From the zero of that set of co-ordinates action does or may take place. All changes within the environment are stated in terms of distance experience with reference to that set of co-ordinates. These changes are motions, for it is possible, as in the case of the person in the train, to place one's self either in the train moving in a fixed world or in the fixed environment of the interior of the train, while the landscape moves by. It is the actual contact experience, extended by adjustment to surrounding objects, that determines the co-ordinates. Insofar as we adjust ourselves to these objects whose positions are changing about us, either by the movement of the eye or actual or possible movements of the body, they have the future value of possible acts. They have the values of possible contacts determining action and promising certain results. The experience depends upon what action is taken, not simply upon past positions and relative present positions. These changes are not merely motions in the abstract sense of the doctrine of relativity.

If the promised experience of action is not attained, and action is inhibited by conflicting tendencies, a reconstruction of the field of conduct may take place, in which new objects answering to a different form of action may arise. It is in this situation that motions in their more abstract sense appear. The actual line of conduct is not yet determined. It is only the relative position of things with reference to one another, and their relative changes of position with reference to one another, that may be of interest. This is the situation insofar as we determine the conditions which must obtain for any one of a number of possible acts and so abstract from any specific action. Except in the most extended abstraction, this field of possible activity lies within a world that must condition any alternative course taken. The new objects will still be parts of this bounding, given environment. Our system of co-ordinates is set for this given world that must determine the validity of any hypothesis of action which we adopt. We do not extend the relativity of our attitude to this given unquestioned world. When we present the conditions of possible action within this world, we place ourselves at the imaged completion of the suggested reactions and all the motions that have taken place have the necessity of their dependence upon earlier positions, velocities, accelerations, and directions; but the reorganization of the problematic part of the environment could not be deduced from these, though it is shot through with necessary conditions which belong to the world as given. In the undetermined future of action a new object, a new *terminus ad quem*, can arise, the necessity of which cannot be said to exist in the conditions to which it must conform. Even the inclusion of the physical organism, its elements and their motions, within the conditions of the solution of the problem does not determine the future goal of the act, for the physical organism so stated is a part of the abstraction. It also contains necessary conditions, but not the novel objects that can appear. The novel element can be very slight, especially in comparison with the given world within which it appears, but in the experience of the individual it was not involved as a necessity of its past. The statement of the abstract motions could not have included the necessity of the particular act. This amounts to the affirmation that all the novelties of living experience are as novelties essential parts in the universe; the fact that when they arose they were unpredictable means that in the universe as then existing they were not determinable, nor in the universe as then existing did there exist the conditions that were the sufficient reasons for their appearing.

This statement implies a distinction between a predictable situation that can be deduced from given positions of physical elements and their motions, including their accelerations and directions, and a future concrete situation carrying with it the inevitable novelty which attaches to every event in experience. There seem to be two phases of this novelty. One is found in the difference, shading from almost complete imperceptibility to utter strangeness, between anticipatory imagery of the result of the act and the actual experience. While this difference is unpredictable, we assume that the conditions for it can, after its appearance, be found in the analysis of the situation as it exists. The difference is never of an irrational character, but its rational character does not imply that the conditions of what is novel in it existed in the previous experience, though the structure of that experience can be now assimilated to the structure of the present experience. The other phase of novelty is found in the hypothetical structure of a future situation, when a conflict of the tendencies to action present an essential problem for which a solution is sought. A theoretically complete analysis of the situation as it existed before the problem arose would not involve the reconstruction that takes place, though it would present the conditions to which any such hypothesis must conform. That this hypothetical structure will be found to belong to the future situation depends upon the success of the action it implies, that is, upon experiment. The hypothetical structure itself, however, is a novelty that could not be deduced from the former experience as it existed.

Part V

6

MIND

Social Psychology and Behaviorism

SOCIAL psychology has, as a rule, dealt with various phases of social experience from the psychological standpoint of individual experience. The point of approach which I wish to suggest is that of dealing with experience from the standpoint of society, at least from the standpoint of communication as essential to the social order. Social psychology, on this view, presupposes an approach to experience from the standpoint of the individual, but undertakes to determine in particular that which belongs to this experience because the individual himself belongs to a social structure, a social order.

No very sharp line can be drawn between social psychology and individual psychology. Social psychology is especially interested in the effect which the social group has in the determination of the experience and conduct of the individual member. If we abandon the conception of a substantive soul endowed with the self of the individual at birth, then we may regard the development of the individual's self, and of his self-consciousness within the field of his experience, as the social psychologist's special interest. There are, then, certain phases of psychology which are interested in studying the relation of the individual organism to

First published in *Mind, Self, and Society*, ed. Charles W. Morris (Chicago: University of Chicago Press, 1934), pp. 1–134.

the social group to which it belongs, and these phases constitute social psychology as a branch of general psychology. Thus, in the study of the experience and behavior of the individual organism or self in its dependence upon the social group to which it belongs, we find a definition of the field of social psychology.

While minds and selves are essentially social products, products or phenomena of the social side of human experience, the physiological mechanism underlying experience is far from irrelevant—indeed is indispensable—to their genesis and existence; for individual experience and behavior is, of course, physiologically basic to social experience and behavior: the processes and mechanisms of the latter (including those which are essential to the origin and existence of minds and selves) are dependent physiologically upon the processes and mechanisms of the former and upon the social functioning of these. Individual psychology, nevertheless, definitely abstracts certain factors from the situation with which social psychology deals more nearly in its concrete totality. We shall approach this latter field from a behavioristic point of view.

The common psychological standpoint which is represented by behaviorism is found in John B. Watson. The behaviorism which we shall make use of is more adequate than that of which Watson makes use. Behaviorism in this wider sense is simply an approach to the study of the experience of the individual from the point of view of his conduct, particularly, but not exclusively, the conduct as it is observable by others. Historically, behaviorism entered psychology through the door of animal psychology. There it was found to be impossible to use what is termed introspection. One cannot appeal to the animal's introspection, but must study the animal in terms of external conduct. Earlier animal psychology added an inferential reference to consciousness and even undertook to find the point in conduct at which consciousness appears. This inference had, perhaps, varying degrees of probability, but it was one which could not be tested experimentally. It could be then simply dropped as far as science was concerned. It was not necessary for the study of the conduct of the individual animal. Having taken that behavioristic standpoint for the lower animals, it was possible to carry it over to the human animal.

There remained, however, the field of introspection, of experiences which are private and belong to the individual himself— experiences commonly called subjective. What was to be done with these? John B. Watson's attitude was that of the Queen in *Alice in Wonderland*—"Off with their heads!"—there were no such things. There was no imagery and no consciousness. The field of so-called introspection Watson explained by the use of language symbols.[1] These symbols were not necessarily uttered loudly enough to be heard by others and often only involved the muscles of the throat without leading to audible speech. That was all there was to thought. One thinks, but one thinks in terms of language. In this way Watson explained the whole field of inner experience in terms of external behavior. Instead of calling such behavior subjective, it was regarded as the field of behavior that was accessible only to the individual himself. One could observe his own movements, his own organs of articulation, when other persons could not normally observe them. Certain fields were accessible to the individual alone, but the observation was not different in kind; the difference lay only in the degree of accessibility of others to certain observations. One could be set up in a room by himself and observe something that no one else could observe. What a man observed in the room would be his own experience. Now, in this way something goes on in the throat or the body of the individual which no one else can observe. There are, of course, scientific instruments that can be attached to the throat or the body to reveal the tendency toward movement. There are some movements that are easily observable and others which can be detected only by the individual himself, but there is no qualitative difference in the two cases. It is simply recognized that the apparatus of observation is one that has various degrees of success. That, in brief, is the point of view of Watson's behavioristic psychology. It aims to observe conduct as it takes place, and to utilize that conduct to explain the experience of the individual without bringing in the observation of an inner experience, a consciousness as such.

[1] Especially in *Behavior, an Introduction to Comparative Psychology,* chap. x; *Psychology from the Standpoint of a Behaviorist,* chap. ix; *Behaviorism,* chaps. x, xi.

There was another attack on consciousness, that of William James in his 1904 article entitled, "Does 'Consciousness' Exist?"[2] James pointed out that when a person is in a room the objects of the interior can be looked at from two standpoints. The furniture, for instance, can be considered from the standpoint of the person who bought it and used it, from the point of view of its color values which attach to it in the minds of the persons who observe them, its aesthetic value, its economic value, its traditional value. All of these we can speak of in terms of psychology; they will be put into relationship with the experience of the individual. One man puts one value upon it and another gives it another value. But the same objects can be regarded as physical parts of a physical room. What James insisted upon was that the two cases differ only in an arrangement of certain contents in different series. The furniture, the walls, the house itself, belong to one historical series. We speak of the house as having been built, of the furniture as having been made. We put the house and furniture into another series when one comes in and assesses these objects from the point of view of his own experience. He is talking about the same chair, but the chair is for him now a matter of certain contours, certain colors, taken from his own experience. It involves the experience of the individual. Now one can take a cross-section of both of these two orders so that at a certain point there is a meeting of the two series. The statement in terms of consciousness simply means the recognition that the room lies not only in the historical series but also in the experience of the individual. There has been of late in philosophy a growing recognition of the importance of James's insistence that a great deal has been placed in consciousness that must be returned to the so-called objective world.[3]

Psychology itself cannot very well be made a study of the field of consciousness alone; it is necessarily a study of a more extensive field. It is, however, that science which does make use

[2] *Journal of Philosophy, Psychology, and Scientific Method.* Reprinted in *Essays in Radical Empiricism.*

[3] Modern philosophical realism has helped to free psychology from a concern with a philosophy of mental states (1924).

of introspection, in the sense that it looks within the experience of the individual for phenomena not dealt with in any other sciences—phenomena to which only the individual himself has experiential access. That which belongs (experientially) to the individual *qua* individual, and is accessible to him alone is certainly included within the field of psychology, whatever else is or is not thus included. This is our best clue in attempting to isolate the field of psychology. The psychological datum is best defined, therefore, in terms of accessibility. That which is accessible, in the experience of the individual, only to the individual himself, is peculiarly psychological.

I want to point out, however, that even when we come to the discussion of such "inner" experience, we can approach it from the point of view of the behaviorist, provided that we do not too narrowly conceive this point of view. What one must insist upon is that objectively observable behavior finds expression within the individual, not in the sense of being in another world, a subjective world, but in the sense of being within his organism. Something of this behavior appears in what we may term "attitudes," the beginnings of acts. Now, if we come back to such attitudes we find them giving rise to all sorts of responses. The telescope in the hands of a novice is not a telescope in the sense that it is to those on top of Mount Wilson. If we want to trace the responses of the astronomer, we have to go back into his central nervous system, back to a whole series of neurons; and we find something there that answers to the exact way in which the astronomer approaches the instrument under certain conditions. That is the beginning of the act; it is a part of the act. The external act which we do observe is a part of the process which has started within; the values[4] which we say the instrument has are values through the relationship of the object to the person who has that sort of attitude. If a person did not have that particular nervous system, the instrument would be of no value. It would not be a telescope.

In both versions of behaviorism certain characteristics which

[4]   Value: the future character of the object insofar as it determines your action to it (1924).

things have and certain experiences which individuals have can be stated as occurrences inside of an act.⁵ But part of the act lies within the organism and only comes to expression later; it is that side of behavior which I think Watson has passed over. There is a field within the act itself which is not external, but which belongs to the act, and there are characteristics of that inner organic conduct which do reveal themselves in our own attitudes, especially those connected with speech. Now, if our behavioristic point of view takes these attitudes into account we find that it can very well cover the field of psychology. In any case, this approach is one of particular importance because it is able to deal with the field of communication in a way which neither Watson nor the introspectionist can do. We want to approach language, not from the standpoint of inner meanings to be expressed, but in its larger context of co-operation in the group taking place by means of signals and gestures.⁶ Meaning appears within that process. Our behaviorism is a social behaviorism.

Social psychology studies the activity or behavior of the individual as it lies within the social process; the behavior of an

---

5   An act is an impulse that maintains the life-process by the selection of certain sorts of stimuli it needs. Thus, the organism creates its environment. The stimulus is the occasion for the expression of the impulse.

Stimuli are means, tendency is the real thing. Intelligence is the selection of stimuli that will set free and maintain life and aid in rebuilding it (1927).

The purpose need not be "in view," but the statement of the act includes the goal to which the act moves. This is a natural teleology, in harmony with a mechanical statement (1925).

6   The study of the process of language or speech—its origins and development—is a branch of social psychology, because it can be understood only in terms of the social processes of behavior within a group of interacting organisms; because it is one of the activities of such a group. The philologist, however, has often taken the view of the prisoner in a cell. The prisoner knows that others are in a like position and he wants to get in communication with them. So he sets about some method of communication, some arbitrary affair, perhaps, such as tapping on the wall. Now, each of us, on this view, is shut up in his own cell of consciousness and, knowing that there are other people so shut up, develops ways to set up communication with them.

individual can be understood only in terms of the behavior of the whole social group of which he is a member, since his individual acts are involved in larger, social acts which go beyond himself and which implicate the other members of that group.

We are not, in social psychology, building up the behavior of the social group in terms of the behavior of the separate individuals composing it; rather, we are starting out with a given social whole of complex group activity, into which we analyze (as elements) the behavior of each of the separate individuals composing it. We attempt, that is, to explain the conduct of the individual in terms of the organized conduct of the social group, rather than to account for the organized conduct of the social group in terms of the conduct of the separate individuals belonging to it. For social psychology, the whole (society) is prior to the part (the individual), not the part to the whole; and the part is explained in terms of the whole, not the whole in terms of the part or parts. The social act[7] is not explained by building it up out of stimulus plus response; it must be taken as a dynamic whole—as something going on—no part of which can be considered or understood by itself—a complex organic process implied by each individual stimulus and response involved in it.

In social psychology we get at the social process from the inside as well as from the outside. Social psychology is behavioristic in the sense of starting off with an observable activity—the dynamic, ongoing social process and the social acts which are its component elements—to be studied and analyzed scientifically. But it is not behavioristic in the sense of ignoring the

[7] "A social act may be defined as one in which the occasion or stimulus which sets free an impulse is found in the character or conduct of a living form that belongs to the proper environment of the living form whose impulse it is. I wish, however, to restrict the social act to the class of acts which involve the co-operation of more than one individual, and whose object as defined by the act, in the sense of Bergson, is a social object. I mean by a social object one that answers to all the parts of the complex act, though these parts are found in the conduct of different individuals. The objective of the acts is then found in the life-process of the group, not in those of the separate individuals alone," "The Genesis of the Self and Social Control," *International Journal of Ethics*, XXXV (1925), 263–64.

inner experience of the individual—the inner phase of that process or activity. On the contrary, it is particularly concerned with the rise of such experience within the process as a whole. It simply works from the outside to the inside instead of from the inside to the outside, so to speak, in its endeavor to determine how such experience does arise within the process. The act, then, and not the tract, is the fundamental datum in both social and individual psychology when behavioristically conceived, and it has both an inner and an outer phase, an internal and an external aspect.

These general remarks have had to do with our point of approach. It is behavioristic, but unlike Watsonian behaviorism it recognizes the parts of the act which do not come to external observation, and it emphasizes the act of the human individual in its natural social situation.

The Behavioristic Significance of Attitudes

The problem that presents itself as crucial for human psychology concerns the field that is opened up by introspection; this field apparently could not be dealt with by a purely objective psychology which only studied conduct as it takes place for the observer. In order that this field could be brought within the range of objective psychology, the behaviorist, such as Watson, did what he could to cut down the field itself, to deny certain phenomena supposed to lie only in that field, such as "consciousness" as distinct from conduct without consciousness. The animal psychologist studied conduct without taking up the question as to whether it was conscious conduct or not.[8] But when we

8   Comparative psychology freed psychology in general from being confined solely to the field of the central nervous system, which, through the physiological psychologists, had taken the place of consciousness as such, as the field of psychological investigation. It thus enabled psychology in general to consider the act as a whole, and as including or taking place within the entire social process of behavior. In other words, comparative psychology—and behaviorism as its outgrowth—has extended the field of general psychology beyond the central nervous system of the individual organism alone, and has caused psychologists to consider the individual act as a part of the larger social whole to which it in fact belongs,

reach the field of human conduct we are in fact able to distinguish reflexes which take place without consciousness. There
seems, then, to be a field which the behavioristic psychology
cannot reach. The Watsonian behaviorist simply did what he
could to minimize this difference.

The field of investigation of the behaviorist has been quite
largely that of the young infant, and the methods employed are
just the methods of animal psychology. The behaviorist has endeavored to find out what the processes of behavior are and to
see how the activities of the infant can be used to explain the
activities of the adult. It is here that the psychologist brings in
the conditioned reflexes. He shows that by a mere association
of certain stimuli he can get results which would not follow
from these secondary stimuli alone. This conditioning of reflexes
can be carried over into other fields, such as those of terror on
the part of an infant. The infant can be made to fear something
by associating the object with others producing terror. The same
process can be used for explaining more elaborate conduct in
which we associate elements with certain events which are not
directly connected with them, and by elaborating this conditioning we can, it is believed, explain the more extended processes
of reasoning and inference. In this way a method which belongs
to objective psychology is carried over into the field which is
dealt with ordinarily in terms of introspection. That is, instead
of saying we have certain ideas when we have certain experiences, and that these ideas imply something else, we say that a
certain experience has taken place at the same time that the first
experience has taken place, so that now this secondary experience
arouses the response which belongs to the primary experience.

There remain contents, such as those of imagery, which are
more resistant to such analysis. What shall we say of responses
that do not answer to any given experience? We can say, of
course, that they are the results of past experiences. But take

and from which, in a definite sense, it gets its meaning; though they do
not, of course, lose interest thereby in the central nervous system and the
physiological processes going on in it.

the contents themselves, the actual visual imagery that one has: it has outline; it has color; it has values; and other characters which are isolated with more difficulty. Such experience is one which plays a part, and a very large part, in our perception, our conduct; and yet it is an experience which can be revealed only by introspection. The behaviorist has to make a detour about this type of experience if he is going to stick to the Watsonian type of behavioristic psychology.

Such a behaviorist desires to analyze the act, whether individual or social, without any specific reference to consciousness whatever and without any attempt to locate it either within the field of organic behavior or within the larger field of reality in general. He wishes, in short, to deny its existence as such altogether. Watson insists that objectively observable behavior completely and exclusively constitutes the field of scientific psychology, individual and social. He pushes aside as erroneous the idea of "mind" or "consciousness," and attempts to reduce all "mental" phenomena to conditioned reflexes and similar physiological mechanisms—in short, to purely behavioristic terms. This attempt, of course, is misguided and unsuccessful, for the existence as such of mind or consciousness, in some sense or other, must be admitted—the denial of it leads inevitably to obvious absurdities. But though it is impossible to *reduce* mind or consciousness to purely behavioristic terms—in the sense of thus explaining it away and denying its existence as such entirely— yet it is not impossible to *explain* it in these terms, and to do so without explaining it away, or denying its existence as such, in the least. Watson apparently assumes that to deny the existence of mind or consciousness as a psychical stuff, substance, or entity is to deny its existence altogether and that a naturalistic or behavioristic account of it as such is out of the question. But, on the contrary, we may deny its existence as a psychical entity without denying its existence in some other sense at all; and if we then conceive it functionally, and as a natural rather than a transcendental phenomenon, it becomes possible to deal with it in behavioristic terms. In short, it is not possible to deny the existence of mind or consciousness or mental phenomena, nor is it desirable to do so; but it is possible to account for them or deal with them in behavioristic terms which are precisely similar to those which Watson employs in dealing with non-mental psychological phenomena (phenomena which, according to his definition of the field of psychology, are all the psychological phenomena there are). Mental behavior is not reducible to non-mental behavior. But mental behavior or phenomena can be explained in terms of non-mental behavior or phenomena, as arising out of, and as resulting from complications in, the latter.

If we are going to use behavioristic psychology to explain conscious behavior, we have to be much more thoroughgoing in our statement of the act than Watson was. We have to take into account not merely the complete or social act but what goes on in the central nervous system as the beginning of the individual's act and as the organization of the act. Of course, that takes us beyond the field of our direct observation. It takes us beyond that field because we cannot get at the process itself. It is a field that is more or less shut off, seemingly because of the difficulty of the country itself that has to be investigated. The central nervous system is only partly explored. Present results, however, suggest the organization of the act in terms of attitudes. There is an organization of the various parts of the nervous system that are going to be responsible for acts, an organization which represents, not only that which is immediately taking place, but also the later stages that are to take place. When one approaches a distant object he approaches it with reference to what he is going to do when he arrives there. When one is approaching a hammer he is muscularly all ready to seize the handle of the hammer. The later stages of the act are present in the early stages—not simply in the sense that they are all ready to go off, but in the sense that they serve to control the process itself. They determine how we are going to approach the object, and the steps in our early manipulation of it. We can recognize, then that the innervation of certain groups of cells in the central nervous system can already initiate in advance the later stages of the act. The act as a whole can be there determining the process.

We can also recognize in such a general attitude toward an

object an attitude that represents alternative responses, such as are involved when we talk about our idea of an object. A person who is familiar with a horse approaches it as one who is going to ride it. He moves toward the proper side and is ready to swing himself into the saddle. His approach determines the success of the whole process. But the horse is not simply something that must be ridden. It is an animal that must eat, that belongs to somebody. It has certain economic values. The individual is ready to do a whole series of things with reference to the horse, and that readiness is involved in any one of the many phases of the various acts. It is a horse that he is going to mount; it is a biological animal; it is an economic animal. Those characters are involved in the ideas of a horse. If we seek this ideal character of a horse in the central nervous system we would have to find it in all those different parts of the initiated acts. One would have to think of each as associated with the other processes in which he uses the horse, so that no matter what the specific act is, there is a readiness to act in these different ways with reference to the horse. We can find in that sense in the beginning of the act just those characters which we assign to "horse" as an idea, or if you like, as a concept.

If we are going to look for this idea in a central nervous system, we have to look for it in the neurons, particularly in the connection between the neurons. There are whole sets of connections there which are of such a character that we are able to act in a number of ways, and these possible actions have their effect on the way in which we do act. For example, if the horse belongs to the rider, the rider acts in a different way than if it belongs to someone else. These other processes involved determine the immediate action itself and particularly the later stages of the act, so that the temporal organization of the act may be present in the immediate process. We do not know how that temporal organization takes place in the central nervous system. In some sense these later processes which are going to take place, and are in some sense started, are worked into the immediate process. A behavioristic treatment, if it is made broad enough, if it makes use of the almost indefinite complexities existing in the nervous system, can adjust itself to many fields which were supposed to be confined to an introspective attack. Of course, a great deal of this must be hypothetical. We learn more day by day of what the connections are, but they are largely hypothetical. However, they can at least be stated in a behavioristic form. We can, therefore, in principle, state behavioristically what we mean by an idea.

The Behavioristic Significance of Gestures

The behaviorist of the Watsonian type has been prone to carry his principle of conditioning over into the field of language. By a conditioning of reflexes the horse has become associated with the word "horse," and this in turn releases the set of responses. We use the word, and the response may be that of mounting, buying, selling, or trading. We are ready to do all these different things. This statement, however, lacks the recognition that these different processes which the behaviorist says are identified with the word "horse" must be worked into the act itself, or the group of acts, which gather about the horse. They go to make up that object in our experience, and the function of the word is a function which has its place in that organization; but it is not, however, the whole process. We find that same sort of organization seemingly extended in the conduct of animals lower than man: those processes which go to make up our objects must be present in the animals themselves who have not the use of language. It is, of course, the great value, or one of the great values, of language that it does give us control over this organization of the act. That is a point we will have to consider in detail later, but it is important to recognize that that to which the word refers is something that can lie in the experience of the individual without the use of language itself. Language does pick out and organize this content in experience. It is an implement for that purpose.

Language is a part of social behavior.[9] There are an indefi-

9   What is the basic mechanism whereby the social process goes on? It is the mechanism of gesture, which makes possible the appropriate responses to one another's behavior of the different individual organisms in-

nite number of signs or symbols which may serve the purpose
of what we term "language." We are reading the meaning of
the conduct of other people when, perhaps, they are not aware
of it. There is something that reveals to us what the purpose is—
just the glance of an eye, the attitude of the body which leads
to the response. The communication set up in this way between
individuals may be very perfect. Conversation in gestures may
be carried on which cannot be translated into articulate speech.
This is also true of the lower animals. Dogs approaching each
other in hostile attitude carry on such a language of gestures.
They walk around each other, growling and snapping, and wait-
ing for the opportunity to attack. Here is a process out of which
language might arise, that is, a certain attitude of one individual
that calls out a response in the other, which in turn calls out a
different approach and a different response, and so on indefinitely. In fact, as we shall see, language does arise in just such
a process as that. We are too prone, however, to approach language as the philologist does, from the standpoint of the symbol
that is used.[10] We analyze that symbol and find out what is the
intent in the mind of the individual in using that symbol and
then attempt to discover whether this symbol calls out this intent
in the mind of the other. We assume that there are sets of ideas
in persons' minds and that these individuals make use of certain
arbitrary symbols which answer to the intent which the individ-

---

volved in the social process. Within any given social act, an adjustment
is effected, by means of gestures, of the actions of one organism involved
to the actions of another; the gestures are movements of the first organism
which act as specific stimuli calling forth the (socially) appropriate responses of the second organism. The field of the operation of gestures is
the field within which the rise and development of human intelligence has
taken place through the process of the symbolization of experience which
gestures—especially vocal gestures—have made possible. The specialization of the human animal within this field of the gesture has been responsible, ultimately, for the origin and growth of present human society
and knowledge, with all the control over nature and over the human environment which science makes possible.

10   "The Relations of Psychology and Philology," *Psychological Bulletin,* I (1904), 375 ff.

uals had. But if we are going to broaden the concept of language in the sense I have spoken of, so that it takes in the underlying attitudes, we can see that the so-called intent, the idea we are talking about, is one that is involved in the gesture or attitudes which we are using. The offering of a chair to a person who comes into the room is in itself a courteous act. We do not have to assume that a person says to himself that this person wants a chair. The offering of a chair by a person of good manners is something which is almost instinctive. This is the very attitude of the individual. From the point of view of the observer it is a gesture. Such early stages of social acts precede the symbol proper and deliberate communication.

One of the important documents in the history of modern psychology, particularly for the psychology of language, is Darwin's *Expression of the Emotions in Man and Animals*. Here Darwin carried his theory of evolution into the field of what we call "conscious experience." What Darwin did was to show that there was a whole series of acts or beginnings of acts which called out certain responses that do express emotions. When one animal attacks another, or is on the point of attacking, or of taking the bone of another dog, that action calls out violent responses which express the anger of the second dog. There we have a set of attitudes which express the emotional attitude of dogs; and we can carry this analysis into the human expression of emotion.

The part of our organism that most vividly and readily expresses the emotions is the face, and Darwin studied the face from this point of view. He took, naturally, the actor, the man whose business it is to express the emotions by the movements of the countenance, and studied the muscles themselves; and in studying them he undertook to show what the value of these changes of the face might be in the actual act. We speak of such expressions as those of anger and note the way in which the blood may suffuse the face at one stage and then leave it at another. Darwin studied the blood flow in fear and in terror. In these emotions one can find changes taking place in the blood flow itself. These changes have their value. They represent, of course, changes in the circulation of blood in the acts. These actions are generally actions which are rapid and can only take place when the blood is flowing rapidly. There must be a change in the rhythm of circulation and this generally registers itself in the countenance.

Many of our acts of hostility exhibit themselves in attitudes of the face similar to animals which attack with their teeth. The attitude, or in a more generalized term, the gesture, has been preserved after the value of the act has disappeared. The title of Darwin's work indicates his point of approach. He was dealing with these gestures, these attitudes, as expressive of emotions and assuming at the time that the gesture has this function of expressing the emotions. That attitude has been preserved, on this view, after the value of the act has disappeared. This gesture seems to remain for the purpose of expressing emotions. One naturally assumed there an attitude in the experience of animals which answers in some sense to those of the human animal. One could apply the doctrine of the survival of the fittest here also. The implication in this particular case was that these gestures or attitudes had lost the value which they had in the original acts and yet had survived. The indication was that they had survived because they served certain valuable functions, and the suggestion was that this was the expression of the emotions. That attitude on Darwin's part is reflected in the work of other psychologists, men who were interested, as Darwin was, in the study of the act, in the information that is conveyed by one individual to another by his attitude. They assume that these acts had a reason for existence because they expressed something in the mind of the individual. It is an approach like that of the philologist. They assume that language existed for the purpose of conveying certain ideas, certain feelings.

When one considers, he realizes that this is a false approach. It is quite impossible to assume that animals do undertake to express their emotions. They certainly do not undertake to express them for the benefit of other animals. The most that can be said is that the "expressions" did set free a certain emotion in the individual, an escape valve, so to speak, an emotional attitude which the animal needed, in some sense, to get rid of. They certainly could not exist in these lower animals as means of expressing emotions; we cannot approach them from the point of view of expressing a content in the mind of the individual. We can, of course, see how, for the actor, they may become definitely a language. An actor, for example, may undertake to express his rage, and he may do it by an expression of the countenance and so convey to the audience the emotion he intended. However, he is not expressing his own emotion but simply conveying to the audience the evidence of anger, and if he is successful he may do it more effectively, as far as the audience is concerned, than a person who is in reality angered. There we have these gestures serving the purpose of expression of the emotions, but we cannot conceive that they arose as such a language in order to express emotion. Language, then, has to be studied from the point of view of the gestural type of conduct within which it existed without being as such a definite language. And we have to see how the communicative function could have arisen out of that prior sort of conduct.

The psychology of Darwin assumed that emotion was a psychological state, a state of consciousness, and that this state could not itself be formulated in terms of the attitude or the behavior of the form. It was assumed that the emotion is there and that certain movements might give evidence of it. The evidence would be received and acted upon by other forms that were fashioned like itself. That is, it presupposed the conscious state as against the biological organism. The conscious state was that which was to be expressed in the gesture or the attitude. It was to be expressed in behavior and to be recognized in some fashion as existent in the consciousness of the other form through this medium of expression. Such was the general psychological attitude which Darwin accepted.

Contrary to Darwin, however, we find no evidence for the prior existence of consciousness as something which brings about behavior on the part of one organism that is of such a sort as to call forth an adjustive response on the part of another organism, without itself being dependent on such behavior. We are rather forced to conclude that consciousness is an emergent from such behavior; that so far from being a precondition of the social act, the social act is the precondition of it. The mechanism of the social act can be traced out without introducing into it the conception of consciousness as a separable element within that act; hence the social act, in its more elementary stages or forms, is possible without, or apart from, some form of consciousness.

Rise of Parallelism in Psychology

The psychology which stresses parallelism has to be distinguished from the psychology which regards certain states of consciousness as existing in the mind of the individual and succeeding each other in accordance with their own laws of association. The whole doctrine of the psychology which follows Hume was predominantly associationistic. Given certain states of consciousness, they were supposed to be held together by other similar elements. Among these elements were those of pleasure and pain. Connected with this atomism of associated conscious states was a psychology of action grounded on the association of pleasure and pain with certain other sensations and experiences. The doctrine of association was the dominant psychological doctrine; it dealt with static rather than dynamic experience.

The pushing of the psychological side further and further into the central nervous system revealed that there were whole series of experiences which might be called sensations and yet were very different from those which could be regarded as static, such as sound, odor, taste, and color. Association belonged to this static world. It was increasingly recognized that there was a large part of our experience which was dynamic.[11] The form of actual doing was present in some of the sensations which answered to the innervation of sensory nerves. There was also the study of those tracts which went down to the viscera, and these certainly were aligned with the emotional experiences. The whole process of the circulation of the blood had been opened up, and the action which involved the sudden change of the circulation of the blood. Fear,

11   The lines of association follow the lines of the act (1924).

hostility, anger, which called for sudden movement, or terror, which deprived the individual of the ability to move, reflected themselves in the visceral conditions; and also had their sensory aspects connected with the central nervous system. There was, then, a type of experience which did not fall into place in a static world. Wilhelm Wundt approached his problem from the standpoint of this sort of physiology which offered a clew by means of which one could follow out these various dynamic experiences into the mechanism of the organism itself.

The treatment which had been given to the central nervous system and its motor and sensory nerves had been that of bringing a nerve current to a central nervous system which was then in turn responsible for a sensation that happened in consciousness. To get a complete statement of what we call the act, one had to follow up the sensory side and then follow out the motor results that took place because of what happened in consciousness. The physiology to which I have referred in a certain sense separated itself from the field of consciousness. It was difficult to carry such a mechanism as this into the lower animals. That, at least, took the psychologist out of the field of animal experience. Darwin regarded the animal as that out of which human conduct evolves, as well as the human form, and if this is true then it must be that in some sense consciousness evolves.

The resulting approach is from the point of view of conduct itself, and here the principle of parallelism is brought in. What takes place in consciousness runs parallel with what takes place in the central nervous system. It is necessary to study the content of the form as physiological and also as psychological. The center of consciousness, within which is registered that which affects the sensory nerves and out of which springs the conduct due to sensation and memory images, is to be taken out of the physiological mechanism; and yet one must find a parallel in what takes place in the nervous system for what the physiologist had placed in consciousness as such. What I have referred to in the matter of the emotions seemed to present a physiological counterpart for what takes place in consciousness, a field that seemed to belong peculiarly to the mental side of life. Hate, love, anger—these are seemingly states of mind. How could they be stated in physiological terms? The study of the acts themselves from an evolutionary standpoint and also the study of the changes that take place in the organism itself when it is under the influence of what we call an emotion present analogues to these emotional states. One could find something there that definitely answered to the emotions.

The further development of this lead occurred in James's theory of the emotions. Because we run away when we are afraid and strike when we are angry, we can find something in the physiological organism that answers to fear and to anger. It is an attitude in the organism which answers to these emotional states, especially these visceral conditions to which I have referred, and the sudden changes in the circulation which are found associated with emotions. It becomes possible to relate the psychical conditions with physiological ones. The result was that one could make a much more complete statement of the conduct of the individual in physiological terms, could find a parallel for that which is stated in terms of consciousness in the mechanism of the body and in the operation of that mechanism. Such a psychology was called, naturally enough, a physiological psychology. It was a statement in terms of what went on in the organism of the content with which the psychologist had been dealing. What is there in the act of the animal which answers to these different so-called psychological categories? What is there that answers to the sensations, to the motor responses? When these questions were answered physiologically, they, of course, involved mechanisms located inside of the act, for all that takes place in the body is action. It may be delayed action, but there is nothing there that is itself simply a state, a physiological state that could be compared with a static state. We come then to the sensations and undertake to state them in terms of complete reflex action. We deal with the sensation from the standpoint of the stimulus, and when we come to deal with the various emotional states, we deal with them in terms of the preparation for action and the act itself as it is going on.[12] That is, it becomes now essential to relate a

[12]   Thus John Dewey added to James's doctrine the necessity of conflict in action in order for emotions to arise.

set of psychical states with the different phases of the act. Parallelism, then, is an attempt to find analogues between action and experienced contents.

The inevitable result of this analysis was to carry psychology from a static to a dynamic form. It was not simply a question of relating what was found in introspection with what is found in the organism; it became a question of relating together those things which were found in introspection in the dynamic way in which the physiological elements were related to the life of the organism. Psychology became in turn associational, motor, functional, and finally behavioristic.

The historical transformation of psychology was a process which took place gradually. Consciousness was' something which could not be simply dispensed with. In early psychology there was a crude attempt to account for consciousness as a certain secretion in the brain, but this was only a ridiculous phase of the transformation. Consciousness was something that was there, but it was something that could be brought into closer and closer relationship with what went on in the body. What went on there had a certain definite order. Everything that took place in the body was part of an act. The earlier conception of the central nervous system assumed that one could locate certain faculties of the mind in certain parts of the brain, but a study of the central nervous system did not reveal any such correlation. It became evident that there were nothing but paths in the central nervous system.[13] The cells of the brain were seen to be parts of the nervous paths provided with material for carrying on the system, but nothing was found there to carry on the preservation of an idea as such. There was nothing in the central nervous system which would enable one to locate a tract given over to abstractions. There was a time when the frontal lobe was regarded as the locus of thought-processes—but the frontal lobe also represents nothing but paths. The paths make very complicated conduct possible, they complicate the act enormously through the mechanism of the brain; but they do not set up any structure which functionally answers to

13   Among philosophers, Henri Bergson especially stressed this point. See his *Matière et Mémoire*.

ideas. So the study of consciousness from the standpoint of the organism inevitably led men to look at consciousness itself from the point of view of action.

What, for example, is our experience that answers to clenching of the fist? Physiological psychology followed the action out through the nerves that came from the muscles of the arm and hand. The experience of the act would then be the sensation of what was going on; in consciousness as such there is an awareness of what the organ was doing; there is a parallelism between what goes on in the organ and what takes place in consciousness. This parallelism is, of course, not a complete parallelism. There seems to be consciousness corresponding only to the sensory nerves.[14] We are conscious of some things and not conscious of others, and attention seems to play a very great part in determining which is the case. The parallelism which we carry over does not seem to be complete, but one which occurs only at various points. The thing that is interesting here is that it is the organism that now provides the clew for the analysis. Only portions of the response appear in consciousness as such. The organism has assumed the primary place. Experimental psychology started off from what it could get hold of in the physiological system, and then undertook to find out what in consciousness seemed to answer to it. The scientist felt that he had the same assurance that the physiologist had in identifying these facts in the nervous system, and given those facts he could look into consciousness. It was simpler to start with the neurosis and then register what was found in the psychosis. Thus, the acceptance of some sort of a parallelism between the contents of consciousness and the physiological processes of the central nervous system led to a conception of those contents dynamically, in terms of acts, instead of statically, in terms of states. In this way the contents of consciousness were approached from below (naturalistically) rather than from above (transcenden-

[14] We are conscious always of what we have done, never of doing it. We are always conscious directly only of sensory processes, never of motor processes; hence we are conscious of motor processes only through sensory processes, which are their resultants. The contents of consciousness have, therefore, to be correlated with or fitted into a physiological system in dynamic terms, as processes going on.

tally), by a study of the physiological processes of the central nervous system to determine what in the mind answers to the activities of the physiological organism.

There was a question as to the directive centers for unified action. We are apt to think of the central nervous system from the point of view of the telephone board, with calls coming in and responses going out. Certain centers come to be conceived as principal centers. When you go back to the base of the brain, to that portion which is the essence of the central nervous system of lower forms, you do find an organization there which controls in its activity other activities; but when you come to conduct in the human form, you fail to find any such system in which there is a single directive center or group of centers. One can see that the various processes which are involved in running away from danger can be processes which are so interrelated with other activities that the control comes in the organization. One sees the tree as a possible place of escape if a bull is after him; and in general, one sees things which will enable the ongoing activity to be carried out. A varying group of centers may be the determining factor in the whole activity of the individual. That is the concept which has also been carried into the field of growth. Certain parts of the embryo start growing and control growth until some other process comes into control. In the cortex, that organ which in some sense answers to human intelligence, we fail to find any exclusive and unvarying control, that is, any evidence of it in the structure of the form itself. In some way we can assume that the cortex acts as a whole, but we cannot come back to certain centers and say that this is where the mind is lodged in thinking and in action. There are an indefinite number of cells connected with each other, and their innervation in some sense leads to a unitary action, but what that unity is in terms of the central nervous system it is almost impossible to state. All the different parts of the cortex seem to be involved in everything that happens. All the stimuli that reach the brain are reflected into all parts of the brain, and yet we do get a unitary action. There remains, then, a problem which is by no means definitely solved: the unity of the action of the central nervous system. Wundt undertook to find certain centers which would be responsible for this sort of unity, but there is nothing in the structure of the brain itself which iso- lated any parts of the brain as those which direct conduct as a whole. The unity is a unity of integration, though just how this integration takes place in detail we cannot say.

What I wanted to bring out is that the approach to psycho- logical theory from the standpoint of the organism must inevita- bly be through an emphasis upon conduct, upon the dynamic rather than the static. It is, of course, possible to work in the other direction, that is, to look at experience from the point of view of the psychologist and to draw conclusions as to what must go on in the central nervous system. It is possible to recognize, for ex- ample, that we are not simply at the mercy of the different stimuli that play in the central nervous system—the natural view of the physiologist. We can see these organs adjust themselves to differ- ent types of stimuli. When air waves come in they affect the par- ticular organs of the ear; when tastes and odors come in, the stimuli get to tracts in the proper organs that respond. There may seem to be merely a response of the organism to the stimuli. This position is taken over into the psychology of Spencer, who ac- cepted the Darwinian principle of evolution. The influence of en- vironment is exercised over the form, and the adaptation of the form results from the influences of the environment on it. Spencer conceived of the central nervous system as being continually played upon by stimuli which set up certain paths, so that it was the environment which was fashioning the form.

The phenomena of attention, however, give a different picture of conduct. The human animal is an attentive animal, and his at- tention may be given to stimuli that are relatively faint. One can pick out sounds at a distance. Our whole intelligent process seems to lie in the attention which is selective of certain types of stim- uli.[15] Other stimuli which are bombarding the system are in some fashion shunted off. We give our attention to one particular thing. Not only do we open the door to certain stimuli and close it to others, but our attention is an organizing process as well as a se-

15   George Herbert Mead, *Mind, Self, and Society*, ed. Charles W. Morris (Chicago: University of Chicago, 1934), pp. 90–109.

lective process. When giving attention to what we are going to do, we are picking out the whole group of stimuli which represent successive activity. Our attention enables us to organize the field in which we are going to act. Here we have the organism as acting and determining its environment. It is not simply a set of passive senses played upon by the stimuli that come from without. The organism goes out and determines what it is going to respond to and organizes that world. One organism picks out one thing and another picks out a different one, since each is going to act in a different way. Such is an approach to what goes on in the central nervous system which comes to the physiologist from the psychologist.

The physiology of attention is a field which is still a dark continent. The organism itself fits itself to certain types of conduct, and this is of considerable importance in determining what the animal will do. There also lie back in the organism responses, such as those of escape from danger, that represent a peculiar sensitivity. A sound in some other direction would not have the same effect. The eye is very sensitive to motions that lie outside of the field of central vision, even though this area of the retina of the eye is not so sensitive to form and distinctions of color. You look for a book in a library and you carry a sort of mental image of the back of the book; you render yourself sensitive to a certain image of a friend you are going to meet. We can sensitize ourselves to certain types of stimuli, and we can build up the sort of action we are going to take. In a chain set of responses the form carries out one instinctive response and then finds itself in the presence of another stimulus, and so forth; but as intelligent beings we build up such organized reactions ourselves. The field of attention is one in which there must be a mechanism in which we can organize the different stimuli with reference to others so that certain responses can take place. The description of this is something we can reach through a study of our own conduct, and at present that is the most that we can say.

Parallelism in psychology was very largely under the control of the study of the central nervous system, and that led on inevitably to functional, motor, voluntaristic, and finally behavioristic

psychology. The more one could state of the processes of the individual in terms of the central nervous system, the more one
would use the pattern which one found in the central nervous system to interpret conduct. What I am insisting upon is that the
patterns which one finds in the central nervous system are patterns of action—not of contemplation, not of appreciation as
such, but patterns of action. On the other hand I want to point
out that one is able to approach the central nervous system from
the psychologist's point of view and set certain problems to the
physiologist. How is the physiologist to explain attention? When
the physiologist attempts that he is bound to do so in terms of the
various paths. If he is going to explain why one path is selected
rather than another he must go back to these terms of paths and
actions. You cannot set up in the central nervous system a selective principle which can be generally applied throughout; you
cannot say there is a specific something in the central nervous system that is related to attention; you cannot say that there is a
general power of attention. You have to state it specifically, so
that even when you are directing your study of the central nervous
system from the point of view of psychology, the type of explanation that you are going to get will have to be in terms of paths
which represent action.

Such, in brief, is the history of the appearance of physiological psychology in its parallelistic form, a psychology which had
moved to the next stage beyond that of associationalism. Attention is ordinarily stressed in tracing this transition, but the emphasis on attention is one which is derived largely from the study
of the organsm as such, and it accordingly should be seen in the
larger context we have presented.

Parallelism and the Ambiguity of "Consciousness"

"Consciousness" is a very ambiguous term. One often
identifies consciousness with a certain something that is there under certain conditions and is not there under other conditions.
One approaches this most naturally by assuming that it is some-

thing that happens under certain conditions of the organism, something, then, that can be conceived of as running parallel to certain phenomena in the nervous system, but not parallel to others. There seems to be no consciousness that answers to the motor processes as such; the consciousness we have of our action is sensory in type and answers to the current coming from the sensory nerves which are affected by the contraction of the muscles. We are not conscious of the actual motor processes, but we have a sensory process that runs parallel to it. This is the situation out of which parallelistic psychology arises. It implies an organism which is a going concern, that seemingly can run without consciousness. A person continues to live when he is under a general anesthetic. Consciousness leaves and consciousness returns, but the organism itself runs on. And the more completely one is able to state the psychological processes in terms of the central nervous system, the less important does this consciousness become.

The extreme statement of that sort was given by Hugo Münsterberg.[16] He assumed the organism itself simply ran on, but that answering to certain nervous changes there were conscious states. If one said that he did something, what that amounted to was a consciousness of the movement of the muscles of his body in doing it; the consciousness of the beginning of the act is that which he interpreted as his own volition to act. There is only a consciousness of certain processes that are going on. Parallelism in this extreme form, however, excluded just such processes as those of attention and the selective character of consciousness. If the physiologist had been able to point out the mechanism of the central nervous system by which we organize our action, there might still be dominant such a statement in terms of this extreme parallelism which would regard the individual as simply conscious of the selection which the organism made. But the process of selection itself is so complex that it becomes almost impossible to state it, especially in such terms. Consciousness as such is peculiarly selective, and the processes of selection, of sensitizing the organ to stimuli, are something very difficult to isolate in the central nervous system. William James points out that the amount of

16   See *Die Willenshandlung.*

difference which you have to give to a certain stimulus to make it dominant is very slight, and he could conceive of an act of volition which holds onto a certain stimulus and just gives it a little more emphasis than it otherwise would have. Wundt tried to make parallelism possible by assuming the possibility of certain centers which could perform this selective function. But there was no satisfactory statement of the way in which one could get this interaction between an organism and a consciousness, of the way in which consciousness could act upon a central nervous system. So that we get, at this stage of the development of psychology, parallelism rather than interactionism.

The parallelistic phase of psychology reveals itself, not simply as one of the passing forms which has appeared in psychological investigation, but as one which has served a very evident purpose and met a very evident need.

We do distinguish, in some sense, the experiences that we call conscious from those going on in the world around us. We see a color and give it a certain name. We find that we are mistaken, due to a defect in our vision, and we go back to the spectral colors and analyze it. We say there is something that is independent of our immediate sensory process. We are trying to hold that part of experience that can be taken as independent of one's own immediate response. We want to get hold of that so that we can deal with the problem of error. When error is involved, we do not draw the line. When we discover that a tree seen at a distance is not there when we reach the spot, we have mistaken something else for a tree. Thus, we have to have a field to which we can refer our own experience; and also we require objects which are recognized to be independent of our own vision. We want the mechanism which will make that distinction at any time, and we generalize it in this way. We work out the theory of sense perception in terms of the external stimulus, so that we can get hold of that which can be depended upon in order to distinguish it from that which cannot be depended upon in the same way. Even an object that is actually there can still be so resolved. In the laboratory we can distinguish between the stimulus and the sense experience. The experimenter turns on a certain light, and he knows just what that light is. He can tell what takes place in the retina and in the central nervous system, and then he asks what the experiences are. He puts all sorts of elements in the process so that the subject will mistake what it is. He gets on the one side conscious data and on the other side the physical processes that are going on. He carries this analysis only into a field which is of importance for his investigation; and he himself has objects out there which could be analyzed in the same fashion.

We want to be able to distinguish what belongs to our own experience from that which can be stated, as we say, in scientific terms. We are sure of some processes, but we are not sure as to the reaction of people to these processes. We recognize that there are all sorts of differences among individuals. We have to make this distinction, so we have to set up a certain parallelism between things which are there and have a uniform value for everybody, and things which vary with certain individuals. We seem to get a field of consciousness and a field of physical things which are not conscious.

I want to distinguish the differences in the use of the term "consciousness" to stand for accessibility to certain contents and as synonymous with certain contents themselves. When you shut your eyes you shut yourself off from certain stimuli. When one takes an anesthetic, the world is inaccessible to him. Similarly, sleep renders one inaccessible to the world. Now I want to distinguish this use of consciousness, that of rendering one accessible and inaccessible to certain fields, from these contents themselves which are determined by the experience of the individual. We want to be able to deal with an experience which varies among the different individuals, to deal with the different contents which in some sense represent the same object. We want to be able to separate those contents which vary from contents which are in some sense common to all of us. Our psychologists undertake definitely to deal with experience as it varies with individuals. Some of these experiences are dependent upon the perspective of the individual, and some are peculiar to a particular organ. When one is color-blind he has a different experience from a person with a normal eye.

When we use "consciousness," then, with reference to those conditions which are variable with the experience of the individual, this usage is a quite different one from that of rendering ourselves inaccessible to the world.[17] In one case we are dealing with the situation of a person going to sleep, distracting his attention or centering his attention—a partial or complete exclusion of certain parts of a field. The other use is in application to the experience of the individual that is different from the experience of anybody else, and not only different in that way, but different from his own experience at different times. Our experience varies not simply with our own organism but from moment to moment, and yet it is an experience which is of something which has not varied as our experiences vary, and we want to be able to study that experience in this variable form, so that some sort of parallelism has to be set up. One might attempt to set up the parallelism outside of the body, but the study of the stimuli inevitably takes us over into the study of the body itself.

Different positions will lead to different experiences in regard to such an object as a penny placed on a certain spot. There are other phenomena that are dependent upon the character of the eye, or the effect of past experiences. What the penny would be experienced as depends upon the past experiences that may have occurred to the different individuals. It is a different penny to one person from what it is to another; yet the penny is there as an entity by itself. We want to be able to deal with these spatially perspectival differences in individuals. Still more important from a psychological standpoint is the perspective of memory, by means of which one person sees one penny and another sees another penny. These are characters which we want to separate, and it is here that the legitimacy of our parallelism lies, namely, in that distinction between the object as it can be determined, physically and physiologically, as common to all, and the experience which is peculiar to a particular organism, a particular person.

[17]   Also from a third use in which "consciousness" is restricted to the level of the operation of symbols. On consciousness *see* "The Definition of the Psychical," *University of Chicago Decennial Publications*, III (1903), 77 ff.; "What Social Objects Must Psychology Presuppose?" *Journal of Philosophy*, VII (1910), 174 ff.

Setting this distinction up as a psychological doctrine gives the sort of psychology that Wundt has most effectively and exhaustively presented. He has tried to present the organism and its environment as identical physical objects for any experience, although the reflection of them in the different experiences are all different. Two persons studying the same central nervous system at the dissecting table will see it a little differently; yet they see the same central nervous system. Each of them has a different experience in that process. Now, put on one side the organism and its environment as a common object and then take what is left, so to speak, and put that into the experience of the separate individuals, and the result is a parallelism: on the one side the physical world, and on the other side consciousness.

The basis for this distinction is, as we have seen, a familiar and a justifiable one, but when put into the form of a psychology, as Wundt did, it reaches its limits; and when carried beyond leads into difficulty. The legitimate distinction is that which enables a person to identify that phase of an experience which is peculiar to himself, which has to be studied in terms of a moment in his biography. There are facts which are important only insofar as they lie in the biography of the individual. The technique of that sort of a separation comes back to the physiological environment on one side and to the experience on the other. In this way an experience of the object itself is contrasted with the individual's experience, consciousness on one side with the unconscious world on the other.

When we follow this distinction down to its limits, we reach a physiological organism that is the same for all people, played upon by a set of stimuli which is the same to all. We want to follow the effects of such stimuli in the central nervous system up to the point where a particular individual has a specific experience. When we have done that for a particular case, we use this analysis as a basis for generalizing that distinction. We can say that there are physical things on one side and mental events on the other. We assume that the experienced world of each person is looked upon as a result of a causal series that lies inside of his brain. We follow stimuli into the brain, and there we say consciousness flashes out. In this way we have ultimately to locate all experience in the brain, and then old epistemological ghosts arise. Whose brain is it? How is the brain known? Where does that brain lie? The whole world comes to lie inside of the observer's brain; and his brain lies in everybody else's brain, and so on without end. All sorts of difficulties arise if one undertakes to erect this parallelistic division into a metaphysical one. The essentially practical nature of this division must now be pointed out.

The Program of Behaviorism

We have seen that a certain sort of parallelism is involved in the attempt to state the experience of the individual insofar as it is peculiar to him as an individual. What is accessible only to that individual, what takes place only in the field of his own inner life, must be stated in its relationship to the situation within which it takes place. One individual has one experience and another has another experience, and both are stated in terms of their biographies; but there is in addition that which is common to the experience of all. And our scientific statement correlates that which the individual himself experiences, and which can ultimately be stated only in terms of his experience, with the experience which belongs to everyone. This is essential in order that we may interpret what is peculiar to the individual. We are always separating that which is peculiar to our own reaction, that which we can see that other persons cannot see, from that which is common to all. We are referring what belongs to the experience just of the individual to a common language, to a common world. And when we carry out this relationship, this correlation, into what takes place physically and physiologically, we get a parallelistic psychology.

The particular color or odor that any one of us experiences is a private affair. It differs from the experience of other individuals, and yet there is the common object to which it refers. It is the same light, the same rose, that is involved in these experiences. What we try to do is to follow these common stimuli in through the nervous system of each of these individuals. We aim to get the statement in universal terms which will answer to those particular conditions. We want to control them as far as we can, and it is that determination of the conditions under which the particular experience takes place that enables us to carry out that control.[18]

When one says that his experience of an object is made up of different sensations and then undertakes to state the conditions under which those sensations take place, he may say that he is stating those conditions in terms of his own experience. But they are conditions which are common to all. He measures, he determines just what is taking place, but this apparatus with which he measures is, after all, made up of his sensuous experience. Things that are hot or cold, rough or smooth, the objects themselves, are stated in terms of sensations; but they are stated in terms of sensations which we can make universal, and we take these common characters of experience and find in terms of them those experiences which are peculiar to the different individuals.

Psychology is interested in this correlation, in finding out what the relationship is between what goes on in the physical world and what goes on in the organism when a person has a sensory experience. That program was carried out by Hermann Helmholtz.[19] The world was there in terms which could be stated in the laws of science, that is, the stimuli were stated in physical terms. What goes on in the nervous system could be stated more and more exactly, and this could be correlated with certain definite experiences which the individual found in his own life. The psychologist is interested in learning the correlation between the conditions under which the experience takes place and that which is peculiar to the individual. He wishes to make these statements as universal as possible and is scientific in that respect. He wants to state the experience of an individual just as closely as he can in terms of the field which he can control, those conditions under which it appears. He naturally tries to state the conduct of the individual in terms of his reflexes, and he carries back as far as he can the more complex reflexes of the individual to the simpler

[18]   The following methodological interpretation of parallelism is further discussed in Mead, *op. cit.*, pp. 109 ff.

[19]   *Die Lehre von dem Tonempfindungen; Handbuch der physiologischen Optik.*

forms of action. He uses, as far as he is able to use, a behavioristic statement, because that can be formulated in terms of this same field he controls.

The motive back of modern psychology gets an expression in the field of mental testing, where one is getting correlations between certain situations and certain responses. It is characteristic of this psychology that, not only is it as behavioristic as it can be (in that it states the experience of the individual as completely as it can in objective terms), but it also is interested in getting such statements and correlations so that it can control conduct as far as possible. We find modern psychology interested in practical problems, especially those of education. We have to lead the intelligences of infants and children into certain definite uses of media and certain definite types of responses. How can we take the individual with his peculiarities and bring him over into a more nearly uniform type of response? He has to have the same language as others, and the same units of measurement; and he has to take over a certain definite culture as a background for his own experience. He has to fit himself into certain social structures and make them a part of himself. How is that to be accomplished? We are dealing with separate individuals and yet these individuals have to become a part of a common whole. We want to get the correlation between this world which is common and that which is peculiar to the individual. So we have psychology attacking the questions of learning, and the problems of the school, and trying to analyze different intelligences so that we can state them in terms which are as far as possible common; we want something which can correlate with the task which the child has to carry out. There are certain definite processes involved in speech. What is there that is uniform by means of which we are able to identify what the individual can do and what particular training he may have to take? Psychology also goes over into the field of business questions, of salesmanship, personnel questions; it goes over into the field of that which is abnormal and tries to get hold of that which is peculiar in the abnormal individual and to bring it into relation with the normal and with the structures which get their expression in these abnormalities. It is interesting to see that psychology starts with this problem of getting correlations between the experience of individuals and conditions under which it takes place and undertakes to state this experience in terms of behavior; and that it at once endeavors to make a practical use of this correlation it finds for the purposes of training and control. It is becoming essentially a practical science and has pushed to one side the psychological and philosophical problems which have been tied up with earlier dogma under associational psychology. Such are the influences which work in the behavioristic psychology.

This psychology is not, and should not be regarded as, a theory which is to be put against an associational doctrine. What it is trying to do is to find what the conditions are under which the experience of the individual arises. That experience is of the sort that takes us back to conduct in order that we can follow it. It is that which gives a distinctive mark to a psychological investigation. History and all the social sciences deal with human beings, but they are not primarily psychological. Psychology can be of great importance in dealing with, say, economics, the problem of value, of desire, the problems of political science, the relation of the individual to the state, and the personal relations which have to be considered in terms of individuals. All of the social sciences can be found to have a psychological phase. History is nothing but biography, a whole series of biographies; and yet all of these social sciences deal with individuals in their common characters; and when the individual stands out as different, he is looked at from the point of view of that which he accomplishes in the whole society, or in terms of the destructive effect which he may have. But we are not primarily occupied as social scientists in studying his experience as such. Psychology does undertake to work out the technique which will enable it to deal with these experiences which any individual may have at any moment in his life and which are peculiar to that individual. And the method of dealing with such an experience is in knowing the conditions under which that experience of the individual took place. We should undertake to state the experience of the individual just as far as we can in terms of the conditions under which it arises. It is essentially a control problem to which the psychologist is turning. It has, of course, its aspect of research for knowledge. We want to increase our knowledge, but there is back of that an attempt to get control through the knowledge which we obtain; and it is very interesting to see that our modern psychology is going farther and farther into those fields within which control can be so realized. It is successful insofar as it can work out correlations which can be tested. We want to get hold of those factors in the nature of the individual which can be recognized in the nature of all members of society but which can be identified in the particular individual. Those are problems which are forcing themselves more and more to the front.

There is another phase of recent psychology which I should refer to, namely, configuration or *gestalt* psychology, which has been of interest in recent years. There we have the recognition of elements or phases of experience which are common to the experience of the individual and to those conditions under which this experience arises.[20] There are certain general forms in the field of perception in the experience of the individual as well as in the objects themselves. They can be identified. One cannot take such a thing as a color and build it up out of certain sets of sensations. Experience, even that of the individual, must start with some whole. It must involve some whole in order that we may get the elements we are after. What is of peculiar importance to us is this recognition of an element which is common in the perception of the individual and that which is regarded as a condition under which that perception arises—a position in opposition to an analysis of experience which proceeds on the assumption that the whole we have in our perception is simply an organization of these separate elements. *Gestalt* psychology gives us another element which is common to the experience of the individual and the world which determines the conditions under which that experience arises. When before one was concerned with the stimuli and what could be traced in the central nervous system which was then correlated with the experience of the individual, now we have a certain struc-

[20]   W. Köhler, *Die physischen Gestalten in Ruhe und im stationaren Zustand; Gestalt Psychology.*

ture that has to be recognized both in the experience of the individual and the conditioning world.

A behavioristic psychology represents a definite tendency rather than a system, a tendency to state as far as possible the conditions under which the experience of the individual arises. Correlation gets its expression in parallelism. The term is unfortunate in that it carries with it the distinction between mind and body, between the psychical and the physical. It is true that all the operations of stimuli can be traced through to the central nervous system, so we seem to be able to take the problem inside of our skins and get back to something in the organism, the central nervous system, which is representative of everything that happens outside. When we speak of a light as influencing us, we must remember it does not influence us until it strikes the retina of the eye. Sound does not exert influence until it reaches the ear, and so on, so that we can say the whole world can be stated in terms of what goes on inside of the organism itself. And we can say that what we are trying to correlate are the happenings in the central nervous system on the one side and the experience of the individual on the other.

But we have to recognize that we have made an arbitrary cut there. We cannot take the central nervous system by itself, nor the physical objects by themselves. The whole process is one which starts from a stimulus and involves everything that takes place. Thus, psychology correlates the difference of perceptions with the physical intensity of the stimulus. We could state the intensity of a weight we were lifting in terms of the central nervous system, but that would be a difficult way of stating it. That is not what psychology is trying to do. It is not trying to relate a set of psychoses to a set of neuroses. It is trying to state the experiences of the individual in terms of the conditions under which they arise, and such conditions can very seldom be stated in terms of the neuroses. Occasionally we can follow the process into the central nervous system, but it is quite impossible to state most of the conditions in those terms. We control experiences in the intensity of the light, in the noises that we produce—control them in terms of the effects which are produced on us by heat and cold. That is where we get our control. We may be able to change these by dealing with actual organisms, but in general we are trying to correlate the experience of the individual with the situation under which it arises. In order that we can get that sort of control, we have to have a generalized statement. We want to know the conditions under which experience may appear. We are interested in finding the most general laws of correlation we can find. But the psychologist is interested in finding that sort of condition which can be correlated with the experience of the individual. We are trying to state the experience of the individual and situations in just as common terms as we can, and it is this which gives the importance to what we call behavioristic psychology. It is not a new psychology that comes in and takes the place of an old system.

An objective psychology is not trying to get rid of consciousness, but trying to state the intelligence of the individual in terms which will enable us to see how that intelligence is exercised and how it can be improved. It is natural, then, that such a psychology as this should seek for a statement which would bring these two phases of the experience as close to each other as possible or translate them into language which is common to both fields. We do not want two languages, one of certain physical facts and one of certain conscious facts. When you push that analysis to the limit, you say that everything that takes place in consciousness in some way has to be located in the head, because you are following up a certain sort of causal relation which affects consciousness. The head you talk about is not stated in terms of the head you are observing. Bertrand Russell says the real head he is referring to is not the head that the physiologist is looking at, but the physiologist's own head. Whether that is the case or not, it is a matter of infinite indifference to psychologists. That is not a problem in the present psychology, and behaviorism is not to be regarded as legitimate to a certain point and as then breaking down. Behavioristic psychology only undertakes to get a common statement that is significant and makes our correlation successful. The history of psychology has been a history which moved in this direction, and anyone who looks at what takes place in the psychological associations at the present time and the ways in which psychology is being carried over into other fields, sees that the interest, the impulse that lies behind it, is in getting just such a correlation which will enable science to get a control over the conditions of experience.

The term "parallelism" has an unfortunate implication: it is historically and philosophically bound up with the contrast of the physical over against the psychical, with consciousness over against the unconscious world. Actually, we simply state what an experience is as compared to those conditions under which it arises. The fact lies behind parallelism, and to carry out the correlation one has to state both fields in as common a language as possible, and behaviorism is simply a movement in that direction. Psychology is not something that deals with consciousness; psychology deals with the experience of the individual in relation to the conditions under which the experience goes on. It is social psychology when the conditions are social ones. It is behavioristic when the approach to experience is made through conduct.[21]

21 By way of further avoiding certain metaphysical implications I wish to say that it does not follow that because we have on the one side individual experience which can be perhaps private in the sense to which I have referred to privacy, and have on the other a common world, that we have then two separate levels of existence or reality which are to be distinguished metaphysically from each other. A great deal that appears simply as the experience of an individual, as his own sensation or perception, becomes public later. Every discovery as such begins with experiences which have to be stated in terms of the biography of the discoverer. The man can note exceptions and implications which other people do not see and can only record them in terms of his own experience. He puts them in that form in order that other persons may get a like experience, and then he undertakes to find out what the explanation of these strange facts is. He works out hypotheses and tests them and they become common property thereafter. That is, there is a close relationship between these two fields of the psychical and the physical, the private and the public. We make distinctions between these, recognizing that the same factor may now be only private and yet later may become public. It is the work of the discoverer through his observations and through his hypotheses and experiments to be continually transforming what is his own private experience into a universal form. The same may be said of other fields, as in the work of the great artist who takes his own emotions and gives them a universal form so that others may enter into them.

Wundt and the Concept of the Gesture

The particular field of social science with which we are concerned is one which was opened up through the work of Darwin and the more elaborate presentation of Wundt.

When we take Wundt's parallelistic statement, we get a point of view from which we can approach the problem of social experience. Wundt undertook to show the parallelism between what goes on in the body as represented by processes of the central nervous system and what goes on in those experiences which the individual recognizes as his own. He had to find that which was common to these two fields—what in the psychical experience could be referred to in physical terms.[22]

Wundt isolated a very valuable conception of the gesture as that which becomes later a symbol, but which is to be found in its earlier stages as a part of a social act.[23] It is that part of the social act which serves as a stimulus to other forms involved in the same social act. I have given the illustration of the dogfight as a method of presenting the gesture. The act of each dog becomes the stimulus to the other dog for his response. There is then a relationship between these two; and as the act is responded to by the other dog; it, in turn, undergoes change. The very fact that the dog is ready to attack another becomes a stimulus to the other dog to change his own position or his own attitude. He has no sooner done this than the change of attitude in the

22 Cf. *Grundzüge der physiologischen Psychologie.* The fundamental defect of Wundt's psychophysical parallelism is the fundamental defect of all psychophysical parallelism: the required parallelism is not in fact complete on the psychical side, since only the sensory and not the motor phase of the physiological process of experience has a psychic correlate; hence the psychical aspect of the required parallelism can be completed only physiologically, thus breaking it down. And this fundamental defect of his psychophysical parallelism vitiates the analysis of social experiences —and especially of communication—which he bases upon the assumption of that parallelism.

23 *Völkerpsychologie,* Vol. I. For Mead's treatment of Wundt compare "The Relations of Psychology and Philology," *Psychological Bulletin,* I (1904), 375 ff., with the more critical "The Imagination in Wundt's Treatment of Myth and Religion," *ibid.,* III (1906), 393 ff.

second dog in turn causes the first dog to change his attitude. We have here a conversation of gestures. They are not, however, gestures in the sense that they are significant. We do not assume that the dog says to himself, "If the animal comes from this direction, he is going to spring at my throat, and I will turn in such a way." What does take place is an actual change in his own position due to the direction of the approach of the other dog.

We find a similar situation in boxing and in fencing, as in the feint and the parry that is initiated on the part of the other. And then the first one of the two in turn changes his attack; there may be considerable play back and forth before actually a stroke results. This is the same situation as in the dogfight. When the individual is successful a great deal of his attack and defense must be not considered, it must take place immediately. He must adjust himself "instinctively" to the attitude of the other individual. He may, of course, think it out. He may deliberately feint in order to open up a place of attack. But a great deal has to be without deliberation.

In this case we have a situation in which certain parts of the act become a stimulus to the other form to adjust itself to those responses; and that adjustment in turn becomes a stimulus to the first form to change his own act and start a different one. There are a series of attitudes, movements, on the part of these forms which belong to the beginnings of acts that are the stimuli for the responses that take place. The beginning of a response becomes the stimulus to the first form to change his attitude, to adopt a different act. The term "gesture" may be identified with these beginnings of social acts which are stimuli for the response of other forms. Darwin was interested in such gestures because they expressed emotions, and he dealt with them very largely as though this were their sole function. He looked at them as serving the function with reference to the other forms which they served with reference to his own observation. The gestures expressed emotions of the animal to Darwin; he saw in the attitude of the dog the joy with which he accompanied his master in taking a walk. And he left his treatment of the gestures largely in these terms.

It was easy for Wundt to show that this was not a legitimate point of attack on the problem of these gestures. They did not at bottom serve the function of expression of the emotions: that was not the reason why they were stimuli, but rather because they were parts of complex acts in which different forms were involved. They became the tools through which the other forms responded. When they did give rise to a certain response, they were themselves changed in response to the change which took place in the other form. They are part of the organization of the social act and highly important elements in that organization. To the human observer they are expressions of emotion, and that function of expressing emotion can legitimately become the field of the work of the artist and of the actor. The actor is in the same position as the poet; he is expressing emotions through his own attitude, his tones of voice, through his gestures, just as the poet through his poetry is expressing his emotions and arousing that emotion in others. We get in this way a function which is not found in the social act of these animals or in a great deal of our own conduct, such as that of the boxer and the fencer. We have this interplay with the gestures serving their functions, calling out the responses of the others, these responses becoming themselves stimuli for readjustment until the final social act itself can be carried out. Another illustration of this is in the relation of parent-form to the infant —the stimulating cry, the answering tone on the part of the parent-form and the consequent change in the cry of the infant-form. Here we have a set of adjustments of the two forms carrying out a common social act involved in the care of the child. Thus we have, in all these instances, a social process in which one can isolate the gesture which has its function in the social process and which can become an expression of emotions or later can become the expression of a meaning, an idea.

The primitive situation is that of the social act which involves the interaction of different forms, which involves, therefore, the adjustment of the conduct of these different forms to each other, in the social process. Within that process one can find what we term the gestures, those phases of the act which bring about the adjustment of the response of the other form. These phases of the act carry with them the attitude as the observer recognizes it and also what we call the inner attitude. The animal may be angry or afraid. There are such emotional attitudes which lie back of these acts, but these are only part of the whole process that is going on. Anger expresses itself in attack; fear expresses itself in flight. We can see, then, that the gestures mean these attitudes on the part of the form, that is, they have that meaning for us. We see that an animal is angry and that he is going to attack. We know that that is in the action of the animal and is revealed by the attitude of the animal. We cannot say the animal means it in the sense that he has a reflective determination to attack. A man may strike another before he means it; a man may jump and run away from a loud sound behind his back before he knows what he is doing. If he has the idea in his mind, then the gesture not only means this to the observer but it also means the idea which the individual has. In one case the observer sees that the attitude of the dog means attack, but he does not say that it means a conscious determination to attack on the part of the dog. However, should somebody shake his fist in your face you assume that he has not only a hostile attitude but that he has some idea behind it. You assume that it means not only a possible attack, but that the individual has an idea in his experience.

When, now, that gesture means this idea behind it and it arouses that idea in the other individual, then we have a significant symbol. In the case of the dogfight we have a gesture which calls out appropriate response; in the present case we have a symbol which answers to a meaning in the experience of the first individual and which also calls out that meaning in the second individual. Where the gesture reaches that situation it has become what we call "language." It is now a significant symbol, and it signifies a certain meaning.[24]

The gesture is that phase of the individual act to which adjustment takes place on the part of other individuals in the

[24] See "A Behavioristic Account of the Significant Symbol," *Journal of Philosophy*, XIX (1922), 157 ff.

social process of behavior. The vocal gesture becomes a significant symbol (unimportant, as such, on the merely affective side of experience) when it has the same effect on the individual making it that it has on the individual to whom it is addressed or who explicitly responds to it, and thus involves a reference to the self of the individual making it. The gesture in general, and the vocal gesture in particular, indicates some object or other within the field of social behavior, an object of common interest to all the individuals involved in the given social act thus directed toward or upon that object. The function of the gesture is to make adjustment possible among the individuals implicated in any given social act with reference to the object or objects with which that act is concerned; and the significant gesture or significant symbol affords far greater facilities for such adjustment and readjustment than does the non-significant gesture, because it calls out in the individual making it the same attitude toward it (or toward its meaning) that it calls out in the other individuals participating with him in the given social act. Thus it makes him conscious of their attitude toward it (as a component of his behavior) and enables him to adjust his subsequent behavior to theirs in the light of that attitude. In short, the conscious or significant conversation of gestures is a much more adequate and effective mechanism of mutual adjustment within the social act—involving, as it does, the taking, by each of the individuals carrying it on, of the attitudes of the others toward himself—than is the unconscious or non-significant conversation of gestures.

When, in any given social act or situation, one individual indicates by a gesture to another individual what this other individual is to do, the first individual is conscious of the meaning of his own gesture—or the meaning of his gesture appears in his own experience—insofar as he takes the attitude of the second individual toward that gesture and tends to respond to it implicitly in the same way that the second individual responds to it explicitly. Gestures become significant symbols when they implicitly arouse in an individual making them the same responses which they explicitly arouse, or are supposed to arouse, in other individuals, the individuals to whom they are addressed. In all conversations of gestures within the social process, whether external (between different individuals) or internal (between a given individual and himself), the individual's consciousness of the content and flow of meaning involved depends on his thus taking the attitude of the other toward his own gestures. In this way every gesture within a given social group or community comes to stand for a particular act or response, namely, the act or response which it calls forth explicitly in the individual to whom it is addressed and implicitly in the individual who makes it; and this particular act or response for which it stands is its meaning as a significant symbol. Only in terms of gestures as significant symbols is the existence of mind or intelligence possible; for only in terms of gestures which are significant symbols can thinking—which is simply an internalized or implicit conversation of the individual with himself by means of such gestures—take place. The internalization in our experience of the external conversations of gestures which we carry on with other individuals in the social process is the essence of thinking; and the gestures thus internalized are significant symbols because they have the same meanings for all individual members of the given society or social group, that is, they respectively arouse the same attitudes in the individuals making them that they arouse in the individuals responding to them. Otherwise the individual could not internalize them or be conscious of them and their meanings. As we shall see, the same procedure which is responsible for the genesis and existence of mind or consciousness—namely, the taking of the attitude of the other toward one's self, or toward one's own behavior—also necessarily involves the genesis and existence at the same time of significant symbols, or significant gestures.

In Wundt's doctrine, the parallelism between the gesture and the emotion or the intellectual attitude of the individual, makes it possible to set up a like parallelism in the other individual. The gesture calls out a gesture in the other form which will arouse or call out the same emotional attitude and the same idea. When this has taken place the individuals have begun to talk to each other. What I referred to before was a conversation of gestures which did not involve significant symbols or gestures. The dogs are not talking to each other; there are no ideas in the minds of the dogs; nor do we assume that the dog is trying to convey an idea to the other dog. But if the gesture, in the case of the human individual, has parallel to it a certain psychical state which is the idea of what the person is going to do, and if this gesture calls out a like gesture in the other individual and calls out a similar idea, then it becomes a significant gesture. It stands for the ideas in the minds of both of them.

There is some difficulty in carrying out this analysis if we accept Wundt's parallelism. When a person shakes his fist in your face, that is a gesture in the sense in which we use the term, the beginning of an act that calls out a response on your part. Your response may vary: it may depend on the size of the man, it may mean shaking your fist, or it may mean flight. A whole series of different responses are possible. In order that Wundt's theory of the origin of language may be carried out, the gesture which the first individual makes use of must in some sense be reproduced in the experience of the individual in order that it may arouse the same idea in his mind. We must not confuse the beginning of language with its later stages. It is quite true that as soon as we see the attitude of the dog we say that it means an attack, or that when we see a person looking around for a chair that it means he would like to sit down. The gesture is one which means these processes, and that meaning is aroused by what we see. But we are supposed to be at the beginning of these developments of language. If we assume that there is a certain psychical state answering a physical state, how are we going to get to the point when the gesture will arouse the *same* gesture in the attitude of the other individual? In the very beginning the other person's gesture means what you are going to do about it. It does not mean what he is thinking about or even his emotion. Supposing his angry attack aroused fear in you, then you are not going to have anger in your mind, but fear.

His gesture means fear as far as you are concerned. That is the primitive situation. Where the big dog attacks the little dog, the little dog puts his tail between his legs and runs away, but the gesture does not call out in the second individual what it did in the first. The response is generally of a different kind from the stimulus in the social act, a different action is aroused. If you assume that there is a certain idea answering to that act, you want at a later stage to get the idea of the first form, but originally your idea will be your own idea which answers to a certain end. If we say that gesture "A" has idea "a" as answering to it, gesture "A" in the first form calls out gesture "B" and its related idea "b" in the second form. Here the idea that answers to gesture "A" is not idea "a" but idea "b." Such a process can never arouse in one mind just the idea which the other person has in his.

How, in terms of Wundt's psychological analysis of communication, does a responding organism get or experience the same idea or psychical correlate of any given gesture that the organism making this gesture has? The difficulty is that Wundt presupposes selves as antecedent to the social process in order to explain communication within that process, whereas, on the contrary, selves must be accounted for in terms of the social process, and in terms of communication; and individuals must be brought into essential relation within that process before communication, or the contact between the minds of different individuals, becomes possible. The body is not a self, as such; it becomes a self only when it has developed a mind within the context of social experience. It does not occur to Wundt to account for the existence and development of selves and minds within, or in terms of, the social process of experience; and his presupposition of them as making possible that process, and communication within it, invalidates his analysis of that process. For if, as Wundt does, you presuppose the existence of mind at the start, as explaining or making possible the social process of experience, then the origin of minds and the interaction among minds become mysteries. But if, on the other hand, you regard the social process of experience as prior (in a rudimentary form) to the existence of mind and explain the origin of minds in terms of the interaction among individuals within that process, then not only the origin of minds, but also the interaction among minds (which is thus seen to be internal to their very nature and presupposed by their existence or development at all) cease to seem mysterious or miraculous. Mind arises through communication by a conversation of gestures in a social process or context of experience—not communication through mind.

Wundt thus overlooks the important fact that communication is fundamental to the nature of what we term "mind"; and it is precisely in the recognition of this fact that the value and advantage of a behavioristic account of mind is chiefly to be found. Thus, Wundt's analysis of communication presupposes the existence of minds which are able to communicate, and this existence remains an inexplicable mystery on his psychological basis; whereas the behavioristic analysis of communication makes no such presupposition, but instead explains or accounts for the existence of minds in terms of communication and social experience. By regarding minds as phenomena which have arisen and developed from the process of communication and of social experience generally (phenomena which therefore presuppose that process, rather than being presupposed by it), we say this analysis is able to throw real light on their nature. Wundt preserves a dualism or separation between gesture (or symbol) and idea, between sensory process and psychic content, because his psychophysical parallelism commits him to this dualism; and though he recognizes the need for establishing a functional relationship between them in terms of the process of communication within the social act, yet the only relationship of this sort which can be established on his psychological basis is one which entirely fails to illuminate the bearing that the context of social experience has upon the existence and development of mind. Such illumination is provided only by the behavioristic analysis of communication and by the statement of the nature of mind in terms of communication to which that analysis leads.

Meaning[25]

We are particularly concerned with intelligence on the human level, that is, with the adjustment to one another of the acts of different human individuals within the human social process. This adjustment takes place through communication—by gestures on the lower planes of human evolution and by significant symbols (gestures which possess meanings and are hence more than mere substitute stimuli) on the higher planes of human evolution.

The central factor in such adjustment is "meaning." Meaning arises and lies within the field of the relation between the gesture of a given human organism and the subsequent behavior of this organism as indicated to another human organism by that gesture. If that gesture does so indicate to another organism the subsequent (or resultant) behavior of the given organism, then it has meaning. In other words, the relationship between a given stimulus—as a gesture—and the later phases of the social act of which it is an early (if not the initial) phase constitutes the field within which meaning originates and exists. Meaning is thus a development of something objectively there as a relation between certain phases of the social act; it is not a psychical addition to that act and it is not an "idea" as traditionally conceived. A gesture by one organism, the resultant of the social act in which the gesture is an early phase, and the response of another organism to the gesture, are the relata in a threefold relationship of gesture to first organism, of gesture to second organism, and of gesture to subsequent phases of the given social act; and this threefold relationship constitutes the matrix within which meaning arises or which develops into the field of meaning. The gesture stands for a certain resultant of the social act, a resultant to which there is a definite response on the part of the individuals involved therein; so that meaning is given or stated in terms of response. Meaning is implicit—if

25   See also "Social Consciousness and the Consciousness of Meaning," *Psychological Bulletin*, VII (1910), 397 ff.; "The Mechanism of Social Consciousness," *Journal of Philosophy*, IX (1912), 401 ff.

not always explicit—in the relationship among the various phases of the social act to which it refers and out of which it develops. And its development takes place in terms of symbolization at the human evolutionary level.

We have been concerning ourselves, in general, with the social process of experience and behavior as it appears in the calling out by the act of one organism of an adjustment to that act in the responsive act of another organism. We have seen that the nature of meaning is intimately associated with the social process as it thus appears—that meaning involves this threefold relation among phases of the social act as the context in which it arises and develops: this relation of the gesture of one organism to the adjustive response of another organism (also implicated in the given act) and to the completion of the given act—is a relation such that the second organism responds to the gesture of the first as indicating or referring to the completion of the given act. For example, the chick's response to the cluck of the mother hen is a response to the meaning of the cluck; the cluck refers to danger or to food, as the case may be, and has this meaning or connotation for the chick.

The social process, as involving communication, is in a sense responsible for the appearance of new objects in the field of experience of the individual organisms implicated in that process. Organic processes or responses in a sense constitute the objects to which they are responses; that is to say, any given biological organism is in a way responsible for the existence (the meanings they have for it) of the objects to which it physiologically and chemically responds. There would, for example, be no food— no edible objects—if there were no organisms which could digest it. And similarly, the social process in a sense constitutes the objects to which it responds or to which it is an adjustment. That is to say, objects are constituted in terms of meanings within the social process of experience and behavior through the mutual adjustment to one another of the responses or actions of the various individual organisms involved in that process, an adjustment made possible by means of a communication which takes the form of a conversation of gestures in the earlier evolutionary stages of that process and of language in its later stages.

Awareness or consciousness is not necessary for meaning in the process of social experience. A gesture on the part of one organism in any given social act calls out a response on the part of another organism which is directly related to the action of the first organism and its outcome; and a gesture is a symbol of the result of the given social act of one organism (the organism making it) insofar as it is responded to by another organism (thereby also involved in that act) as indicating that result. The mechanism of meaning is thus present in the social act before the emergence of consciousness or awareness of meaning occurs. The act or adjustive response of the second organism gives to the gesture of the first organism the meaning which it has.

Symbolization constitutes objects not constituted before, objects which would not exist except for the context of social relationships wherein symbolization occurs. Language does not simply symbolize a situation or object which is already there in advance; it makes possible the existence or the appearance of that situation or object, for it is a part of the mechanism whereby that situation or object is created. The social process relates the responses of one individual to the gestures of another, as the meanings of the latter, and is thus responsible for the rise and existence of new objects in the social situation, objects dependent upon or constituted by these meanings. Meaning is thus not to be conceived, fundamentally, as a state of consciousness or as a set of organized relations existing or subsisting mentally outside the field of experience into which they enter; on the contrary, it should be conceived objectively, as having its existence entirely within this field itself.[26] The response of one organism to the gesture of another in any given social act is the meaning of that gesture and also is in a sense responsible for the appearance or coming into being of the new object—or new content of an old object—to which that gesture refers through the outcome of the given social act in which it is an early phase. For, to re-

26 Nature has meaning and implication but not indication by symbols. The symbol is distinguishable from the meaning it refers to. Meanings are in nature, but symbols are the heritage of man (1924).

peat, objects are in a genuine sense constituted within the social process of experience by the communication and mutual adjustment of behavior among the individual organisms which are involved in that process and which carry it on. Just as in fencing the parry is an interpretation of the thrust, so, in the social act, the adjustive response of one organism to the gesture of another is the interpretation of that gesture by that organism. Indeed, it is the meaning of that gesture.

At the level of self-consciousness such a gesture becomes a symbol, a significant symbol. But the interpretation of gestures is not, basically, a process going on in a mind as such or one necessarily involving a mind; it is an external, overt, physical, or physiological process in the actual field of social experience. Meaning can be described, accounted for, or stated in terms of symbols or language at its highest and most complex stage of development (the stage it reaches in human experience), but language simply lifts out of the social process a situation which is logically or implicitly there already. The language symbol is simply a significant or conscious gesture.

Two main points are being made here: (1) that the social process, through the communication which it makes possible among the individuals implicated in it, is responsible for the appearance of a whole set of new objects in nature which exist in relation to it (objects, namely, of "common sense"); and (2) that the gesture of one organism and the adjustive response of another organism to that gesture within any given social act bring out the relationship that exists between the gesture as the beginning of the given act and the completion or resultant of the given act, to which the gesture refers. These are the two basic and complementary logical aspects of the social process.

The result of any given social act is definitely separated from the gesture indicating it by the response of another organism to that gesture, a response which points to the result of that act as indicated by that gesture. This situation is all there—is completely given—on the non-mental, non-conscious level before the analysis of it on the mental or conscious level. Dewey says that meaning arises through communication.[27] It is to the content to which the social process gives rise that this statement refers, not to bare ideas or printed words as such, but to the social process which has been so largely responsible for the objects constituting the daily environment in which we live—a process in which communication plays the main part. That process can give rise to these new objects in nature only insofar as it makes possible communication among the individual organisms involved in it. And the sense in which it is responsible for their existence—indeed for the existence of the whole world of common-sense objects—is the sense in which it determines, conditions, and makes possible their abstraction from the total structure of events, as identities which are relevant for everyday social behavior; and in that sense, or as having that meaning, they are existent only relative to that behavior. In the same way, at a later, more advanced stage of its development, communication is responsible for the existence of the whole realm of scientific objects as well as identities abstracted from the total structure of events by virtue of their relevance for scientific purposes.

The logical structure of meaning, we have seen, is to be found in the threefold relationship of gesture to adjustive response and to the resultant of the given social act. Response on the part of the second organism to the gesture of the first is the interpretation—and brings out the meaning—of that gesture, as indicating the resultant of the social act which it initiates, and in which both organisms are thus involved. This threefold or triadic relation between gesture, adjustive response, and resultant of the social act which the gesture initiates is the basis of meaning; for the existence of meaning depends upon the fact that the adjustive response of the second organism is directed toward the resultant of the given social act as initiated and indicated by the gesture of the first organism. The basis of meaning is thus objectively there in social conduct or in nature in its relation to such conduct. Meaning is a content of an object which is dependent upon the relation of an organism or group of organisms to it. It is not essentially or primarily a psychical content (a content

27   See *Experience and Nature*, chap. v.

of mind or consciousness), for it need not be conscious at all, and is not in fact until significant symbols are evolved in the process of human social experience. Only when it becomes identified with such symbols does meaning become conscious. The meaning of a gesture on the part of one organism is the adjustive response of another organism to it, as indicating the resultant of the social act it initiates, the adjustive response of the second organism being itself directed toward or related to the completion of that act. In other words, meaning involves a reference of the gesture of one organism to the resultant of the social act it indicates or initiates, as adjustively responded to in this reference by another organism; and the adjustive response of the other organism is the meaning of the gesture.

Gestures may be either conscious (significant) or unconscious (non-significant). The conversation of gestures is not significant below the human level, because it is not conscious, that is, not *self*-conscious (though it is conscious in the sense of involving feelings or sensations). An animal as opposed to a human form, in indicating something to, or bringing out a meaning for, another form, is not at the same time indicating or bringing out the same thing or meaning to or for himself; for the animal has no mind, no thought, and hence there is no meaning here in the significant or self-conscious sense. A gesture is not significant when the response of another organism to it does not indicate to the first organism what the second organism is responding to.[28]

28   There are two characters which belong to that which we term "meanings," one is participation and the other is communicability. Meaning can arise only insofar as some phase of the act which the individual is arousing in the other can be aroused in himself. There is always, to this extent, participation. And the result of this participation is communicability, that is, the individual can indicate to himself what he indicates to others. There is communication without significance where the gesture of the individual calls out the response in the other without calling out or tending to call out the same response in the individual himself. Significance from the standpoint of the observer may be said to be present in the gesture which calls out the appropriate response in the other or others within a co-operative act, but it does not become significant to the individuals who are involved in the act unless the tendency to the act is aroused

Much subtlety has been wasted on the problem of the meaning of meaning. It is not necessary, in attempting to solve this problem, to have recourse to psychical states, for the nature of meaning, as we have seen, is found to be implicit in the structure of the social act, implicit in the relations among its three basic individual components: namely, in the triadic relation of a gesture of one individual, a response to that gesture by a second individual, and completion of the given social act initiated by the gesture of the first individual. And the fact that the nature of meaning is thus found to be implicit in the structure of the social act provides additional emphasis upon the necessity, in social psychology, of starting with the initial assumption of an ongoing social process of experience and behavior in which any given group of human individuals is involved, and upon which the existence and development of their minds, selves, and self-consciousness depend.

The Nature of Reflective Intelligence

In the type of temporary inhibition of action which signifies thinking, or in which reflection arises, we have presented in the experience of the individual, tentatively and in advance and for his selection among them, the different possibilities or alternatives of future action open to him within the given social situation—the different or alternative ways of completing the given social act wherein he is implicated, or which he has already initiated. Reflection or reflective behavior arises only under the conditions of self-consciousness and makes possible the purposive control and organization by the individual organism of its conduct, with reference to its social and physical environment, that is, with reference to the various social and physical situations in which it becomes involved and to which it reacts. The organization of the self is simply the organization, by the individual organism, of the set of attitudes toward its social environment—

---

within the individual who makes it and unless the individual who is directly affected by the gesture puts himself in the attitude of the individual who makes the gesture (MS).

and toward itself from the standpoint of that environment, or as a functioning element in the process of social experience and behavior constituting that environment—which it is able to take. It is essential that such reflective intelligence be dealt with from the point of view of social behaviorism.

There is something involved in our statement of the meaning of an object which is more than the mere response, however complex that may be. We may respond to a musical phrase and there may be nothing in the experience beyond the response; we may not be able to say why we respond or what it is we respond to. Our attitude may simply be that we like some music and do not like other music. Most of our recognitions are of this sort. We pick the book we want but could not say what the character of the book is. We probably could give a more detailed account of the countenance of a man we meet for the first time than of our most intimate friends. With our friends we are ready to start our conversation the moment they are there; we do not have to make sure who they are. But if we try to pick out a man who has been described to us, we narrowly examine the person to make sure he answers to the account that is given to us. With a person with whom we are familiar we carry on our conversation without thinking of these things. Most of our processes of recognition do not involve this identification of the characters which enable us to identify the objects. We may have to describe a person, and we find we cannot do it—we know him too well. We may have to pick those details out, and then if we are taking a critical attitude, we have to find out what it is in the object that calls out this complex response. When we are doing that, we are getting a statement of what the nature of the object is, or if you like, its meaning. We have to indicate to ourselves what it is that calls out this particular response. We recognize a person, say, because of the character of his physique. If one should come into the room greatly changed by a long attack of sickness, or by exposure to the tropical sun, his friends would not be able to recognize him immediately. There are certain elements which enable us to recognize a friend. We may have to pick out the characters which make recognition successful, to indicate those characters to somebody or to ourselves. We may have to determine what the stimuli are that call out a response of this complex character. That is often a very difficult thing to do, as is evidenced by musical criticism. A whole audience can be swept away by a composition and perhaps not a person there will be able to state what it is in the production that calls out this particular response, or to tell what the various reactions are in these individuals. It is an unusual gift which can analyze that sort of an object and pick what the stimulus is for so complex an action.

What I want to call attention to is the process by which there is an indication of those characters which do call out the response. Animals of a type lower than man respond to certain characters with a nicety that is beyond human capacity, such as odor in the case of a dog. But it would be beyond the capacity of a dog to indicate to another dog what the odor was. Another dog could not be sent by the first dog to pick out this odor. A man may tell how to identify another man. He can indicate what the characters are that will bring about a certain response. That ability absolutely distinguishes the intelligence of such a reflective being as man from that of the lower animals, however intelligent they may be. We generally say that man is a rational animal and lower animals are not. What I wanted to show, at least in terms of behavioristic psychology, is that what we have in mind in this distinction is the indication of those characters which lead to the sort of response which we give to an object. Pointing out the characters which lead to the response is precisely that which distinguishes a detective office that sends a man from a bloodhound which runs down a man. Here are two types of intelligence, each one specialized; the detective could not do what the bloodhound does, and the bloodhound could not do what the detective does. Now, the intelligence of the detective over the intelligence of the bloodhound lies in this capacity to indicate what the particular characters are which will call out his response of taking the man.[29]

29 Intelligence and knowledge are inside the process of conduct. Thinking is an elaborate process of . . . presenting the world so that it will be favorable for conduct, so that the ends of the life of the form can be reached (MS).

Thinking is pointing out—to think about a thing is to point it out before acting (1924).

Such would be a behaviorist's account of what is involved in reason. When you are reasoning you are indicating to yourself the characters that call out certain responses—and that is all you are doing. If you have the angle and a side you can determine the area of a triangle; given certain characters, there are certain responses indicated. There are other processes, not exactly rational, out of which you can build up new responses from old ones. You may pick responses which are there in other reactions and put them together. A book of directions may provide a set of stimuli which lead to a certain set of responses, and you pick them out of your other complex responses, perhaps as they have not been picked out before. When you write on a typewriter you may be instructed as to the way in which to use it. You can build up a fairly good technique to start, but even that is a process which still involves the indication of the stimuli to call out the various responses. You unite stimuli which have not been united in the past, and then these stimuli take with them the compound responses. It may be a crude response at first and must be freed from the responses had in the past. The way in which you react toward the doubling of letters when you write is different from the way you react in writing the letters on a typewriter. You make mistakes because the responses you utilize have been different, have been connected with a whole set of other responses. A drawing teacher will sometimes have pupils draw with the left hand rather than the right because the habits of the right hand are very difficult to get rid of. This is what you are doing when you act in a rational fashion; you are indicating to yourself what the stimuli are that will call out a complex response, and by the order of the stimuli, you are determining what the whole of the response will be. Now, to be able to indicate those stimuli to other persons or to yourself is what we call rational conduct as distinct from the unreasoning intelligence of the lower animals and from a good deal of our own conduct.

Man is distinguished by that power of analysis of the field of stimulation which enables him to pick one stimulus rather than another and so to hold on to the response that belongs to that stimulus, picking it out from the others, and recombining it with others. You cannot get a lock to work. You notice certain elements, each of which brings out a certain sort of response; and what you are doing is holding onto these processes of response by giving attention to the stimuli. Man can combine not only the responses already there, which is the thing an animal lower than man can do, but the human can get into his activities and break them up, giving attention to specific elements, holding the responses that answer to these particular stimuli, and then combining them to build up another act. That is what we mean by learning or by teaching a person to do a thing. You indicate to him certain specific phases or characters of the object which call out certain sorts of responses. We state that generally by saying consciousness accompanies only the sensory process and not the motor process. We can directly control the sensory but not the motor processes; we can give our attention to a particular element in the field and by giving such attention and so holding onto the stimulus, we can get control of the response. That is the way we get control of our action; we do not directly control our response through the motor paths themselves.

There is no capacity in the lower forms to give attention to some analyzed element in the field of stimulation which would enable them to control the response. But one can say to a person, "Look at this, just see this thing"; and he can fasten his attention on the specific object. He can direct attention and so isolate the particular response that answers to it. That is the way in which we break up our complex activities and thereby make learning possible. What takes place is an analysis of the process by giving attention to the specific stimuli that call out a particular act, and this analysis makes possible a reconstruction of the act. An animal makes combinations, as we say, only by trial and error, and the combination that is successful simply maintains itself.

The gesture as worked out in the conduct of the human group serves definitely to indicate just these elements and thus to bring them within the field of voluntary attention. There is, of course, a fundamental likeness between voluntary attention and involuntary attention. A bright light or a peculiar odor may be something which takes complete control of the organism and insofar inhibits other activity. A voluntary action, however, is dependent upon the indication of a certain character, pointing it out, holding onto it, and so holding onto the response that belongs to it. That sort of an analysis is essential to what we call human intelligence, and it is made possible by language.

The psychology of attention ousted the psychology of association. An indefinite number of associations were found which lie in our experience with reference to anything that comes before us, but associational psychology never explained why one association rather than another was the dominant one. It laid down rules that when a certain association had been intense, recent, and frequent, it would be dominant, but often there are situations in which what seems to be the weakest element in the situation occupies the mind. It was not until the psychologist took up the analysis of attention that he was able to deal with such situations and to realize that voluntary attention is dependent upon indication of some character in the field of stimulation. Such indication makes possible the isolation and recombination of responses.

In the case of the vocal gesture there is a tendency to call out the response in one form that is called out in the other, so that the child plays the part of parent, of teacher, or of preacher. The gesture, under those conditions, calls out certain responses in the individual which it calls out in the other person, and carrying it out in the individual isolates that particular character of the stimulus. The response of the other is there in the individual isolating the stimulus. If one calls out quickly to a person in danger, then he himself is in the attitude of jumping away, though the act is not performed. He is not in danger, but he has those particular elements of the response in himself, and we speak of them as meanings. Stated in terms of the central nervous system, this means that he has stirred up its upper tracts which would lead to the actual jumping away. A person picks out the different responses involved in escape when he enters the theater and notices the signs on the program cautioning him to choose the nearest exit in case of fire. He has all the different responses, so to speak, listed before him, and he prepares what he is going to do by picking out the different elements and putting them together in the way required. The efficiency engineer comes in to pick out this, that, or the other thing, and chooses the order in which they should be carried out. One is doing the same himself insofar as he is self-conscious. When we have to determine what will be the order of a set of responses, we are putting them together in a certain fashion, and we can do this because we can indicate the order of the stimuli which are going to act upon us. That is what is involved in the human intelligence as distinguished from the intelligence type of the lower forms. We cannot tell an elephant that he is to take hold of the other elephant's tail; the stimulus will not indicate the same thing to the elephant as to ourselves. We can create a situation which is a stimulus to the elephant, but we cannot get the elephant to indicate to itself what this stimulus is so that he has the response to it in his own system.

The gesture provides a process by means of which one does arouse in himself the reaction that might be aroused in another, and this is not a part of his immediate reaction insofar as his immediate physical environment is concerned. When we tell a person to do something, the response we have is not the doing of the actual thing, but the beginning of it. Communication gives to us those elements of response which can be held in the mental field. We do not carry them out, but they are there constituting the meanings of these objects which we indicate. Language is a process of indicating certain stimuli and changing the response to them in the system of behavior. Language, as a social process, has made it possible for us to pick out responses and hold them in the organism of the individual, so that they are there in relation to that which we indicate. The actual gesture is, within limits, arbitrary. Whether one points with his finger, or points with the glance of the eye, or motion of the head, or the attitude of the body, or by means of a vocal gesture in one language or another, is indifferent, provided it does call out the response that belongs to that thing which is indicated. That is the essential part of language. The gesture must be one that calls out the response in the individual or at least tends to call out the response in the individual, which its utilization will bring out in another's response. Such is the material with which the mind works. However slight, there must be some sort of gesture. To have the response isolated without an indication of a stimulus is almost a contradiction in terms. I have been trying to point out what this process of communication does in the way of providing us with the material that exists in our mind. It does this by furnishing those gestures which, in affecting us as they affect others, call out the attitude which the other takes, and that we take insofar as we assume his role. We get the attitude, the meaning, within the field of our own control, and that control consists in combining all these various possible responses to furnish the newly constructed act demanded by the problem. In such a way we can state rational conduct in terms of a behavioristic psychology.

I wish to add one further factor to our account: the relation of the temporal character of the nervous system to foresight and choice.

The central nervous system makes possible the implicit initiation of a number of possible alternative responses with reference to any given object or objects for the completion of any already initiated act, in advance of the actual completion of that act; and thus it makes possible the exercise of intelligent or reflective choice in the acceptance of that one among these possible alternative responses which is to be carried into overt effect.[30]

Human intelligence, by means of the psychological mechanism of the human central nervous system, deliberately selects one from among the several alternative responses which are possible in the given problematic environmental situation; and when the given response which it selects is complex—is a set or chain or group or succession of simple responses—it can organize this

---

[30] It is an advantage to have these responses ready before we get to the object. If our world were right on top of us, in contact with us, we would have no time for deliberation. There would be only one way of responding to that world.

Through his distance organs and his capacity for delayed responses the individual lives in the future with the possibility of planning his life with reference to that future (1931).

set or chain of simple responses in such a way as to make possible the most adequate and harmonious solution by the individual of the given environmental problem.

It is the entrance of the alternative possibilities of future response into the determination of present conduct in any given environmental situation, and their operation, through the mechanism of the central nervous system, as part of the factors or conditions determining present behavior, which decisively contrasts intelligent conduct or behavior with reflex, instinctive, and habitual conduct or behavior—delayed reaction with immediate reaction. That which takes place in present organic behavior is always in some sense an emergent from the past and never could have been precisely predicted in advance—never could have been predicted on the basis of a knowledge, however complete, of the past, and of the conditions in the past which are relevant to its emergence; and in the case of organic behavior which is intelligently controlled, this element of spontaneity is especially prominent by virtue of the present influence exercised over such behavior by the possible future results or consequences which it may have. Our ideas of or about future conduct are our tendencies to act in several alternative ways in the presence of a given environmental situation—tendencies or attitudes which can appear, or be implicitly aroused, in the structure of the central nervous system in advance of the overt response or reaction to that situation, and which thus can enter as determining factors into the control or selection of this overt response. Ideas, as distinct from acts, or as failing to issue in overt behavior, are simply what we do not do; they are possibilities of overt responses which we test out implicitly in the central nervous system and then reject in favor of those which we do in fact act upon or carry into effect. The process of intelligent conduct is essentially a process of selection from among various alternatives; intelligence is largely a matter of selectivity.

Delayed reaction is necessary to intelligent conduct. The organization, implicit testing, and final selection by the individual of his overt responses or reactions to the social situations which confront him and which present him with problems of adjustment, would be impossible if his overt responses or reactions could not in such situations be delayed until this process of organizing, implicitly testing, and finally selecting is carried out, that is, would be impossible if some overt response or other to the given environmental stimuli had to be immediate. Without delayed reaction, or except in terms of it, no conscious or intelligent control over behavior could be exercised; for it is through this process of selective reaction—which can be selective only because it is delayed—that intelligence operates in the determination of behavior. Indeed, it is this process which constitutes intelligence. The central nervous system provides, not only the necessary physiological mechanism for this process, but also the necessary physiological condition of delayed reaction which this process presupposes. Intelligence is essentially the ability to solve the problems of present behavior in terms of its possible future consequences as implicated on the basis of past experience— the ability, that is, to solve the problems of present behavior in the light of, or by reference to, both the past and the future; it involves both memory and foresight. And the process of exercising intelligence is the process of delaying, organizing, and selecting a response or reaction to the stimuli of the given environmental situation. The process is made possible by the mechanism of the central nervous system, which permits the individual's taking of the attitude of the other toward himself and thus becoming an object to himself. This is the most effective means of adjustment to the social environment, and indeed to the environment in general, that the individual has at his disposal.

An attitude of any sort represents the beginning, or potential initiation, of some composite act or other, a social act in which, along with other individuals, the individual taking the given attitude is involved or implicated. The traditional supposition has been that the purposive element in behavior must ultimately be an idea, a conscious motive, and hence must imply or depend upon the presence of a mind. But the study of the nature of the central nervous system shows that in the form of physiological attitudes (expressed in specific physiological sets) different possible completions to the given act are there in advance of its actual completion, and that through them the earlier parts of the given act are affected or influenced (in present conduct) by its later phases; so that the purposive element in behavior has a physiological seat, a behavioristic basis, and is not fundamentally nor necessarily conscious or psychical.

Mind and the Symbol

I have attempted to point out that the meanings of things, our ideas of them, answer to the structure of the organism in its conduct with reference to things. The structure which makes this possible was found primarily in the central nervous system. One of the peculiarities of this system is that it has, in a sense, a temporal dimension; the things we are going to do can be arranged in a temporal order so that the later processes can in their inception be present determining the earlier processes; what we are going to do can determine our immediate approach to the object.

The mechanism of the central nervous system enables us to have now present, in terms of attitudes or implicit responses, the alternative possible overt completions of any given act in which we are involved; and this fact must be realized and recognized, in virtue of the obvious control which later phases of any given act exert over its earlier phases. More specifically, the central nervous system provides a mechanism of implicit response which enables the individual to test out implicitly the various possible completions of an already initiated act in advance of the actual completion of the act and thus to choose for himself, on the basis of this testing, the one which it is most desirable to perform explicitly or carry into overt effect. The central nervous system, in short, enables the individual to exercise conscious control over his behavior. It is the possibility of delayed response which principally differentiates reflective conduct from non-reflective conduct in which the response is always immediate. The higher centers of the central nervous system are involved in the former type of behavior by making possible the interposition, between stimulus and response in the simple stimulus-response arc, of a process of selecting one or another of a whole set of possible responses and combinations of responses to the given stimulus.

Mental processes take place in this field of attitudes as expressed by the central nervous system, and this field is hence the field of ideas—the field of the control of present behavior in terms of its future consequences or in terms of future behavior and the field of that type of intelligent conduct which is peculiarly characteristic of the higher forms of life and especially of human beings. The various attitudes expressible through the central nervous system can be organized into different types of subsequent acts; and the delayed reactions or responses thus made possible by the central nervous system are the distinctive feature of mentally controlled or intelligent behavior.[31]

What is the mind as such, if we are to think in behavioristic terms? Mind, of course, is a very ambiguous term, and I want to avoid ambiguities. What I suggested as characteristic of the mind is the reflective intelligence of the human animal which can be distinguished from the intelligence of lower forms. Should we try to regard reason as a specific faculty which deals with that which is universal, we should find responses in lower forms which are universal. We can also point out that their conduct is purposive and that types of conduct which do not lead up to certain ends are eliminated. This would seem to answer to what we term "mind" when we talk about the animal mind, but what we refer to as reflective intelligence we generally recognize as belonging only to the human organism. The non-human animal acts with reference to a future in the sense that it has impulses which are seeking expression that can only be satisfied in later experience,

31   In considering the role or function of the central nervous system —important though it is—in intelligent human behavior, we must nevertheless keep in mind the fact that such behavior is essentially and fundamentally social; that it involves and presupposes an ever ongoing social life-process; and that the unity of this ongoing social process—or of any one of its component acts—is irreducible, and in particular cannot be adequately analyzed simply into a number of discrete nerve elements. This fact must be recognized by the social psychologist. These discrete nerve elements lie within the unity of this ongoing social process, or within the unity of any one of the social acts in which this process is expressed or embodied; and the analysis which isolates them—the analysis of which they are the results or end-products—does not and cannot destroy that unity.

and however this is to be explained, this later experience does determine what the present experience shall be. If one accepts a Darwinian explanation, he says that only those forms survive whose conduct has a certain relationship to a specific future, such as belongs to the environment of the specific form. The forms whose conduct does insure the future will naturally survive. In such a statement, indirectly at least, one is making the future determine the conduct of the form through the structure of things as they now exist as a result of past happenings.

When, on the other hand, we speak of reflective conduct we very definitely refer to the presence of the future in terms of ideas. The intelligent man as distinguished from the intelligent animal presents to himself what is going to happen. The animal may act in such a way as to insure its food tomorrow. A squirrel hides nuts, but we do not hold that the squirrel has a picture of what is going to happen. The young squirrel is born in the summer time and has no directions from other forms, but he will start hiding nuts as well as the older ones. Such action shows that experience could not direct the activity of the specific form. The provident man, however, does definitely pursue a certain course, pictures a certain situation, and directs his own conduct with reference to it. The squirrel follows certain blind impulses, and the carrying-out of his impulses leads to the same result that the storing of grain does for the provident man. It is this picture, however, of what the future is to be as determining our present conduct that is the characteristic of human intelligence—the future as present in terms of ideas.

When we present such a picture it is in terms of our reactions, in terms of what we are going to do. There is some sort of a problem before us, and our statement of the problem is in terms of a future situation which will enable us to meet it by our present reactions. That sort of thinking characterizes the human form, and we have endeavored to isolate its mechanism. What is essential to this mechanism is a way of indicating characters of things which control responses and which have various values to the form itself, so that such characters will engage the attention of the organism and bring about a desired result. The odor of the victim engages the attention of the beast of prey, and by attention to that odor he does satisfy his hunger and insure his future. What is the difference between such a situation and the conduct of the man who acts, as we say, rationally? The fundamental difference is that the latter individual in some way indicates this character, whatever it may be, to another person and to himself; and the symbolization of it by means of this indicative gesture is what constitutes the mechanism that gives the implements, at least, for intelligent conduct. Thus, one points to a certain footprint and says that it means bear. Now to identify that sort of a trace by means of some symbol so that it can be utilized by the different members of the group, but particularly by the individual himself later, is the characteristic thing about human intelligence. To be able to identify "this as leading to that" and to get some sort of a gesture, vocal or otherwise, which can be used to indicate the implication to others and to himself so as to make possible the control of conduct with reference to it, is the distinctive thing in human intelligence which is not found in animal intelligence.

Such symbols pick out particular characteristics of the situation so that the response to them can be present in the experience of the individual. We can say they are present in ideal form, as in a tendency to run away, in a sinking of the stomach when we come on the fresh footprints of a bear. The indication that this is a bear calls out the response of avoiding the bear, or when one is on a bear hunt, it indicates the further progress of the hunt. One gets the response into experience before that response is overtly carried out through indicating and emphasizing the stimulus that instigates it. When this symbol is utilized for the thing itself, one is, in Watson's terms, conditioning a reflex. The sight of the bear would lead one to run away, the footprint conditioned that reflex, and the word "bear" spoken by one's self or a friend can also condition the reflex, so that the sign comes to stand for the thing so far as action is concerned.

What I have been trying to bring out is the difference between the foregoing type of conduct and the type which I have illustrated by the experiment on the baby with the white rat and the noise behind its head. In the latter situation there is a conditioning of the reflex in which there is no holding apart of the different elements. But when there is a conditioning of the reflex which involves the word "bear," or the sight of the footprint, there is in the experience of the individual the separation of the stimulus and the response. Here the symbol means bear, and that in turn means getting out of the way, or furthering the hunt. Under these circumstances the person who stumbles on the footprints of the bear is not afraid of the footprints—he is afraid of the bear. The footprint means a bear. The child is afraid of the rat, so that the response of fear is to the sight of the white rat; the man is not afraid of the footprint but of the bear. The footprint and the symbol which refers to the bear in some sense may be said to condition or set off the response, but the bear and not the sign is the object of the fear. The isolation of the symbol, as such, enables one to hold onto these given characters and to isolate them in their relationship to the object, and consequently in their relation to the response. It is that, I think, which characterizes our human intelligence to a peculiar degree. We have a set of symbols by means of which we indicate certain characters, and in indicating those characters hold them apart from their immediate environment, and keep simply one relationship clear. We isolate the footprint of the bear and keep only that relationship to the animal that made it. We are reacting to that, nothing else. One holds onto it as an indication of the bear and of the value that object has in experience as something to be avoided or to be hunted. The ability to isolate these important characters in their relationship to the object and to the response which belongs to the object is, I think, what we generally mean when we speak of a human being thinking a thing out, or having a mind. Such ability makes the world-wide difference between the conditioning of reflexes in the case of the white rat and the human process of thinking by means of symbols.[32]

[32] The meanings of things or objects are actual inherent properties or qualities of them; the locus of any given meaning is in the thing which, as we say, "has it." We refer to the meaning of a thing when we make use of the symbol. Symbols stand for the meanings of those things or objects which have meanings; they are given portions of experience which point

What is there in conduct that makes this level of experience possible, this selection of certain characters with their relationship to other characters and to the responses which these call out? My own answer, it is clear, is in terms of such a set of symbols as arise in our social conduct, in the conversation of gestures—in terms of language. When we get into conduct these symbols, which indicate certain characters and their relationship to things and to responses, they enable us to pick out these characters and hold them insofar as they determine our conduct.

A man walking across country comes upon a chasm which he cannot jump. He wants to go ahead, but the chasm prevents this from being carried out. In that kind of a situation there arises a sensitivity to all sorts of characters which he has not noticed before. When he stops, mind, we say, is freed. He does not simply look for the indication of the path going ahead. The dog and the man would both try to find a point where they could cross. But what the man could do that the dog could not would be to note that the sides of the chasm seem to be approaching each other in one direction. He picks out the best places to try, and that approach which he indicates to himself determines the way in which he is going to go. If the dog saw at a distance a narrow place he would

---

to, indicate, or represent other portions of experience not directly present or given at the time when, and in the situation in which, any one of them is thus present (or is immediately experienced). The symbol is thus more than a mere substitute stimulus—more than a mere stimulus for a conditioned response or reflex. For the conditioned reflex—the response to a mere substitute stimulus—does not or need not involve consciousness; whereas the response to a symbol does and must involve consciousness. Conditioned reflexes plus consciousness of the attitudes and meanings they involve are what constitute language, and hence lay the basis or comprise the mechanism for thought and intelligent conduct. Language is the means whereby individuals can indicate to one another what their responses to objects will be, and hence what the meanings of objects are; it is not a mere system of conditioned reflexes. Rational conduct always involves a reflexive reference to self, that is, an indication to the individual of the significances which his actions or gestures have for other individuals. And the experiential or behavioristic basis for such conduct—the neurophysiological mechanism of thinking—is to be found in the central nervous system.

run to it, but probably he would not be affected by the gradual approach which the human individual symbolically could indicate to himself.

The human individual would see other objects about him and have other images appear in his experience. He sees a tree which might serve as a bridge across the space ahead of him. He might try various sorts of possible actions which would be suggested to him in such a situation and present them to himself by means of the symbols he uses. He has not simply conditioned certain responses by certain stimuli. If he had, he would be bound to those. What he does do by means of these symbols is to indicate certain characters which are present, so that he can have these responses ready to go off. He looks down the chasm and thinks he sees the edges drawing together, and he may run toward that point. Or he may stop and ask if there is not some other way in which he can hasten his crossing. What stops him is a variety of other things he can do. He notes all the possibilities of getting across. He can hold onto them by means of symbols and relate them to each other so that he can get a final action. The beginning of the act is there in his experience. He already has a tendency to go in a certain direction and what he would do is already determining him. And not only is that determination in his attitude, but he has that which is picked out by means of: "that is narrow, I can jump it." He is ready to jump, and that reflex is ready to determine what he is doing. These symbols, instead of being a mere conditioning of reflexes, are ways of picking out the stimuli so that the various responses can organize themselves into a form of action.[33]

[33] The reflective act consists in a reconstruction of the perceptual field so that it becomes possible for impulses which were in conflict to inhibit action no longer. This may take place by such a temporal readjustment that one of the conflicting impulses finds a later expression. In this case there has entered into the perceptual field other impulses which postpone the expression of that which had inhibited action. Thus, the width of the ditch inhibits the impulse to jump. There enters into the perceptual field the image of a narrower stretch and the impulse to go ahead finds its place in a combination of impulses, including that of movement toward the narrower stretch.

The reconstruction can take place through the appearance of

The situation in which one seeks conditioning responses is, I think, as far as effective intelligence is concerned, always present in the form of a problem. When a man is just going ahead, he seeks the indications of the path, but he does it unconsciously. He just sees the path ahead of him; he is not aware of looking for it under those conditions. But when he reaches the chasm, this onward movement is stopped by the very process of drawing back from the chasm. That conflict, so to speak, sets him free to see a whole set of other things. Now, the sort of things he will see will be the characters which represent various possibilities of action under the circumstances. The man holds onto these different possibilities of response in terms of the different stimuli which present themselves, and it is his ability to hold them there that constitutes his mind.

We have no evidence of such a situation in the case of the lower animals, as is made fairly clear by the fact that we do not find in any animal behavior that we can work out in detail any symbol, any method of communication, anything that will answer to these different responses so that they can all be held there in the experience of the individual. It is that which differentiates the action of the reflectively intelligent being from the conduct of the lower forms; and the mechanism that makes that possible is language. We have to recognize that language is a part of conduct. Mind involves, however, a relationship to the characters of things. Those characters are in the things, and while the stimuli call out the response which is in one sense present in the organism, the

---

other sensory characters in the field ignored before. A board long enough to bridge the ditch is recognized. Because the individual has already the complex of impulses which lead to lifting it and placing it across the ditch, it becomes a part of the organized group of impulses that carry the man along toward his destination. In neither case would he be ready to respond to the stimulus (in the one case the image of the narrower stretch of the ditch, in the other the sight of the board) if he had not reactions in his nature answering to these objects, nor would these tendencies to response sensitize him to their stimuli if they were not freed from firmly organized habits. It is this freedom, then, that is the prerequisite of reflection, and it is our social self-reflective conduct that gives this freedom to human individuals in their group life (MS).

responses are to things out there. The whole process is not a mental product, and you cannot put it inside of the brain. Mentality is that relationship of the organism to the situation which is mediated by sets of symbols.

Relation of Mind to Response and Environment

We have seen that mental processes have to do with the meanings of things, and that these meanings can be stated in terms of highly organized attitudes of the individual. These attitudes involve not only situations in which the elements are simultaneous, but also ones which involve other temporal relationships, that is, the adjustment of the present response to later responses which are in some sense already initiated. Such an organization of attitudes with reference to what we term objects is what constitutes for us the meanings of things. These meanings in logical terminology are considered as universals, and this universality, we have seen, attaches in a certain sense to a habitual response in contrast to the particular stimuli which elicit this response. The universality is reflected in behavioristic terms in the identity of the response, although the stimuli that call out this response are all different. We can throw this statement into a logical form and say that the response is universal while the stimuli are particulars which are brought under such a universal.

These relations of attitudes to each other throw light upon the relation of a "substance" to its attributes. We speak of a house as, in a certain sense, a substance to which the attribute of color can be applied. The color is an accident which inheres in a certain substance, as such. This relationship of the inherence of a certain character in a certain substance is a relationship of a specific response, such as that of ornamenting objects about us, to the group of actions involved in dwelling in a house. The house must protect us; it must provide for us when we are asleep and when we are awake; it must carry the requisites of a family life—these are essentials that stand for a set of responses in which one inevitably implies the other. There are other responses, however, that vary. We can satisfy, not simply our taste, but also our whims in the ornaments we use. Those are not essential. There are certain responses that vary, whereas there is a certain body of more or less standardized responses that remain unchanged. The organized sets of responses answer to the meanings of things, answer to them in their universality, that is, in the habitual response that is called out by a great variety of stimuli. They answer to things in their logical relationships.

I have referred just now to the relationship of the substance as reflected in the body of habits, to the varied responses answering to the attributes. In the relationship of cause and effect there is the relation of the responses to each other in the sense of dependence, involving the adjustment of the steps to be taken with reference to the thing to be carried out. The arrangement which can appear at one time in terms of means and end appears at another time in terms of cause and effect. We have here a relationship of dependence of one response on another, a necessary relation that lies inside of a larger system.[34] It depends upon what we are going to do whether we select this means or another one, one causal series or another. Our habits are so adjusted that if we decide to take a journey, for instance, we have a body of related habits that begin to operate—packing our bags, getting our railroad tickets, drawing out money for use, selecting books to read on the journey, and so on. There are a whole set of organized responses which at once start to go off in their proper relationship to each other when a person makes up his mind that he will take a journey. There must be such an organization in our habits in order that many may have the sort of intelligence which he in fact has.

We have, then, in the behavioristic statement, a place for that which is supposed to be the peculiar content of mind, that is, the meanings of things. I have referred to these factors as attitudes. There is, of course, that in the world which answers to the group of attitudes. We are here avoiding logical and metaphysical problems, just as modern psychology does. What this psychology is seeking to do is to get control; it is not seeking to settle meta-

[34] Representation involves relation of earlier to later acts. This relation of responses gives implication (1924).

physical questions. Now, from the point of view of behavioristic psychology, we can state in terms of attitudes what we call the meanings of things; the organized attitude of the individual is that which the psychologist gets hold of in this situation. It is at least as legitimate for him to state meaning in terms of attitudes as it was for an earlier psychologist to state it in terms of a static concept that had its place in the mind.

What I have pointed out is that in the central nervous system one can find, or at least justifiably assume, just such complexities of responses, or the mechanism of just such complexities of response, as we have been discussing. If we speak of a person going through the steps to which I have referred, in preparing for a journey, we then have to assume that, not only are the nervous elements essential to the steps, but that the relation of those responses in the central nervous system is such that if the person carries out one response, then he is inevitably ready to find the stimulus which will set free another related response. There must be an organization in the central nervous system in the way of its elements, its neurons, for all the combinations which can possibly enter into a mind and for just such a relationship of responses which are interdependent upon each other. Some of these have been identified in the physiological study of the nervous system, while others have to be assumed on the basis of such study. As I have said before, it is not the specific physiological process which is going on inside of the neurons that answers to meaning. Earlier physiological psychologists had spoken of a specific psychical process, but there is nothing in the mechanical, electrical, and physical activity that goes on in the nerve which answers to what we term an idea. What is going on in the nerve in a particular situation is the innervation of a certain response which means this, that, and the other thing, and here is where the specificity of a certain nervous organization is found. It is in the central nervous system that organization takes place. In a certain sense you can say that it is in the engineer's office that the organization of the concern is carried out. But what is found there in the blueprints and body of statistics is not the actual production that is going on in the factory, even though that office does organize and co-ordinate those various branches of the concern. In the same way the central nervous system co-ordinates all the various processes that the body carries out. If there is anything in the organism as a purely physiological mechanism which answers to what we call experience, when that is ordinarily termed conscious, it is the total organic process for which these nervous elements stand. These processes are, as we have seen, attitudes of response, adjustments of the organism to a complex environment, attitudes which sensitize the form to the stimuli which will set the response free.

The point I want to emphasize is the way that these attitudes determine the environment. There is an organized set of responses which first send certain telegrams, then select the means of transportation, then send us to the bank to get money, and then see to it that we get something to read on the train. As we advance from one set of responses to another we find ourselves picking out the environment which answers to this next set of responses. To finish one response is to put ourselves in a position where we see other things. The appearance of the retinal elements has given the world color; the development of the organs in the ear has given the world sound. We pick an organized environment in relationship to our response, so that these attitudes, as such, not only represent our organized responses, but they also represent what exists for us in the world; the particular phase of reality that is there for us is picked out for us by our response. We can recognize that it is the sensitizing of the organism to the stimuli which will set free its responses that is responsible for one's living in this sort of an environment rather than in another. We see things in their temporal relationship which answer to the temporal organization found in the central nervous system. We see things as distant from us not only spatially but temporally; when we do this, we can do that. Our world is definitely mapped out for us by the responses which are going to take place.[35]

35   The structure of the environment is a mapping out of organic responses to nature; any environment, whether social or individual, is a mapping out of the logical structure of the act to which it answers, an act seeking overt expression.

It is a difficult matter to state just what we mean by dividing up a certain situation between the organism and its environment. Certain objects come to exist for us because of the character of the organism. Take the case of food. If an animal that can digest grass, such as an ox, comes into the world, then grass becomes food. That object did not exist before, that is, grass as food. The advent of the ox brings in a new object. In that sense, organisms are responsible for the appearance of whole sets of objects that did not exist before.[36] The distribution of meaning to the organism and the environment has its expression in the organism as well as in the thing, and that expression is not a matter of psychical or mental conditions. There is an expression of the reaction of the organism's organized response to the environment, and that reaction is not simply a determination of the organism by the environment, since the organism determines the environment as fully as the environment determines the organs. The organic reaction is responsible for the appearance of a whole set of objects which did not exist before.

There is a definite and necessary structure or *gestalt* of sensitivity within the organism, which determines selectively and relatively the character of the external object it perceives. What we term consciousness needs to be brought inside just this relation between an organism and its environment. Our constructive selection of an environment—colors, emotional values, and the like —in terms of our physiological sensitivities, is essentially what we mean by consciousness. This consciousness we have tended historically to locate in the mind or in the brain. The eye and related processes endow objects with color in exactly the same sense that an ox endows grass with the character of food, that is, not in the sense of projecting sensations into objects, but rather of putting itself into a relation with the object which makes the appearance and existence of the color possible, as a quality of the object. Colors inhere in objects only by virtue of their relations to given percipient organisms. The physiological or sensory structure of

36   It is objectionable to speak of the food-process in the animal as constituting the food-object. They are certainly relative to each other (MS).

the percipient organism determines the experienced content of the object.

The organism, then, is in a sense responsible for its environment. And since organism and environment determine each other and are mutually dependent for their existence, it follows that the life-process, to be adequately understood, must be considered in terms of their interrelations.

The social environment is endowed with meanings in terms of the process of social activity; it is an organization of objective relations which arises in relation to a group of organisms engaged in such activity, in processes of social experience and behavior. Certain characters of the external world are possessed by it only with reference to or in relation to an interacting social group of individual organisms; just as other characters of it are possessed by it only with reference to or in relation to individual organisms themselves. The relation of the social process of behavior—or the relation of the social organism—to the social environment is analogous to the relation of the processes of individual biological activity—or the relation of the individual organism—to the physical-biological environment.[37]

The parallelism I have been referring to is the parallelism of the set of the organism and the objects answering to it. In the ox there is hunger and also the sight and odor which bring in the food. The whole process is not found simply in the stomach, but in all the activities of grazing, chewing the cud, and so on. This process is one which is intimately related to the so-called food. The organism sets up a bacteriological laboratory, such as the ox carries around to take care of the grass. Within that parallelism what we term the meaning of the object is found, specifically, in the organized attitude of response on the part of the organism to the characters and the things. The meanings are there, and the mind is occupied with these meanings. The organized stimuli answer to the organized responses.

37   A social organism—a social group of individual organisms—constitutes or creates its own special environment of objects just as, and in the same sense as, an individual organism constitutes or creates its own special environment of objects (which, however, is much more rudimentary than the environment constructed by a social organism).

It is the organization of the different responses to each other in their relationship to the stimuli they are setting free that is the peculiar subject matter of psychology in dealing with what we term "mind." We generally confine the term "mental," and so "mind," to the human organism, because there we find that body of symbols that enables us to isolate these characters, these meanings. We try to distinguish the meaning of a house from the stone, the cement, the bricks that make it up as a physical object, and in doing so we are referring to the use of it. That is what makes the house a mental affair.[38] We are isolating, if you like, the building materials from the standpoint of the physicist and the architect. There are various standpoints from which one can look at a house. The burrow in which some animal lives is in one sense the house of the animal, but when the human being lives in a house the house takes on what we term a mental character for him which it presumably has not for the mole that lives in the burrow. The human individual has the ability to pick out the elements in a house which answer to his responses so that he can control them. He reads the advertisement of a new form of a boiler and can then have more warmth, have a more comfortable dressing room than before. Man is able to control the process from the standpoint of his own responses. He gets meanings and so controls his responses. His ability to pick those out is what makes the house a mental affair. The mole, too, has to find his food, meet his enemies, and avoid them, but we do not assume that the mole is able to indicate to himself the peculiar advantages of his burrow over another one. His house has no mental

38   Nature—the external world—is objectively there, in opposition to our experience of it or in opposition to the individual thinker himself. Although external objects are there, independent of the experiencing individual, nevertheless they possess certain characteristics by virtue of their relations to his experiencing or to his mind, which they would not possess otherwise or apart from those relations. These characteristics are their meanings for him, or in general, for us. The distinction between physical objects or physical reality and the mental or self-conscious experience of those objects or that reality—the distinction between external and internal experience—lies in the fact that the latter is concerned with or constituted by meanings. Experienced objects have definite meanings for the individuals thinking about them.

characteristics. Mentality resides in the ability of the organism to indicate those things in the environment which answer to his responses, so that he can control those responses in various ways. This ability, from the point of view of behavioristic psychology, is what mentality consists in. There are in the mole and other animals complex elements of behavior related to the environment, but the human animal is able to indicate to itself and to others what the characters are in the environment which call out these complex, highly organized responses and by such indication is able to control the responses. The human animal has the ability over and above the adjustment which belongs to the lower animal to pick out and isolate the stimulus. The biologist recognizes that food has certain values, and while the human animal responds to these values as other animals do, it can also indicate certain characters in the food which mean certain things in its digestive responses to these foods. Mentality consists in indicating these values to others and to one's self so that one can control one's responses.

Mentality on our approach simply comes in when the organism is able to point out meanings to others and to himself. This is the point at which mind appears, or if you like, emerges. What we need to recognize is that we are dealing with the relationship of the organism to the environment selected by its own sensitivity. The psychologist is interested in the mechanism which the human species has evolved to get control over these relationships. The relationships have been there before the indications are made, but the organism has not in its own conduct controlled that relationship. It originally has no mechanism by means of which it can control it. The human animal, however, has worked out a mechanism of language communication by means of which it can get this control. Now, it is evident that much of that mechanism does not lie in the central nervous system but in the relation of things to the organism. The ability to pick these meanings out and to indicate them to others and to the organism is an ability which gives peculiar power to the human individual. The control has been made possible by language. It is that mechanism of control over meaning in this sense which has, I say, constituted what we term "mind." The mental processes do not, however, lie in words any more than the intelligence of the organism lies in the elements of the central nervous system. Both are part of a process that is going on between organism and environment. The symbols serve their part in this process, and it is that which makes communication so important. Out of language emerges the field of mind.

It is absurd to look at the mind simply from the standpoint of the individual human organism; for, although it has its focus there, it is essentially a social phenomenon; even its biological functions are primarily social. The subjective experience of the individual must be brought into relation with the natural, sociobiological activities of the brain in order to render an acceptable account of mind possible at all; and this can be done only when the social nature of mind is recognized. The meagerness of individual experience in isolation from the processes of social experience—in isolation from its social environment—should, moreover, be apparent. We must regard mind, then, as arising and developing within the social process, within the empirical matrix of social interactions. We must, that is, get an inner individual experience from the standpoint of social acts which include the experiences of separate individuals in a social context wherein those individuals interact. The processes of experience which the human brain makes possible are made possible only for a group of interacting individuals—only for individual organisms which are members of a society, not for the individual organism in isolation from other individual organisms.

Mind arises in the social process only when that process as a whole enters into, or is present in, the experience of any one of the given individuals involved in that process. When this occurs the individual becomes self-conscious and has a mind; he becomes aware of his relations to that process as a whole, and to the other individuals participating in it with him; he becomes aware of that process as modified by the reactions and interactions of the individuals—including himself—who are carrying it on. The evolutionary appearance of mind or intelligence takes place when the whole social process of experience and behavior is brought within the experience of any one of the separate individuals implicated therein and when the individual's adjustment to the process is modified and refined by the awareness or consciousness which he thus has of it. It is by means of reflexiveness—the turning-back of the experience of the individual upon himself—that the whole social process is thus brought into the experience of the individuals involved in it; it is by such means, which enable the individual to take the attitude of the other toward himself, that the individual is able consciously to adjust himself to that process, and to modify the resultant of that process in any given social act in terms of his adjustment to it. Reflexiveness, then, is the essential condition, within the social process, for the development of mind.

Part VI

7

SELF

The Self and the Organism

IN OUR statement of the development of intelligence we have already suggested that the language process is essential for the development of the self. The self has a character which is different from that of the physiological organism proper. The self is something which has a development; it is not initially there at birth but arises in the process of social experience and activity, that is, develops in the given individual as a result of his relations to that process as a whole and to other individuals within that process. The intelligence of the lower forms of animal life, like a great deal of human intelligence, does not involve a self. In our habitual actions, for example, in our moving about in a world that is simply there and to which we are so adjusted that no thinking is involved, there is a certain amount of sensuous experience such as persons have when they are just waking up, a bare "thereness" of the world. Such characters about us may exist in experience without taking their place in relationship to the self. One must, of course, under those conditions, distinguish between the experience that immediately takes place and our own organization of it into the experience of the self. One says upon analysis that a certain item had its place in his

---

First published in *Mind, Self, and Society,* ed. Charles W. Morris (Chicago: University of Chicago Press, 1934), pp. 135–226.

experience, in the experience of his self. We inevitably do tend at a certain level of sophistication to organize all experience into that of a self. We do so intimately identify our experiences, especially our affective experiences, with the self that it takes a moment's abstraction to realize that pain and pleasure can be there without being the experience of the self. Similarly, we normally organize our memories upon the string of our self. When we date things we always date them from the point of view of our past experiences. We frequently have memories that we cannot date, that we cannot place. A picture comes before us suddenly, and we are at a loss to explain when that experience originally took place. We remember perfectly distinctly the picture, but we do not have it definitely placed, and until we can place it in terms of our past experience we are not satisfied. Nevertheless, I think it is obvious, when one comes to consider it, that the self is not necessarily involved in the life of the organism, nor involved in what we term our sensuous experience, that is, experience in a world about us for which we have habitual reactions.

We can distinguish very definitely between the self and the body. The body can be there and can operate in a very intelligent fashion without there being a self involved in the experience. The self has the characteristic that it is an object to itself, and that characteristic distinguishes it from other objects and from the body. It is perfectly true that the eye can see the foot, but it does not see the body as a whole. We cannot see our backs; we can feel certain portions of them, if we are agile, but we cannot get an experience of our whole body. There are, of course, experiences which are somewhat vague and difficult of location, but the bodily experiences are for us organized about a self. The foot and hand belong to the self. We can see our feet, especially when we look at them from the wrong end of an opera glass, as strange things which we have difficulty in recognizing as our own. The parts of the body are quite distinguishable from the self. We can lose parts of the body without any serious invasion of the self. The mere ability to experience different parts of the body is not different from the experience of a table. The table presents a different feel from what the hand does when one hand feels another, but it is an experience of something with which we come definitely into contact. The body does not experience itself as a whole, in the sense in which the self in some way enters into the experience of the self.

It is the characteristic of the self as an object to itself that I want to bring out. This characteristic is represented in the word "self," which is a reflexive, and indicates that which can be both subject and object. This type of object is essentially different from other objects, and in the past it has been distinguished as conscious, a term which indicates an experience with, an experience of, one's self. It was assumed that consciousness in some way carried this capacity of being an object to itself. In giving a behavioristic statement of consciousness we have to look for some sort of experience in which the physical organism can become an object to itself.[1]

When one is running away from someone who is chasing him, he is entirely occupied in this action, and his experience may be swallowed up in the objects about him, so that he has, at the time being, no consciousness of self at all. We must be, of course, very completely occupied to have that take place, but we can, I think, recognize that sort of a possible experience in which the self does not enter. We can, perhaps, get some light on that situation through those experiences in which during very intense action there appear in the experience of the individual, back of this intense action, memories and anticipations. Tolstoi as an officer in the war gives an account of having pictures of his past experience in the midst of his most intense action. There are also the pictures that flash into a person's mind when he is drowning. In such instances there is a contrast between an experience

[1] Man's behavior is such in his social group that he is able to become an object to himself, a fact which makes him a more advanced product of evolutionary development than are the lower animals. Fundamentally it is this social fact—and not his alleged possession of a soul or mind with which he, as an individual, has been mysteriously and supernaturally endowed, and with which the lower animals have not been endowed—that differentiates him from them.

that is absolutely wound up in outside activity in which the self as an object does not enter, and an activity of memory and imagination in which the self is the principal object. The self is then entirely distinguishable from an organism that is surrounded by things and acts with reference to things, including parts of its own body. These latter may be objects like other objects, but they are just objects out there in the field, and they do not involve a self that is an object to the organism. This is, I think, frequently overlooked. It is that fact which makes our anthropomorphic reconstructions of animal life so fallacious. How can an individual get outside himself (experientially) in such a way as to become an object to himself? This is the essential psychological problem of selfhood or of self-consciousness; and its solution is to be found by referring to the process of social conduct or activity in which the given person or individual is implicated. The apparatus of reason would not be complete unless it swept itself into its own analysis of the field of experience or unless the individual brought himself into the same experiential field as that of the other individual selves in relation to whom he acts in any given social situation. Reason cannot become impersonal unless it takes an objective, non-affective attitude toward itself; otherwise we have just consciousness, not *self*-consciousness. And it is necessary to rational conduct that the individual should thus take an objective, impersonal attitude toward himself, that he should become an object to himself. For the individual organism is obviously an essential and important fact or constituent element of the empirical situation in which it acts; and without taking objective account of itself as such, it cannot act intelligently or rationally.

The individual experiences himself as such, not directly, but only indirectly, from the particular standpoints of other individual members of the same social group or from the generalized standpoint of the social group as a whole to which he belongs. For he enters his own experience as a self or individual, not directly or immediately, not by becoming a subject to himself, but only insofar as he first becomes an object to himself just as other individuals are objects to him or are in his experience; and he becomes an object to himself only by taking the attitudes of other individuals toward himself within a social environment or context of experience and behavior in which both he and they are involved.

The importance of what we term "communication" lies in the fact that it provides a form of behavior in which the organism or the individual may become an object to himself. It is that sort of communication which we have been discussing—not communication in the sense of the cluck of the hen to the chickens, or the bark of a wolf to the pack, or the lowing of a cow, but communication in the sense of significant symbols, communication which is directed not only to others but also to the individual himself. So far as that type of communication is a part of behavior, it at least introduces a self. Of course, one may hear without listening; one may see things that he does not realize; do things that he is not really aware of. But it is when one does respond to that which he addresses to another and when that response of his own becomes a part of his conduct, when he not only hears himself but responds to himself, talks and replies to himself as truly as the other person replies to him, that we have behavior in which the individuals become objects to themselves.

Such a self is not, I would say, primarily the physiological organism. The physiological organism is essential to it,[2] but we

2   *a*) All social interrelations and interactions are rooted in a certain common socio-physiological endowment of every individual involved in them. These physiological bases of social behavior—which have their ultimate seat or locus in the lower part of the individual's central nervous system—are the bases of such behavior, precisely because they in themselves are also social; that is, because they consist in drives or instincts or behavior tendencies, on the part of the given individual, which he cannot carry out or give overt expression and satisfaction to without the co-operative aid of one or more other individuals. The physiological processes of behavior of which they are the mechanisms are processes which necessarily involve more than one individual, processes in which other individuals besides the given individual are perforce implicated. Examples of the fundamental social relations to which these physiological bases of social behavior give rise are those between the sexes (expressing the reproductive instinct), between parent and child (expressing the parental

are at least able to think of a self without it. Persons who believe in immortality, or believe in ghosts, or in the possibility of the self leaving the body, assume a self which is quite distinguishable from the body. How successfully they can hold these conceptions is an open question, but we do, as a fact, separate the self and the organism. It is fair to say that the beginning of the self as an object, so far as we can see, is to be found in the experiences of people that lead to the conception of a "double." Primitive people assume that there is a double, located presumably in the diaphragm, that leaves the body temporarily in sleep and completely in death. It can be enticed out of the body of one's enemy and perhaps killed. It is represented in infancy by the imaginary playmates which children create and through which they come to control their experiences in their play.

The self, as that which can be an object to itself, is essentially a social structure, and it arises in social experience. After a self has arisen, it in a certain sense provides for itself its social experiences, and so we can conceive of an absolutely solitary self. But it is impossible to conceive of a self arising outside of social experience. When it has arisen, we can think of a person in solitary confinement for the rest of his life, but who still has himself as a companion and is able to think and to converse with him-

---

instinct), and between neighbors (expressing the gregarious instinct). These relatively simple and rudimentary physiological mechanisms or tendencies of individual human behavior, besides constituting the physiological bases of all human social behavior, are also the fundamental biological materials of human nature; so that when we refer to human nature, we are referring to something which is essentially social.

b) Sexually and parentally, as well as in its attacks and defenses, the activities of the physiological organism are social in that the acts begun within the organism require their completion in the actions of others. . . . But while the pattern of the individual act can be said to be in these cases social, it is only so insofar as the organism seeks for the stimuli in the attitudes and characters of other forms for the completion of its own responses, and by its behavior tends to maintain the other as a part of its own environment. The actual behavior of the other or the others is not initiated in the individual form as a part of its own pattern of behavior (MS).

self as he had communicated with others. That process to which I have just referred, of responding to one's self as another responds to it, taking part in one's own conversation with others, being aware of what one is saying and using that awareness of what one is saying to determine what one is going to say thereafter—that is a process with which we are all familiar. We are continually following up our own address to other persons by an understanding of what we are saying and using that understanding in the direction of our continued speech. We are finding out what we are going to say, what we are going to do, by saying and doing, and in the process we are continually controlling the process itself. In the conversation of gestures what we say calls out a certain response in another and that in turn changes our own action, so that we shift from what we started to do because of the reply the other makes. The conversation of gestures is the beginning of communication. The individual comes to carry on a conversation of gestures with himself. He says something and that calls out a certain reply in himself which makes him change what he was going to say. One starts to say something, we will presume an unpleasant something, but when he starts to say it he realizes it is cruel. The effect on himself of what he is saying checks him; there is here a conversation of gestures between the individual and himself. By significant speech we mean that the action is one that affects the individual himself and that the effect upon the individual himself is part of the intelligent carrying-out of the conversation with others. Now we, so to speak, amputate that social phase and dispense with it for the time being, so that one is talking to one's self as one would talk to another person.[3]

---

[3]   It is generally recognized that the specifically social expressions of intelligence, or the exercise of what is often called "social intelligence," depend upon the given individual's ability to take the roles of, or "put himself in the place of," the other individuals implicated with him in given social situations and upon his consequent sensitivity to their attitudes toward himself and toward one another. These specifically social expressions of intelligence acquire unique significance in terms of our view that the whole nature of intelligence is social to the very core—that this putting of one's self in the places of others, this taking by one's self of their roles or attitudes, is not merely one of the various aspects or expressions

This process of abstraction cannot be carried on indefinitely. One inevitably seeks an audience, has to pour himself out to somebody. In reflective intelligence one thinks to act, and to act solely so that this action remains a part of a social process. Thinking becomes preparatory to social action. The very process of thinking is, of course, simply an inner conversation that goes on, but it is a conversation of gestures which in its completion implies the expression of that which one thinks to an audience. One separates the significance of what he is saying to others from the actual speech and gets it ready before saying it. He thinks it out and perhaps writes it in the form of a book; but it is still a part of social intercourse in which one is addressing other persons and at the same time addressing one's self, and in which one controls the address to other persons by the response made to one's own gesture. That the person should be responding to himself is necessary to the self, and it is this sort of social conduct which provides behavior within which that self appears. I know of no other form of behavior than the linguistic in which the individual is an object to himself, and, so far as I can see, the individual is not a self in the reflective sense unless he is an object to himself. It is this fact that gives a critical importance to communication, since this is a type of behavior in which the individual does so respond to himself.

We realize in everyday conduct and experience that an individual does not mean a great deal of what he is doing and saying. We frequently say that such an individual is not himself. We come away from an interview with a realization that we have left out important things, that there are parts of the self that

---

of intelligence or of intelligent behavior, but is the very essence of its character. Spearman's "X factor" in intelligence—the unknown factor which, according to him, intelligence contains—is simply (if our social theory of intelligence is correct) this ability of the intelligent individual to take the attitude of the other, or the attitudes of others, thus realizing the significations or grasping the meanings of the symbols or gestures in terms of which thinking proceeds; and thus being able to carry on with himself the internal conversation with these symbols or gestures which thinking involves.

did not get into what was said. What determines the amount of the self that gets into communication is the social experience itself. Of course, a good deal of the self does not need to get expression. We carry on a whole series of different relationships to different people. We are one thing to one man and another thing to another. There are parts of the self which exist only for the self in relationship to itself. We divide ourselves up in all sorts of different selves with reference to our acquaintances. We discuss politics with one and religion with another. There are all sorts of different selves answering to all sorts of different social reactions. It is the social process itself that is responsible for the appearance of the self; it is not there as a self apart from this type of experience.

A multiple personality is in a certain sense normal, as I have just pointed out. There is usually an organization of the whole self with reference to the community to which we belong and the situation in which we find ourselves. What the society is, whether we are living with people of the present, people of our own imaginations, or people of the past, varies of course, with different individuals. Normally, within the sort of community as a whole to which we belong, there is a unified self, but that can be broken up. To a person who is somewhat unstable nervously and in whom there is a line of cleavage, certain activities become impossible, and that set of activities may separate and evolve another self. Two separate "me's" and "I's," two different selves, result, and that is the condition under which there is a tendency to break up the personality. There is an account of a professor of education who disappeared, was lost to the community, and later turned up in a logging camp in the West. He freed himself of his occupation and turned to the woods where he felt, if you like, more at home. The pathological side of it was the forgetting, the leaving out of the rest of the self. This result involved getting rid of certain bodily memories which would identify the individual to himself. We often recognize the lines of cleavage that run through us. We would be glad to forget certain things, get rid of things the self is bound up with in past experiences. What we have here is a situation in which there can be different selves, and it is dependent upon the set of social reactions that is involved as to which self we are going to be. If we can forget everything involved in one set of activities, then obviously we relinquish that part of the self. Take a person who is unstable, get him occupied by speech, and at the same time get his eye on something you are writing so that he is carrying on two separate lines of communication, and if you go about it in the right way, you can get those two currents going so that they do not run into each other. You can get two entirely different sets of activities going on. You can bring about in that way the dissociation of a person's self. It is a process of setting up two sorts of communication which separate the behavior of the individual. For one individual it is this thing said and heard, and for the other individual there exists only that which he sees written. You must, of course, keep one experience out of the field of the other. Dissociations are apt to take place when an event leads to emotional upheavals. That which is separated goes on in its own way.

The unity and structure of the complete self reflects the unity and structure of the social process as a whole; and each of the elementary selves of which it is composed reflects the unity and structure of one of the various aspects of that process in which the individual is implicated. In other words, the various elementary selves which constitute, or are organized into, a complete self are the various aspects of the structure of that complete self answering to the various aspects of the structure of the social process as a whole; the structure of the complete self is thus a reflection of the complete social process. The organization and unification of a social group is identical with the organization and unification of any one of the selves arising within the social process in which that group is engaged or which it is carrying on.[4]

---

4   The unity of the mind is not identical with the unity of the self. The unity of the self is constituted by the unity of the entire relational pattern of social behavior and experience in which the individual is implicated and which is reflected in the structure of the self; but many of the aspects or features of this entire pattern do not enter into consciousness, so that the unity of the mind is in a sense an abstraction from the more inclusive unity of the self.

The phenomenon of dissociation of personality is caused by a breaking up of the complete, unitary self into the component selves of which it is composed, and which respectively correspond to different aspects of the social process in which the person is involved, and within which his complete or unitary self has arisen; these aspects being the different social groups to which he belongs within that process.

The Background of the
Genesis of the Self

The problem is how, in detail, a self arises. We have to note something of the background of its genesis. First of all there is the conversation of gestures between animals involving some sort of co-operative activity. There the beginning of the act of one is a stimulus to the other to respond in a certain way, while the beginning of this response becomes again a stimulus to the first to adjust his action to the oncoming response. Such is the preparation for the completed act, and ultimately it leads to the conduct which is the outcome of this preparation. The conversation of gestures, however, does not carry with it the reference of the individual, the animal, the organism, to itself. It is not acting in a fashion which calls for a response from the form itself, although it is conduct with reference to the conduct of others. We have seen, however, that there are certain gestures that do affect the organism as they affect other organisms and may, therefore, arouse in the organism responses of the same character as aroused in the other. Here, then, we have a situation in which the individual may at least arouse responses in himself and reply to these responses, the condition being that the social stimuli have an effect on the individual which is like that which they have on the other. That, for example, is what is implied in language; otherwise language as significant symbol would disappear, since the individual would not get the meaning of that which he says.

The peculiar character possessed by our human social environment belongs to it by virtue of the peculiar character of human social activity. That character is found in the process of communication, and more particularly in the triadic relation on which the existence of meaning is based. That is the relation of the gesture of one organism to the adjustive response made to it by another organism, in its indicative capacity as pointing to the completion or resultant of the act it initiates (the meaning of the gesture being thus the response of the second organism to it as such, or as a gesture). What, as it were, takes the gesture out of the social act and isolates it as such—what makes it something more than just an early phase of an individual act—is the response of another organism, or of other organisms, to it. Such a response is its meaning, or gives it meaning. The social situation and process of behavior are here presupposed by the acts of the individual organisms implicated therein. The gesture arises as a separable element in the social act, since it is selected by the sensitivities of other organisms to it; it does not exist as a gesture merely in the experience of the single individual. The meaning of a gesture by one organism, to repeat, is found in the response of another organism to what would be the completion of the act of the first organism which that gesture initiates and indicates.

We sometimes speak as if a person could build an entire argument in his mind, and then put it into words to convey it to someone else. Actually, our thinking always takes place by means of some sort of symbols. It is possible that one could have the meaning of "chair" in his experience without there being a symbol, but we would not be thinking about it in that case. We may sit down in a chair without thinking about what we are doing, that is, the approach to the chair is presumably already aroused in our experience, so that the meaning is there. But if one is thinking about the chair, he must have some sort of a symbol for it. It may be the form of the chair, it may be the attitude that somebody else takes in sitting down, but it is more apt to be some language symbol that arouses this response. In a thought process there has to be some sort of a symbol that can refer to this meaning, that is, tend to call out this response, and also serve this purpose for other persons as well. It would not be a thought process if that were not the case.

Our symbols are all universal.[5] You cannot say anything that is absolutely particular; anything you say that has any meaning at all is universal. You are saying something that calls out a specific response in anybody else provided that the symbol exists for him in his experience as it does for you. There is the language of speech and the language of hands, and there may be the language of the expression of the countenance. One can register grief or joy and call out certain responses. There are primitive people who can carry on elaborate conversations just by expressions of the countenance. Even in these cases the person who communicates is affected by that expression just as he expects somebody else to be affected. Thinking always implies a symbol which will call out the same response in another that it calls out in the thinker. Such a symbol is a universal of discourse; it is universal in its character. We always assume that the symbol we use is one which will call out in the other person the same response, provided it is a part of his mechanism of conduct. A person who is saying something is saying to himself what he says to others; otherwise he does not know what he is talking about.

There is, of course, a great deal in one's conversation with others that does not arouse in one's self the same response it arouses in others. That is particularly true in the case of emotional attitudes. One tries to bully somebody else; he is not trying to bully himself. There is, further, a whole set of values given in speech which are not of a symbolic character. The actor is conscious of these values; that is, when he assumes a certain

5 Thinking proceeds in terms of or by means of universals. A universal can be interpreted behavioristically as simply the social act as a whole, involving the organization and interrelation of the attitudes of all the individuals implicated in the act, as controlling their overt responses. This organization of the different individual attitudes and interactions in a given social act, with reference to their interrelations as realized by the individuals themselves, is what we mean by a universal; and it determines what the actual overt responses of the individuals involved in the given social act will be, whether that act be concerned with a concrete project of some sort (such as the relation of physical and social means to ends desired) or with some purely abstract discussion, say the theory of relativity or the Platonic ideas.

attitude he is, as we say, aware that this attitude represents grief. When it does, he is able to respond to his own gesture in some sense as his audience does. It is not a natural situation; one is not an actor all of the time. We do at times act and consider just what the effect of our attitude is going to be, and we may deliberately use a certain tone of voice to bring about a certain result. Such a tone arouses the same response in ourselves that we want to arouse in somebody else. But a very large part of what goes on in speech has not this symbolic status.

It is the task not only of the actor but of the artist as well to find the sort of expression that will arouse in others what is going on in himself. The lyric poet has an experience of beauty with an emotional thrill to it, and as an artist using words he is seeking for those words which will answer to his emotional attitude and which will call out in others the attitude he himself has. He can only test his results in himself by seeing whether these words do call out in him the response he wants to call out in others. He is in somewhat the same position as that of the actor. The first direct and immediate experience is not in the form of communication. We have an interesting light on this from such a poet as Wordsworth, who was very much interested in the technique of the poet's expression; and he has told us in his prefaces and also in his own poetry how his poems, as poems, arose—and uniformly the experience itself was not the immediate stimulus to the poetic expression. A period of ten years might lie between the original experience and the expression of it. This process of finding the expression in language which will call out the emotion once had is more easily accomplished when one is dealing with the memory of it than when one is in the midst of the trance-like experiences through which Wordsworth passed in his contact with nature. One has to experiment and see how the expression that is given does answer to the responses which are now had in the fainter memories of experience. Someone once said that he had very great difficulty in writing poetry; he had plenty of ideas but could not get the language he needed. He was rightly told that poetry was written in words, not in ideas.

A great deal of our speech is not of this genuinely aesthetic character; in most of it we do not deliberately feel the emotions which we arouse. We do not normally use language stimuli to call out in ourselves the emotional response which we are calling out in others. One does, of course, have sympathy in emotional situations; but what one is seeking for there is something which is, after all, that in the other which supports the individual in his own experience. In the case of the poet and actor, the stimulus calls out in the artist that which it calls out in the other, but this is not the natural function of language; we do not assume that the person who is angry is calling out the fear in himself that he is calling out in someone else. The emotional part of our act does not directly call out in us the response it calls out in the other. When a person is hostile, the attitude of the other that he is interested in, an attitude which flows naturally from his angered tones, is not one that he definitely recognizes in himself. We are not frightened by a tone which we may use to frighten somebody else. On the emotional side, which is a very large part of the vocal gesture, we do not call out in ourselves in any such degree the response we call out in others as we do in the case of significant speech. Here we should call out in ourselves the type of response we are calling out in others; we must know what we are saying, and the attitude of the other which we arouse in ourselves should control what we do say. Rationality means that the type of the response which we call out in others should be so called out in ourselves and that this response should in turn take its place in determining what further thing we are going to say and do.

What is essential to communication is that the symbol should arouse in one's self what it arouses in the other individual. It must have that sort of universality to any person who finds himself in the same situation. There is a possibility of language whenever a stimulus can affect the individual as it affects the other. With a blind person such as Helen Keller, it is a contact experience that could be given to another as it is given to herself. It is out of that sort of language that the mind of Helen Keller was built. As she has recognized, it was not until she could get into communication with other persons through symbols which could arouse in herself the responses they arouse in other people that she could get what we term a mental content, or a self.

Another set of background factors in the genesis of the self is represented in the activities of play and the game.

Among primitive people, as I have said, the necessity of distinguishing the self and the organism was recognized in what we term the "double": the individual has a thing-like self that is affected by the individual as it affects other people and which is distinguished from the immediate organism in that it can leave the body and come back to it. This is the basis for the concept of the soul as a separate entity.

We find in children something that answers to this double, namely, the invisible, imaginary companions which a good many children produce in their own experience. They organize in this way the responses which they call out in other persons and call out also in themselves. Of course, this playing with an imaginary companion is only a peculiarly interesting phase of ordinary play. Play in this sense, especially the stage which precedes the organized games, is a play at something. A child plays at being a mother, at being a teacher, at being a policeman; that is, it is taking different roles, as we say. We have something that suggests this in what we call the play of animals: a cat will play with her kittens and dogs play with each other. Two dogs playing with each other will attack and defend, in a process which, if carried through, would amount to an actual fight. There is a combination of responses which checks the depth of the bite. But we do not have in such a situation the dogs taking a definite role in the sense that a child deliberately takes the role of another. This tendency on the part of the children is what we are working with in the kindergarten where the roles which the children assume are made the basis for training. When a child does assume a role he has in himself the stimuli which call out that particular response or group of responses. He may, of course, run away when he is chased, as the dog does, or he may turn around and strike back just as the dog does in his play. But that is not the same as playing at something. Children get together to "play Indian." This means that the child has a certain set of stimuli which call out in itself the responses that they would call out in others and which answer to an Indian. In the play period the child utilizes his own responses to these stimuli which he makes use of in building a self. The response which he has a tendency to make to these stimuli organizes them. He plays that he is, for instance, offering himself something, and he buys it; he gives a letter to himself and takes it away; he addresses himself as a parent or as a teacher; he arrests himself as a policeman. He has a set of stimuli which call out in himself the sort of responses they call out in others. He takes this group of responses and organizes them into a certain whole. Such is the simplest form of being another to one's self. It involves a temporal situation. The child says something in one character and responds in another character, and then his responding in another character is a stimulus to himself in the first character, and so the conversation goes on. A certain organized structure arises in him and in his other which replies to it, and these carry on the conversation of gestures between themselves.

When we contrast play with the situation in an organized game, we note the essential difference that the child who plays in a game must be ready to take the attitude of everyone else involved in that game and that these different roles must have a definite relationship to each other. Take a very simple game such as hide-and-seek. Everyone with the exception of the one who is hunting is a person who is hiding. A child does not require more than the person who is hunted and the one who is hunting. When a child is playing in the first sense he just goes on playing, but there is no basic organization gained. In that early stage he passes from one role to another just as the whim takes him. But in a game when a number of individuals are involved, the child taking one role must be ready to take the role of everyone else. When he gets in a baseball game, he must have the responses of each position involved in his own position. He must know what everyone else is going to do in order to carry out his own play. He has to take all of these roles. They do not all have to be present in consciousness at the same time, but at some moments he has to have three or four individuals present in his own attitude, such as the one who is going to throw the ball, the one who is going to catch it, and so on. These responses must be, in some degree, present in his own make-up. In the game, then, there is a set of responses of such others so organized that the attitude of one calls out the appropriate attitudes of the other.

This organization is put in the form of the rules of the game. Children take a great interest in rules. They make rules on the spot in order to help themselves out of difficulties. Part of the enjoyment of the game is to get these rules. Now, the rules are the set of responses which a particular attitude calls out. You can demand a certain response in others if you take a certain attitude. These responses are all in yourself as well. There you get an organized set of such responses as that to which I have referred, which is something more elaborate than the roles found in play. Here there is just a set of responses that follow on each other indefinitely. At such a stage we speak of a child as not yet having a fully developed self. The child responds in a fairly intelligent fashion to the immediate stimuli that come to him, but they are not organized. He does not organize his life as we would like to have him do, namely, as a whole. There is just a set of responses of the type of play. The child reacts to a certain stimulus, and the reaction is in himself that is called out in others, but he is not a whole self. In his game he has to have an organization of these roles; otherwise he cannot play the game. The game represents the passage in the life of the child from taking the role of others in play to the organized part that is essential to self-consciousness in the full sense of the term.

Play, the Game, and the Generalized Other

We were speaking of the social conditions under which the self arises as an object. In addition to language we found two illustrations, one in play and the other in the game, and I wish to summarize and expand my account on these points. I have spoken of these from the point of view of children. We can, of course, refer also to the attitudes of more primitive people out of which our civilization has arisen. A striking illustration of play as distinct from the game is found in the myths and the various plays which primitive people carry out, especially in religious pageants. The pure play attitude which we find in the case of little children may not be found here, since the participants are adults, and undoubtedly the relationship of these play processes to that which they interpret is more or less in the minds of even the most primitive people. In the process of interpretation of such rituals, there is an organization of play which perhaps might be compared to that which is taking place in the kindergarten in dealing with the plays of little children, where these are made into a set that will have a definite structure or relationship. At least something of the same sort is found in the play of primitive people. This type of activity belongs, of course, not to the everyday life of the people in their dealing with the objects about them—there we have a more or less definitely developed self-consciousness—but in their attitudes toward the forces about them, the nature upon which they depend; in their attitude toward this nature which is vague and uncertain, there we have a much more primitive response; and that response finds its expression in taking the role of the other, playing at the expression of their gods and their heroes, going through certain rites which are the representation of what these individuals are supposed to be doing. The process is one which develops, to be sure, into a more or less definite technique and is controlled; and yet we can say that it has arisen out of situations similar to those in which little children play at being a parent, at being a teacher—vague personalities that are about them and which affect them and on which they depend. These are personalities which they take, roles they play, and insofar control the development of their own personality. This outcome is just what the kindergarten works toward. It takes the characters of these various vague beings and gets them into such an organized social relationship to each other that they build the character of the little child.[6] The very introduction of organization from outside supposes a lack of organization at this

[6] "The Relation of Play to Education," *University of Chicago Record,* I (1896–97), 140 ff.

period in the child's experience. Over against such a situation of the little child and primitive people, we have the game as such.

The fundamental difference between the game and play is that in the former the child must have the attitude of all the others involved in that game. The attitudes of the other players which the participant assumes organize into a sort of unit, and it is that organization which controls the response of the individual. The illustration used was of a person playing baseball. Each one of his own acts is determined by his assumption of the action of the others who are playing the game. What he does is controlled by his being everyone else on that team, at least insofar as those attitudes affect his own particular response. We get then an "other" which is an organization of the attitudes of those involved in the same process.

The organized community or social group which gives to the individual his unity of self can be called "the generalized other." The attitude of the generalized other is the attitude of the whole community.[7] Thus, for example, in the case of such a social group as a ball team, the team is the generalized other insofar as it enters—as an organized process on social activity—into the experience of any one of the individual members.

[7] It is possible for inanimate objects, no less than for other human organisms, to form parts of the generalized and organized—the completely socialized—other for any given human individual, insofar as he responds to such objects socially or in a social fashion (by means of the mechanism of thought, the internalized conversation of gestures). Any thing—any object or set of objects, whether animate or inanimate, human or animal, or merely physical—toward which he acts, or to which he responds, socially, is an element in what for him is the generalized other; by taking the attitudes of which toward himself, he becomes conscious of himself as an object or individual, and thus develops a self or personality. Thus, for example, the cult, in its primitive form, is merely the social embodiment of the relation between the given social group or community and its physical environment—an organized social means, adopted by the individual members of that group or community, of entering into social relations with that environment, or (in a sense) of carrying on conversations with it; and in this way that environment becomes part of the total generalized other for each of the individual members of the given social group or community.

If the given human individual is to develop a self in the fullest sense, it is not sufficient for him merely to take the attitudes of other human individuals toward himself and toward one another within the human social process and to bring that social process as a whole into his individual experience merely in these terms. He must also, in the same way that he takes the attitudes of other individuals toward himself and toward one another, take their attitudes toward the various phases or aspects of the common social activity or set of social undertakings in which, as members of an organized society or social group, they are all engaged. He must then, by generalizing these individual attitudes of that organized society or social group itself as a whole, act toward different social projects which at any given time it is carrying out, or toward the various larger phases of the general social process which constitutes the group's life and of which these projects are specific manifestations. Getting these broad activities of any given social whole or organized society within the experiential field of any one of the individuals involved or included in that whole is, in other words, the essential basis and prerequisite of the fullest development of that individual's self—only insofar as he takes the attitudes of the organized social group to which he belongs toward the organized, co-operative social activity or set of such activities in which that group as such is engaged, does he develop a complete self or possess the sort of complete self he has developed. And on the other hand, the complex co-operative processes and activities and institutional functionings of organized human society are also possible only insofar as every individual involved in them or belonging to that society can take the general attitudes of all other such individuals with reference to these processes and activities and institutional functionings and to the organized social whole of experiential relations and interactions thereby constituted—and can direct his own behavior accordingly.

It is in the form of the generalized other that the social process influences the behavior of the individuals involved in it and carrying it on, that is, that the community exercises control over the conduct of its individual members; for it is in this form that the social process or community enters as a determining factor into the individual's thinking. In abstract thought the individual takes the attitude of the generalized other[8] toward himself, without reference to its expression in any particular other individuals; and in concrete thought, he takes that attitude insofar as it is expressed in the attitudes toward his behavior of those other individuals with whom he is involved in the given social situation or act. But only by taking the attitude of the generalized other toward himself, in one or another of these ways, can he think at all; for only thus can thinking—or the internalized conversation of gestures which constitutes thinking—occur. And only through the taking by individuals of the attitude or attitudes of the generalized other toward themselves is the existence of a universe of disclosure, as that system of common or social meanings which thinking presupposes at its context, rendered possible.

The self-conscious human individual, then, takes or assumes the organized social attitudes of the given social group or community (or of some one section thereof) to which he belongs, toward the social problems of various kinds which confront that group or community at any given time and which arise in connection with the correspondingly different social projects or organized co-operative enterprises in which that group of community as such is engaged; and as an individual participant in

[8]   We have said that the internal conversation of the individual with himself in terms of words or significant gestures—the conversation which constitutes the process or activity of thinking—is carried on by the individual from the standpoint of the "generalized other." And the more abstract that conversation is, the more abstract thinking happens to be, the further removed is the generalized other from any connection with particular individuals. It is especially in abstract thinking that the conversation involved is carried on by the individual with the generalized other, rather than with any particular individuals. Thus it is, for example, that abstract concepts are concepts stated in terms of the attitudes of the entire social group or community; they are stated on the basis of the individual's consciousness of the attitudes of the generalized other toward them, as a result of his taking these attitudes of the generalized other and then responding to them. And thus it is also that abstract propositions are stated in a form which anyone—any other intelligent individual—will accept.

these social projects or co-operative enterprises, he governs his own conduct accordingly. In politics, for example, the individual identifies himself with an entire political party and takes the organized attitudes of that entire party toward the rest of the given social community and toward the problems which confront the party within the given social situation; and he consequently reacts or responds in terms of the organized attitudes of the party as a whole. He thus enters into a special set of social relations with all the other individuals who belong to that political party; and in the same way he enters into various other special sets of social relations, with various other classes of individuals respectively, the individuals of each of these classes being the other members of some one of the particular organized subgroups (determined in socially functional terms) of which he himself is a member within the entire given society or social community. In the most highly developed, organized, and complicated human social communities—those evolved by civilized man—these various socially functional classes or subgroups of individuals to which any given individual belongs (and with the other individual members of which he thus enters into a special set of social relations) are of two kinds. Some of them are concrete social classes or subgroups, such as political parties, clubs, corporations, which are all actually functional social units, in terms of which their individual members are directly related to one another. The others are abstract social classes or subgroups, such as the class of debtors and the class of creditors, in terms of which their individual members are related to one another only more or less indirectly and which only more or less indirectly function as social units, but which afford or represent unlimited possibilities for the widening and ramifying and enriching of the social relations among all the individual members of the given society as an organized and unified whole. The given individual's membership in several of these abstract social classes or subgroups makes possible his entrance into definite social relations (however indirect) with an almost infinite number of other individuals who also belong to or are included within one or another of these abstract social classes or subgroups cutting across functional lines of demarcation which divide different human social communities from one another, and including individual members from several (in some cases from all) such communities. Of these abstract social classes or subgroups of human individuals the one which is most inclusive and extensive is, of course, the one defined by the logical universe of discourse (or system of universally significant symbols) determined by the participation and communicative interaction of individuals; for all such classes or subgroups, it is the one which claims the largest number of individual members and which enables the largest conceivable number of human individuals to enter into some sort of social relation, however indirect or abstract it may be, with one another—a relation arising from the universal functioning of gestures as significant symbols in the general human social process of communication.

I have pointed out, then, that there are two general stages in the full development of the self. At the first of these stages, the individual's self is constituted simply by an organization of the particular attitudes of other individuals toward himself and toward one another in the specific social acts in which he participates with them. But at the second stage in the full development of the individual's self, that self is constituted not only by an organization of these particular individual attitudes, but also by an organization of the social attitudes of the generalized other or the social group as a whole to which he belongs. These social or group attitudes are brought within the individual's field of direct experience and are included as elements in the structure or constitution of his self, in the same way that the attitudes of particular other individuals are; and the individual arrives at them, or succeeds in taking them, by means of further organizing, and then generalizing, the attitudes of particular other individuals in terms of their organized social bearings and implications. So the self reaches its full development by organizing these individual attitudes of others into the organized social or group attitudes, and by thus becoming an individual reflection of the general systematic pattern of social or group behavior in which it and the others are all involved—a pattern which enters as a whole into the individual's experience in terms of these organized group attitudes which, through the mechanism of his central nervous system, he takes toward himself, just as he takes the individual attitudes of others.

The game has a logic, so that such an organization of the self is rendered possible. There is a definite end to be obtained; the actions of the different individuals are all related to each other with reference to that end so that they do not conflict; one is not in conflict with himself in the attitude of another man on the team. If one has the attitude of the person throwing the ball, he can also have the response of catching the ball. The two are related so that they further the purpose of the game itself. They are interrelated in a unitary, organic fashion. There is a definite unity, then, which is introduced into the organization of other selves when we reach such a stage as that of the game, as against the situation of play where there is a simple succession of one role after another, a situation which is, of course, characteristic of the child's own personality. The child is one thing at one time and another at another, and what he is at one moment does not determine what he is at another. That is both the charm of childhood as well as its inadequacy. You cannot count on the child; you cannot assume that all the things he does are going to determine what he will do at any moment. He is not organized into a whole. The child has no definite character, no definite personality.

The game is then an illustration of the situation out of which an organized personality arises. Insofar as the child does take the attitude of the other and allows that attitude of the other to determine the thing he is going to do with reference to a common end, he is becoming an organic member of society. He is taking over the morale of that society and is becoming an essential member of it. He belongs to it insofar as he does allow the attitude of the other that he takes to control his own immediate expression. What is involved here is some sort of an organized process. That which is expressed in terms of the game is, of course, being continually expressed in the social life of the child, but this wider process goes beyond the immediate experience of the child himself. The importance of the game is that it lies entirely inside of the child's own experience, and the importance of our modern type of education is that it is brought as far as possible within this realm. The different attitudes that a child assumes are so organized that they exercise a definite control over his response, as the attitudes in a game control his own immediate response. In the game we get an organized other, a generalized other, which is found in the nature of the child itself, and finds its expression in the immediate experience of the child. And it is that organized activity in the child's own nature controlling the particular response which gives unity, and which builds up his own self.

What goes on in the game goes on in the life of the child all the time. He is continually taking the attitudes of those about him, especially the roles of those who in some sense control him and on whom he depends. He gets the function of the process in an abstract sort of a way at first. It goes over from the play into the game in a real sense. He has to play the game. The morale of the game takes hold of the child more than the larger morale of the whole community. The child passes into the game, and the game expresses a social situation in which he can completely enter; its morale may have a greater hold on him than that of the family to which he belongs or the community in which he lives. There are all sorts of social organizations, some of which are fairly lasting, some temporary, into which the child is entering, and he is playing a sort of social game in them. It is a period in which he likes "to belong," and he gets into organizations which come into existence and pass out of existence. He becomes a something which can function in the organized whole, and thus tends to determine himself in his relationship with the group to which he belongs. That process is one which is a striking stage in the development of the child's morale. It constitutes him a self-conscious member of the community to which he belongs.

Such is the process by which a personality arises. I have spoken of this as a process in which a child takes the role of the other and said that it takes place essentially through the use of language. Language is predominantly based on the vocal gesture by means of which co-operative activities in a community are carried out. Language in its significant sense is that vocal gesture which tends to arouse in the individual the attitude which it

arouses in others, and it is this perfecting of the self by the gesture which mediates the social activities that gives rise to the
process of taking the role of the other. The latter phrase is a little
unfortunate because it suggests an actor's attitude which is actually more sophisticated than that which is involved in our own
experience. To this degree it does not correctly describe that
which I have in mind. We see the process most definitely in a
primitive form in those situations where the child's play takes different roles. Here the very fact that he is ready to pay money, for
instance, arouses the attitude of the person who receives money,
the very process is calling out in him the corresponding activities
of the other person involved. The individual stimulates himself
to the response which he is calling out in the other person, and
then acts in some degree in response to that situation. In play the
child does definitely act the role which he himself has aroused in
himself. It is that which gives, as I have said, a definite content in
the individual which answers to the stimulus that affects him as it
affects somebody else. The content of the other that enters into
one personality is the response in the individual which his gesture
calls out in the other.

We can illustrate our basic concept by a reference to the notion of property. When we say "This is my property. I shall control it," that affirmation calls out a certain set of responses which
must be the same in any community in which property exists. It
involves an organized attitude with reference to property which is
common to all the members of the community. One must have a
definite attitude of control of his own property and respect for the
property of others. Those attitudes (as organized sets of responses) must be there on the part of all, so that when one says
such a thing he calls out in himself the response of the others. He
is calling out the response of what I have called a generalized
other. That which makes society possible is such common responses, such organized attitudes, with reference to what we term
property, the cults of religion, the process of education, and the
relations of the family. Of course, the wider the society, the more
definitely universal these objects must be. In any case, there must
be a definite set of responses, which we can speak of as abstract

and which can belong to a very large group. Property is in itself a very abstract concept. It is that which the individual himself can control and nobody else can control. The attitude is different from that of a dog toward a bone. A dog will fight any other dog trying to take the bone. The dog is not taking the attitude of the other dog. A man who says "This is my property" is taking an attitude of the other person. The man is appealing to his rights because he is able to take the attitude which everybody else in the group has with reference to property, thus arousing in himself the attitude of others.

What makes the organized self is the organization of the attitudes which are common to the group. A person is a personality because he belongs to a community, because he takes over the institutions of that community into his own conduct. He takes its language as a medium by which he gets his personality, and then through a process of taking the different roles that all the others furnish, he comes to get the attitude of the members of the community. Such, in a certain sense, is the structure of a man's personality. There are certain common responses which each individual has toward certain common things, and insofar as those common responses are awakened in the individual when he is affecting other persons, he arouses his own self. The structure, then, on which the self is built is this response which is common to all, for one has to be a member of a community to be a self. Such responses are abstract attitudes, but they constitute just what we term a man's character. They give him what we term his principles, the acknowledged attitudes of all members of the community toward the values of that community. He is putting himself in the place of the generalized other, which represents the organized responses of all the members of the group. It is that which guides conduct controlled by principles, and a person who has such an organized group of responses is a man whom we say has character, in the moral sense.

It is a structure of attitudes, then, which makes a self, as distinct from a group of habits. All of us have, for example, certain groups of habits, such as the particular intonations in speech. This is a set of habits of vocal expression which one has but which one does not know about. The sets of habits which we have of that sort mean nothing to us; we do not hear the intonations of our speech that others hear unless we are paying particular attention to them. The habits of emotional expression which belong to our speech are of the same sort. We may know that we have expressed ourselves in a joyous fashion, but the detailed process is one which does not come back to our conscious selves. There are whole bundles of such habits which do not enter into a conscious self but which help to make up what is termed the unconscious self.

After all, what we mean by self-consciousness is an awakening in ourselves of the group of attitudes which we are arousing in others, especially when it is an important set of responses which go to make up the members of the community. It is unfortunate to fuse or mix up consciousness, as we ordinarily use that term, and self-consciousness. Consciousness, as frequently used, simply has reference to the field of experience, but self-consciousness refers to the ability to call out in ourselves a set of definite responses which belong to the others of the group. Consciousness and self-consciousness are not on the same level. A man alone has, fortunately or unfortunately, access to his own toothache, but that is not what we mean by self-consciousness.

I have so far emphasized what I have called the structures upon which the self is constructed, the framework of the self, as it were. Of course we are not only what is common to all: each one of the selves is different from everyone else; but there has to be such a common structure as I have sketched in order that we may be members of a community at all. We cannot be ourselves unless we are also members in whom there is a community of attitudes which control the attitudes of all. We cannot have rights unless we have common attitudes. That which we have acquired as self-conscious persons makes us members of society and gives us selves. Selves can only exist in definite relationships to other selves. No hard-and-fast line can be drawn between our own selves and the selves of others, since our own selves exist and enter as such into our experience only insofar as the selves of others exist and enter as such into our experience also. The individual possesses a self only in relation to the selves of the other members of his social group; and the structure of his self expresses or reflects the general behavior pattern of this social group to which he belongs, just as does the structure of the self of every other individual belonging to this social group.

The Self and the Subjective

Emphasis should be laid on the central position of thinking when considering the nature of the self. Self-consciousness, rather than affective experience with its motor accompaniments, provides the core and primary structure of the self, which is thus essentially a cognitive rather than an emotional phenomenon. The thinking or intellectual process—the internalization and inner dramatization, by the individual, of the external conversation of significant gestures which constitutes his chief mode of interaction with other individuals belonging to the same society—is the earliest experiential phase in the genesis and development of the self. Cooley and James, it is true, endeavor to find the basis of the self in reflexive affective experiences, that is, experiences involving "self-feeling"; but the theory that the nature of the self is to be found in such experiences does not account for the origin of the self or of the self-feeling which is supposed to characterize such experiences. The individual need not take the attitudes of others toward himself in these experiences, since these experiences merely in themselves do not necessitate his doing so, and unless he does so, he cannot develop a self; and he will not do so in these experiences unless his self has already originated otherwise, namely, in the way we have been describing. The essence of the self, as we have said, is cognitive. It lies in the internalized conversation of gestures which constitutes thinking or in terms of which thought or reflection proceeds. And hence the origin and foundations of the self, like those of thinking, are social.

The "I" and the "Me"

We have discussed at length the social foundations of the self and hinted that the self does not consist simply in the bare organization of social attitudes. We may now explicitly raise the question as to the nature of the "I" which is aware of the social "me." I do not mean to raise the metaphysical question of how a person can be both "I" and "me" but to ask for the significance of this distinction from the point of view of conduct itself. Where in conduct does the "I" come in as over against the "me"? When one determines what his position is in society and feels himself as having a certain function and privilege, these are all defined with reference to an "I," but the "I" is not a "me" and cannot become a "me." We may have a better self and a worse self, but that again is not the "I" as against the "me," because they are both selves. We approve of one and disapprove of the other, but when we bring up one or the other, they are there for such approval as "me's." The "I" does not get into the limelight; we talk to ourselves, but do not see ourselves. The "I" reacts to the self which arises through the taking of the attitudes of others. Through taking those attitudes, we have introduced the "me" and we react to it as an "I."

The simplest way of handling the problem would be in terms of memory. I talk to myself, and I remember what I said and perhaps the emotional content that went with it. The "I" of this moment is present in the "me" of the next moment. There again I cannot turn around quick enough to catch myself. I become a "me" insofar as I remember what I said. The "I" can be given, however, this functional relationship. It is because of the "I" that we say we are never fully aware of what we are, that we surprise ourselves by our own action. It is as we act that we are aware of ourselves. It is in memory that the "I" is constantly present in experience. We can go back directly a few moments in our experience, and then we are dependent upon memory images for the rest. So that the "I" in memory is there as the spokesman of the self of the second, or minute, or day ago. As given, it is a "me," but it is a "me" which was the "I" at the earlier time. If you ask, then, where directly in your own experience the "I" comes in, the answer is that it comes in as a historical figure. It is what you were a second ago that is the "I" of the "me." It is another "me" that has to take that role. You cannot get the immediate response or the "I" in the process.[9] The "I" is in a certain sense that with which we do identify ourselves. The getting of it into experience constitutes one of the problems of most of our conscious experience; it is not directly given in experience.

The "I" is the response of the organism to the attitudes of the others; the "me" is the organized set of attitudes of others which one himself assumes. The attitudes of the others constitute the organized "me," and then one reacts toward that as an "I." I now wish to examine these concepts in greater detail.

There is neither "I" nor "me" in the conversation of gestures; the whole act is not yet carried out, but the preparation takes place in this field of gesture. Now, insofar as the individual arouses in himself the attitudes of the others, there arises an organized group of responses. And it is due to the individual's ability to take the attitudes of these others insofar as they can be organized that he gets self-consciousness. The taking of all of those organized sets of attitudes gives him his "me"; that is the self he is aware of. He can throw the ball to some other member because of the demand made upon him from other members of the team. That is the self that immediately exists for him in his consciousness. He has their attitudes, knows what they want and what the consequence of any act of his will be, and he has assumed responsibility for the situation. Now, it is the presence of those organized sets of attitudes that constitutes that "me" to which he has an "I" is responding. But what that response will be, he does not know and nobody else knows. Perhaps he will make a brilliant play or an error. The response to that situation as it appears in his immediate experience is uncertain, and it is that which constitutes the "I."

The "I" is his action toward that social institution within his own conduct, and it gets into his experience only after he has car-

9   The sensitivity of the organism brings parts of itself into the environment. It does not, however, bring the life-process itself into the environment, and the complete imaginative presentation of the organism is unable to present the living of the organism. It can conceivably present the conditions under which living takes place but not the unitary life-process. The physical organism in the environment always remains a thing (MS).

ried out the act. Then he is aware of it. He had to do such a thing and he did it. He fulfils his duty and he may look with pride at the throw which he made. The "me" arises to do that duty—that is the way in which it arises in his experience. He had in him all the attitudes of others, calling for a certain response; that was the "me" of that situation, and his response is the "I."

I want to call attention particularly to the fact that this response of the "I" is something that is more or less uncertain. The attitudes of others which one assumes as affecting his own conduct constitute the "me," and that is something that is there, but the response to it is as yet not given. When one sits down to think anything out, he has certain data that are there. Suppose that it is a social situation which he has to straighten out. He sees himself from the point of view of one individual or another in the group. These individuals, all related, give him a certain self. Well, what is he going to do? He does not know, and nobody else knows. He can get the situation into his experience because he can assume the attitudes of the various individuals involved in it. He knows how they feel about it by the assumption of their attitudes. He says, in effect, "I have done certain things that seem to commit me to a certain course of conduct." Perhaps if he does so act, it will place him in a false position with another group. The "I" as a response to this situation, in contrast to the "me" which is involved in the attitudes which he takes, is uncertain. And when the response takes place, then it appears in the field of experience largely as a memory image.

Our specious present as such is very short. We do, however, experience passing events; part of the process of the passage of events is directly there in our experience, including some of the past and some of the future. We see a ball falling as it passes, and as it does pass, part of the ball is covered and part is being uncovered. We remember where the ball was a moment ago, and we anticipate where it will be beyond what is given in our experience. So of ourselves; we are doing something, but to look back and see what we are doing involves getting memory images. So the "I" really appears experientially as a part of a "me." But on the basis of this experience, we distinguish that individual who is doing something from the "me" who puts the problem up to him. The response enters into his experience only when it takes place. When he says he knows what he is going to do, even there he can be mistaken. He starts out to do something, and something happens to interfere. The resulting action is always a little different from anything which he could anticipate. This is true even when he is simply carrying out the process of walking. The very taking of his expected steps puts him in a certain situation which has a slightly different aspect from what is expected, which is in a certain sense novel. That movement into the future is the step, so to speak, of the ego, of the "I." It is something that is not given in the "me."

Take the situation of a scientist solving a problem, when he has certain data which call for certain responses. Some of these data call for his applying such and such a law, while others call for another law. Data are there with their implications. He knows what such and such coloration means, and when he has these data before him, they stand for certain responses on his part; but now they are in conflict with each other. If he makes one response, then he cannot make another. What he is going to do he does not know, nor does anybody else. The action of the self is in response to these conflicting sets of data in the form of a problem, with conflicting demands upon him as a scientist. He has to look at it in different ways. That action of the "I" is something the nature of which we cannot tell in advance.

The "I," then, in this relation of the "I" and the "me," is something that is, so to speak, responding to a social situation which is within the experience of the individual. It is the answer which the individual makes to the attitude which others take toward him when he assumes an attitude toward them. Now, the attitudes he is taking toward them are present in his own experience, but his response to them will contain a novel element. The "I" gives the sense of freedom, of initiative. The situation is there for us to act in a self-conscious fashion. We are aware of ourselves, and of what the situation is, but exactly how we will act never gets into experience until after the action takes place.

Such is the basis for the fact that the "I" does not appear in the same sense in experience as does the "me." The "me" represents a definite organization of the community there in our own attitudes and calling for a response, but the response that takes place is something that just happens. There is no certainty in regard to it. There is a moral necessity but no mechanical necessity for the act. When it does take place, we find what has been done. The above account gives us, I think, the relative position of the "I" and "me" in the situation and the grounds for the separation of the two in behavior. The two are separated in the process, but they belong together in the sense of being parts of a whole. They are separated and yet they belong together. The separation of the "I" and the "me" is not fictitious. They are not identical, for, as I have said, the "I" is something that is never entirely calculable. The "me" does call for a certain sort of an "I" insofar as we meet the obligations that are given in conduct itself, but the "I" is always something different from what the situation itself calls for. So there is always that distinction, if you like, between the "I" and the "me." The "I" both calls out the "me" and responds to it. Taken together they constitute a personality as it appears in social experience. The self is essentially a social process going on with these two distinguishable phases. If it did not have these two phases, there could not be conscious responsibility and there would be nothing novel in experience.

The Realization of the Self in the Social Situation

There is still one phase in the development of the self that needs to be presented in more detail—the realization of the self in the social situation in which it arises.

I have argued that the self appears in experience essentially as a "me" with the organization of the community to which it belongs. This organization is, of course, expressed in the particular endowment and particular social situation of the individual. He is a member of the community, but he is a particular part of the community, with a particular heredity and position which distinguishes him from anybody else. He is what he is insofar as he is a member of this community, and the raw materials out of which this particular individual is born would not be a self but for his relationship to others in the community. Thus he is aware of himself as such and, not only in political citizenship or in membership in groups of which he is a part, but also from the point of view of reflective thought. He is a member of the community of the thinkers whose literature he reads and to which he may contribute by his own published thought. He belongs to a society of all rational beings, and the rationality that he identifies with himself involves a continued social interchange. The widest community in which the individual finds himself, that which is everywhere, through and for everybody, is the thought world. He is a member of such a community, and he is what he is because he is a member.

The fact that all selves are constituted by or in terms of the social process and are individual reflections of it—or rather of this organized behavior pattern which it exhibits and which they prehend in their respective structures—is not in the least incompatible with, or destructive of, the fact that every individual self has its own peculiar individuality, its own unique pattern. Because each individual self within that process reflects in its organized structure the behavior pattern of that process as a whole from its own particular and unique standpoint within that process, it thus reflects in its organized structure a different aspect or perspective of this whole social behavior pattern from that which is reflected in the organized structure of any other individual self within that process. This is similar to every monad in the Leibnizian universe which mirrors that universe from a different point of view and thus mirrors a different aspect or perspective of that universe. In other words, the organized structure of every individual self within the human social process of experience and behavior reflects and is constituted by the organized relational pattern of that process as a whole; but each individual self-structure reflects and is constituted by a different aspect or perspective of this relational pattern, because each reflects this relational pattern from its own unique standpoint, so that the common social origin and constitution of individual selves and their structures does not preclude wide individual differences and variations among them or contradict the peculiar and more or less distinctive individuality which each of them in fact possesses. Every individual self within a given society or social community reflects in its organized structure the whole relational pattern of organized social behavior which that society or community exhibits or is carrying on, and its organized structure is constituted by this pattern; but since each of these individual selves reflects a uniquely different aspect or perspective of this pattern in its structure, from its own particular and unique place or standpoint within the whole process of organized social behavior which exhibits this pattern—since, that is, each is differently or uniquely related to that whole process and occupies its own essentially unique focus of relations therein —the structure of each is differently constituted by this pattern from the way in which the structure of any other is so constituted.

The individual, as we have seen, is continually reacting back against this society. Every adjustment involves some sort of change in the community to which the individual adjusts himself. And this change, of course, may be very important. Take even the widest community which we can present, the rational community that is represented in the so-called universal discourse. Up to a comparatively recent time, the form of this was that of an Aristotelian world. But men in America, England, Italy, Germany, and France have very considerably changed the structure of that world, introducing a logic of multiple relations in place of the Aristotelian relation of substance and attribute. Another fundamental change has taken place in the form of the world through the reaction of an individual—Einstein. Great figures in history bring about very fundamental changes. These profound changes which take place through the action of individual minds are only the extreme expression of the sort of changes that take place steadily through reactions which are not simply those of a "me" but of an "I." These changes are changes that take place gradually and more or less imperceptibly. We know that as we pass from one historical period to another there have been fundamental changes, and we know these changes are due to the reactions of different individuals. It is only the ultimate effect that we can recognize, but the differences are due to the gestures of these countless individuals actually changing the situation in which they find themselves, although the specific changes are too minute for us to identify.

As I have pointed out, the ego or "I" that is responsible for changes of that sort appears in experience only after its reaction has taken place. It is only after we have said the word we are saying that we recognize ourselves as the person that has said it, as this particular self that says this particular thing; it is only after we have done the thing that we are going to do that we are aware of what we are doing. However carefully we plan the future it always is different from that which we can previse, and this something that we are continually bringing in and adding to is what we identify with the self that comes into the level of our experience only in the completion of the act.

In some respects, of course, we can determine what that self is going to do. We can accept certain responsibilities in advance. One makes contracts and promises, and one is bound by them. The situation may change, the act may be different from that which the individual himself expected to carry out, but he is held to the contract which he has made. He must do certain things in order to remain a member of the community. In the duties of what we call rational conduct, in adjusting ourselves to a world in which the laws of nature and of economics and of political systems obtain, we can state what is going to happen and take the responsibility for the thing we are going to do, and yet the real self that appears in that act awaits the completion of the act itself. Now, it is this living act which never gets directly into reflective experience. It is only after the act has taken place that we can catch it in our memory and place it in terms of that which we have done. It is that "I" which we may be said to be continually trying to realize, and to realize through the actual conduct itself. One does not ever get it fully before himself. Sometimes somebody else can tell him something about himself that he is not aware of. He is never sure about himself, and he astonishes himself by his conduct as much as he astonishes other people.

The possibilities in our nature, those sorts of energy which

William James took so much pleasure in indicating, are possibilities of the self that lie beyond our own immediate presentation. We do not know just what they are. They are in a certain sense the most fascinating contents that we can contemplate, so far as we can get hold of them. We get a great deal of our enjoyment of romance, of moving pictures, or of art, in setting free, at least in imagination, capacities which belong to ourselves or which we want to belong to ourselves. Inferiority complexes arise from those wants of a self which we should like to carry out but which we cannot—we adjust ourselves to these by the so-called inferiority complexes. The possibilities of the "I" belong to that which is actually going on, taking place, and it is in some sense the most fascinating part of our experience. It is there that novelty arises, and it is there that our most important values are located. It is the realization in some sense of this self that we are continually seeking.

The Contributions of the "Me" and the "I"

I have been undertaking to distinguish between the "I" and the "me" as different phases of the self, the "me" answering to the organized attitudes of the others which we definitely assume and which determine consequently our own conduct so far as it is of a self-conscious character. Now the "me" may be regarded as giving the form of the "I." The novelty comes in the action of the "I," but the structure, the form of the self is one which is conventional.

This conventional form may be reduced to a minimum. In the artist's attitude, where there is artistic creation, the emphasis upon the element of novelty is carried to the limit. This demand for the unconventional is especially noticeable in modern art. Here the artist is supposed to break away from convention; a part of his artistic expression is thought to be in the breakdown of convention. That attitude is, of course, not essential to the artistic function, and it probably never occurs in the extreme form in which it is often proclaimed. Take certain of the artists of the past. In the Greek world the artists were, in a certain sense, the supreme artisans. What they were to do was more or less set by the community, and accepted by themselves, as the expression of heroic figures, certain deities, the erection of temples. Definite rules were accepted as essential to the expression. And yet the artist introduced an originality into it which distinguishes one artist from another. In the case of the artist, the emphasis upon that which is unconventional, that which is not in the structure of the "me," is carried as far, perhaps, as it can be carried.

This same emphasis also appears in certain types of conduct which are impulsive. Impulsive conduct is uncontrolled conduct. The structure of the "me" does not there determine the expression of the "I." If we use a Freudian expression, the "me" is in a certain sense a censor. It determines the sort of expression which can take place, sets the stage, and gives the cue. In the case of impulsive conduct this structure of the "me" involved in the situation does not furnish to any such degree this control. Take the situation of self-assertion where the self simply asserts itself against others, and suppose that the emotional stress is such that the forms of polite society in the performance of legitimate conduct are overthrown, so that the person expresses himself violently. There the "me" is determined by the situation. There are certain recognized fields within which an individual can assert himself, certain rights which he has within these limits. But let the stress become too great, these limits are not observed, and an individual asserts himself in perhaps a violent fashion. Then the "I" is the dominant element against the "me." Under what we consider normal conditions, the way in which an individual acts is determined by his taking the attitude of the others in the group, but if the individual is not given the opportunity to come up against people, as a child is not who is held out of intercourse with other people, then there results a situation in which the reaction is uncontrolled.

Social control[10] is the expression of the "me" against the ex-

---

[10]   On the topic of social control see "The Genesis of the Self and Social Control," *International Journal of Ethics*, XXXV (1924–25), 251 ff.; "The Working Hypothesis in Social Reform," *American Journal of Sociology*, V (1899–1900), 367 ff.; "The Psychology of Punitive Justice," *ibid.*, XXIII (1917–18), 577 ff.

pression of the "I." It sets the limits, it gives the determination that enables the "I," so to speak, to use the "me" as the means of carrying out what is the undertaking that all are interested in. When persons are held outside or beyond that sort of organized expression, there arises a situation in which social control is absent. In the more or less fantastic psychology of the Freudian group, thinkers are dealing with the sexual life and with self-assertion in its violent form. The normal situation, however, is one which involves a reaction of the individual in a situation which is socially determined but to which he brings his own responses as an "I." The response is, in the experience of the individual, an expression with which the self is identified. It is such a response which raises him above the institutionalized individual.

As I have said before, an institution is, after all, nothing but an organization of attitudes which we all carry in us, the organized attitudes of the others that control and determine conduct. Now, this institutionalized individual is, or should be, the means by which the individual expresses himself in his own way, for such individual expression is that which is identified with the self in those values which are essential to the self, and which arise from the self. To speak of them as arising from the self does not attach to them the character of the selfish egoist, for under the normal conditions to which we were referring, the individual is making his contribution to a common undertaking. The baseball player who makes a brilliant play is making the play called for by the nine to which he belongs. He is playing for his side. A man may, of course, play the gallery, be more interested in making a brilliant play than in helping his team to win, just as a surgeon may carry out a brilliant operation and sacrifice the patient. But under normal conditions, the contribution of the individual gets its expression in the social processes that are involved in the act, so that the attachment of the values to the self does not involve egoism or selfishness. The other situation in which the self in its expression does in some sense exploit the group or society to which it belongs is one which sets up, so to speak, a narrow self which takes advantage of the whole group in satisfying itself. Even such a self is still a social affair. We distinguish very definitely between the selfish man and the impulsive man. The man who may lose his temper and knock another down may be a very unselfish man. He is not necessarily a person who would utilize a certain situation for the sake of his own interests. The latter case involves the narrow self that does not relate itself to the whole social group of which it is a part.

Values do definitely attach to this expression of the self which is peculiar to the self; and what is peculiar to the self is what it calls its own. And yet this value lies in the social situation and would not be apart from that social situation. It is the contribution of the individual to the situation, even though it is only in the social situation that the value is obtained.

We seek certainly for that sort of expression which is self-expression. When an individual feels himself hedged in, he recognizes the necessity of a situation in which there will be an opportunity for him to make his addition to the undertaking, and not simply to be the conventionalized "me." In a person who carries out the routine job, it leads to the reaction against the machine and to the demand that that type of routine work fall into its place in the whole social process. There is, of course, a certain amount of real mental and physical health, a very essential part of one's life, that is involved in doing routine work. One can very well just carry out certain processes in which his contribution is very slight, in a more or less mechanical fashion, and find himself in a better position because of it. Such men as John Stuart Mill have been able to carry on routine occupations during a certain part of the day, and then give themselves to original work for the rest of the day. A person who cannot do a certain amount of stereotyped work is not a healthy individual. Both the health of the individual and the stability of society call for a very considerable amount of such work. The reaction to machine industry simply calls for the restriction of the amount of time given to it, but it does not involve its total abolition. Nevertheless, and granting this point, there must be some way in which the individual can express himself. It is the situations in which it is possible to get this sort of expression that seem to be particularly precious, namely, those situations in which the individual is able to do something on his own, where he can take over responsibility and carry out things in his own way, with an opportunity to think his own thoughts. Those social situations in which the structure of the "me" for the time being is one in which the individual gets an opportunity for that sort of expression of the self bring some of the most exciting and gratifying experiences.

These experiences may take place in a form which involves degradation or in a form which involves the emergence of higher values. The mob furnishes a situation in which the "me" is one which simply supports and emphasizes the more violent sort of impulsive expression. This tendency is deeply imbedded in human nature. It is astonishing what part of the "I" of the sick is consti- tuted by murder stories. Of course, in the story itself, it is the tracking-down of the murderer that is the focal point of interest; but that tracking-down of the murderer takes one back to the vengeance attitude of the primitive community. In the murder story one gets a real villain, runs him down, and brings him to justice. Such expressions may involve degradation of the self. In situations involving the defense of the country a mob attitude or a very high moral attitude may prevail, depending upon the in- dividual. The situation in which one can let himself go, in which the very structure of the "me" opens the door for the "I," is favorable to self-expression. I have referred to the situation in which a person can sit down with a friend and say just what he is thinking about someone else. There is a satisfaction in letting one's self go in this way. The sort of thing that under other cir- cumstances you would not say and would not even let yourself think is now naturally uttered. Should you get in a group which thinks as you do, you can go to lengths which may surprise you. The "me" in the above situations is definitely constituted by the social relations. Now if this situation is such that it opens the door to impulsive expression, one gets a peculiar satisfaction, high or low, the source of which is the value that attaches to the expres- sion of the "I" in the social process.

A Contrast of Individualistic and Social Theories of the Self

The differences between the type of social psychology which derives the selves of individuals from the social process in which they are implicated and in which they empirically interact with one another and the type of social psychology which instead derives that process from the selves of the individuals involved in it are clear. The first type assumes a social process or social order as the logical and biological precondition of the appearance of the selves of the individual organisms involved in that process or belonging to that order. The other type, on the contrary, assumes individual selves as the presuppositions, logically and biologically, of the social process or order within which they interact.

The difference between the social and the individual theories of the development of mind, self, and the social process of experience or behavior is analogous to the difference between the evolutionary and the contract theories of the state as held in the past by both rationalists and empiricists.[11] The latter theory takes individuals and their individual experiencing—individual minds and selves—as logically prior to the social process in which they are involved, and explains the existence of that social process in terms of them; whereas the former takes the social process of experience or behavior as logically prior to the individuals and their individual experiencing which are involved in it, and explains their existence in terms of that social process. But the latter type of theory cannot explain that which is taken as logically prior at all, cannot explain the existence of minds and selves; whereas the former type of theory can explain that which it takes as logically prior, namely, the existence of the social process of behavior, in terms of such fundamental biological or physiological relations and interactions as reproduction, or the co-operation of individuals for mutual protection or for the securing of food.

Our contention is that mind can never find expression, and could never have come into existence at all, except in terms of a social environment; that an organized set or pattern of social re-

11   Historically, both the rationalist and the empiricist are committed to the interpretation of experience in terms of the individual (1931).

Other people are there as much as we are there; to be a self requires other selves (1924).

In our experience the thing is there as much as we are here. Our experience is in the thing as much as it is in us (MS).

lations and interactions (especially those of communication by means of gestures functioning as significant symbols and thus creating a universe of discourse) is necessarily presupposed by it and involved in its nature. And this entirely social theory or interpretation of mind[12]—this contention that mind develops and has its being only in and by virtue of the social process of experience and activity, which it hence presupposes, and that in no other way can it develop and have its being—must be clearly distinguished from the partially (but only partially) social view of mind. On this view, though mind can get expression only within or in terms of the environment of an organized social group, yet it is nevertheless in some sense a native endowment—a congenital or hereditary biological attribute—of the individual organism and could not otherwise exist or manifest itself in the social process at all; so that it is not itself essentially a social phenomenon, but rather is biological both in its nature and in its origin and is social only in its characteristic manifestations or expressions. According to this latter view, moreover, the social process presupposes, and in a sense is a product of, mind; in direct contrast is our opposite view that mind presupposes, and is a product of, the social process. The advantage of our view is that it enables us to give a detailed account and actually to explain the genesis and development of mind; whereas the view that mind is a congenital biological endowment of the individual organism does not really enable us to explain its nature and origin at all—neither what sort of biological endowment it is, nor how organisms at a certain

12   In defending a social theory of mind we are defending a functional, as opposed to any form of substantive or entitive, view as to its nature. And in particular, we are opposing all intracranial or intra-epidermal views as to its character and locus. For it follows from our social theory of mind that the field of mind must be co-extensive with, and include all the components of, the field of the social process of experience and behavior, that is, the matrix of social relations and interactions among individuals, which is presupposed by it and out of which it arises or comes into being. If mind is socially constituted, then the field or locus of any given individual mind must extend as far as the social activity or apparatus of social relations which constitutes it extends; and hence that field cannot be bounded by the skin of the individual organism to which it belongs.

level of evolutionary progress come to possess it.[13] Furthermore, the supposition that the social process presupposes, and is in some sense a product of, mind seems to be contradicted by the existence of the social communities of certain of the lower animals, especially the highly complex social organizations of bees and ants, which apparently operate on a purely instinctive or reflex basis, and do not in the least involve the existence of mind or consciousness in the individual organisms which form or constitute them. And even if this contradiction is avoided by the admission that only at its higher levels—only at the levels represented by the social relations and interactions of human beings—does the social process of experience and behavior presuppose the existence of mind or become necessarily a product of mind, still it is hardly plausible to suppose that this already ongoing and developing process should suddenly, at a particular stage in its evolution, become dependent for its further continuance upon an entirely extraneous factor, introduced into it, so to speak, from without.

The individual enters as such into his own experience only as an object, not as a subject; and he can enter as an object only on the basis of social relations and interactions, only by means of his experiential transactions with other individuals in an organized

[13] According to the traditional assumption of psychology, the content of experience is entirely individual and not in any measure to be primarily accounted for in social terms, even though its setting or context is a social one. And for a social psychology like Cooley's—which is founded on precisely this same assumption—all social interactions depend upon the imaginations of the individuals involved, and take place in terms of their direct conscious influences upon one another in the processes of social experience. Cooley's social psychology, as found in his *Human Nature and the Social Order*, is hence inevitably introspective, and his psychological method carries with it the implication of complete solipsism: society really has no existence except in the individual's mind, and the concept of the self as in any sense intrinsically social is a product of imagination. Even for Cooley the self presupposes experience, and experience is a process within which selves arise; but since that process is for him primarily internal and individual rather than external and social, he is committed in his psychology to a subjectivistic and idealistic, rather than an objectivistic and naturalistic, metaphysical position.

social environment. It is true that certain contents of experience (particularly kinaesthetic) are accessible only to the given individual organism and not to any others; and that these private or "subjective," as opposed to public or "objective," contents of experience are usually regarded as being peculiarly and intimately connected with the individual's self, or as being in a special sense self-experiences. But this accessibility solely to the given individual organism of certain contents of its experience does not affect, nor in any way conflict with, the theory as to the social nature and origin of the self that we are presenting. Existence of private or "subjective" contents of experience does not alter the fact that self-consciousness involves the individual's becoming an object to himself by taking the attitudes of other individuals toward himself within an organized setting of social relationships, and that unless the individual had thus become an object to himself he would not be self-conscious or have a self at all. Apart from his social interactions with other individuals, he would not relate the private or "subjective" contents of his experience to himself and he could not become aware of himself as such, that is, as an individual, a person, merely by means or in terms of these contents of his experience; for in order to become aware of himself as such he must, to repeat, become an object to himself, or enter his own experience as an object, and only by social means—only by taking the attitudes of others toward himself— is he able to become an object to himself.[14]

It is true, of course, that once mind has arisen in the social process it makes possible the development of that process into much more complex forms of social interaction among the component individuals than was possible before it had arisen. But there is nothing odd about a product of a given process contrib-

[14]   The human being's physiological capacity for developing mind or intelligence is a product of the process of biological evolution, just as is his whole organism; but the actual development of his mind or intelligence itself, given that capacity, must proceed in terms of the social situations wherein it gets its expression and import; and hence it itself is a product of the process of social evolution, the process of social experience and behavior.

uting to, or becoming an essential factor in, the further development of that process. The social process, then, does not depend for its origin or initial existence upon the existence and interactions of selves, though it does depend upon the latter for the higher stages of complexity and organization which it reaches after selves have arisen within it.

Part VII

8

SOCIETY

The Community and the Institution[1]

THERE are what I have termed "generalized social attitudes" which make an organized self possible. In the community there are certain ways of acting under situations which are essentially identical, and these ways of acting on the part of anyone are those which we excite in others when we take certain steps. When we assert our rights, we are calling for a definite response just because they are rights that are universal—a response which everyone should, and perhaps will, give. Now, that response is present in our own nature; in some degree we are ready to take that same attitude toward somebody else when he makes the appeal. When we call out that response in others, we can take the attitude of the other and adjust our own conduct to it. There are, then, whole series of such common responses in the community in which we live, and such responses are what we term "institutions." The institution represents a common response on the part of all members of the community to a particular situation. This common response is one which, of course, varies with the character of the individual. In the case of theft the response of the sher-

First published in *Mind, Self, and Society*, ed. Charles W. Morris (Chicago: University of Chicago Press, 1934), pp. 260–328.

[1]   See "Natural Rights and the Theory of the Political Institution," *Journal of Philosophy*, XII (1915), 141 ff.

iff is different from that of the attorney-general, from that of the judge and the jurors, and so forth; and yet they all are responses which maintain property, which involve the recognition of the property right in others. There is a common response in varied forms. And these variations, as illustrated in the different officials, have an organization which gives unity to the variety of the responses. One appeals to the policeman for assistance; one expects the state's attorney to act; one expects the court and its various functionaries to carry out the process of the trial of the criminal. One does take the attitude of all of these different officials as involved in the very maintenance of property; all of them as an organized process are in some sense found in our own natures. When we arouse such attitudes, we are taking the attitude of what I have termed a "generalized other." Such organized sets of response are related to each other; if one calls out one such set of responses, he is implicitly calling out others as well.

Thus the institutions of society are organized forms of group or social activity—forms so organized that the individual members of society can act adequately and socially by taking the attitudes of others toward these activities. Oppressive, stereotyped, and ultraconservative social institutions—like the church—which by their more or less rigid and inflexible unprogressiveness crush or blot out individuality or discourage any distinctive or original expressions of thought and behavior in the individual selves or personalities implicated in and subjected to them, are undesirable but not necessarily outcomes of the general social process of experience and behavior. There is no necessary or inevitable reason why social institutions should be oppressive or rigidly conservative, or why they should not rather be, as many are, flexible and progressive, fostering individuality rather than discouraging it. In any case, without social institutions of some sort, without the organized social attitudes and activities by which social institutions are constituted, there could be no fully mature individual selves or personalities at all; for the individuals involved in the general social life-process of which social institutions are organized, manifestations can develop and possess fully mature selves or personalities only insofar as each one of them reflects or prehends in his individual experience these organized attitudes and activities which social institutions embody or represent. Social institutions, like individual selves, are developments within, or particular and formalized manifestations of, the social life-process at its human evolutionary level. As such, they are not necessarily subversive of individuality in the individual members; and they do not necessarily represent or uphold narrow definitions of certain fixed and specific patterns of acting which in any given circumstances should characterize the behavior of all intelligent and socially responsible individuals (in opposition to such unintelligent and socially irresponsible individuals as morons and imbeciles) as members of the given community or social group. On the contrary, they need to define the social, or socially responsible, patterns of individual conduct in only a very broad and general sense, affording plenty of scope for originality, flexibility, and variety of such conduct; and as the main formalized functional aspects or phases of the whole organized structure of the social life-process at its human level, they properly partake of the dynamic and progressive character of that process.[2]

There are a great number of institutionalized responses which are, we often say, arbitrary, such as the manners of a particular community. Manners in their best sense, of course, cannot be distinguished from morals and are nothing but the expression of the courtesy of an individual toward people about him. They ought to express the natural courtesy of everyone to everyone else. There should be such an expression, but of course a great many

---

2   Human society, we have insisted, does not merely stamp the pattern of its organized social behavior upon any one of its individual members, so that this pattern becomes likewise the pattern of the individual's self; it also, at the same time, gives him a mind, as the means or ability of consciously conversing with himself in terms of the social attitudes which constitute the structure of his self and which embody the pattern of human society's organized behavior as reflected in that structure. And his mind enables him in turn to stamp the pattern of his further developing self (further developing through his mental activity) upon the structure or organization of human society, and thus in a degree, to reconstruct and modify in terms of his self the general pattern of social or group behavior in terms of which his self was originally constituted.

habits for the expression of courtesy are quite arbitrary. The ways to greet people are different in different communities; what is appropriate in one may be an offense in another. The question arises whether a certain manner which expresses a courteous attitude may be what we term "conventional." In answer to this we propose to distinguish between manners and conventions. Conventions are isolated social responses which would not come into, or go to make up, the nature of the community in its essential character as this expresses itself in the social reactions. A source of confusion would lie in identifying manners and morals with conventions, since the former are not arbitrary in the sense that conventions are. Thus conservatives identify what is a pure convention with the essence of a social situation; nothing must be changed. But the very distinction to which I have referred is one which implies that these various institutions, as social responses to situations in which individuals are carrying out social acts, are organically related to each other in a way which conventions are not.

Such interrelation is one of the points which is brought out, for example, in the economic interpretation of history. It was first presented more or less as a party doctrine by the Marxian socialists, implying a particular economic interpretation. It has now passed over into the historian's technique with a recognition that if he can get hold of the real economic situation, which is, of course, more accessible than most social expressions, he can work out from that to the other expressions and institutions of the community. Medieval economic institutions enable one to interpret the other institutions of the period. One can get at the economic situation directly and, following that out, can find what the other institutions were, or must have been. Institutions, manners, or words, present in a certain sense the life-habits of the community as such; and when an individual acts toward others in, say, economic terms, he is calling out not simply a single response but a whole group of related responses.

The same situation prevails in a physiological organism. If the balance of a person who is standing is disturbed, this calls for a readjustment which is possible only insofar as the affected parts of the nervous system lead to certain definite and interconnected responses. The different parts of the reaction can be isolated, but the organism has to act as a whole. Now it is true that an individual living in society lives in a certain sort of organism which reacts toward him as a whole, and he calls out by his action this more or less organized response. There is perhaps under his attention only some very minor fraction of this organized response —he considers, say, only the passage of a certain amount of money. But that exchange could not take place without the entire economic organization, and that in turn involves all the other phases of the group life. The individual can go any time from one phase to the others, since he has in his own nature the type of response which his action calls for. In taking any institutionalized attitude, he organizes in some degree the whole social process, in proportion as he is a complete self.

The getting of this social response into the individual constitutes the process of education which takes over the cultural media of the community in a more or less abstract way.[3] Education is definitely the process of taking over a certain organized set of responses to one's own stimulation; and until one can respond to himself as the community responds to him, he does not genuinely belong to the community. He may belong to a small community, as the small boy belongs to a gang rather than to the city in which he lives. We all belong to small cliques, and we may remain simply inside of them. The "organized other" present in ourselves is then a community of a narrow diameter. We are struggling now to get a certain amount of international-mindedness. We are realizing ourselves as members of a larger community. The vivid

[3]   Among some eighteen notes, editorials, and articles on education, attention should be called to the following: "The Relation of Play to Education," *University of Chicago Record*, I (1896), 140 ff.; "The Teaching of Science in College," *Science*, XXIV (1906), 390 ff.; "Psychology of Social Consciousness Implied in Instruction," *ibid.*, XXXI (1910), 688 ff.; "Industrial Education and Trade Schools," *Elementary School Teacher*, VIII (1908), 402 ff.; "Industrial Education and the Working Man and the School," *ibid.*, IX (1909), 369 ff.; "On the Problem of History in the Elementary School," *ibid.*, 433; "Moral Training in the Schools," *ibid.*, 327 ff.; "Science in the High School," *School Review*, XIV (1906), 237 ff.

nationalism of the present period should, in the end, call out an international attitude of the larger community. The situation is analogous to that of the boy and the gang; the boy gets a larger self in proportion as he enters into this larger community. In general, the self has answered definitely to that organization of the social response which constitutes the community as such; the degree to which the self is developed depends upon the community, upon the degree to which the individual calls out that institutionalized group of responses in himself. The criminal as such is the individual who lives in a very small group, and then makes depredations upon the larger community of which he is not a member. He is taking the property that belongs to others, but he himself does not belong to the community that recognizes and preserves the rights of property.

There is a certain sort of organized response to our acts which represents the way in which people react toward us in certain situations. Such responses are in our nature because we act as members of the community toward others, and what I am emphasizing now is that the organization of these responses makes the community possible.

We are apt to assume that our estimate of the value of the community should depend upon its size. The American worships bigness as opposed to qualitative social content. A little community such as that of Athens produced some of the greatest spiritual products which the world has ever seen; contrast its achievements with those of the United States, and there is no need to ask whether the mere bigness of the one has any relationship to the qualitative contents of the achievements of the other. I wish to bring out the implicit universality of the highly developed, highly organized community. Now, Athens as the home of Socrates, Plato, and Aristotle, the seat of a great metaphysical development in the same period, the birthplace of political theorists and great dramatists, actually belongs to the whole world. These qualitative achievements which we ascribe to a little community belong to it only insofar as it has the organization that makes it universal. The Athenian community rested upon slave labor and upon a political situation which was narrow and contracted, and that part of its social organization was not universal and could not be made the basis for a large community. The Roman Empire disintegrated very largely because its whole economic structure was laid on the basis of slave labor. It was not organized on a universal basis. From the legal standpoint and administrative organization, it was universal, and just as Greek philosophy has come down to us so has Roman law. To the degree that any achievement of organization of a community is successful, it is universal and makes possible a bigger community. In one sense there cannot be a community which is larger than that represented by rationality, and the Greek brought rationality to its self-conscious expression.[4] In that same sense the gospel of Jesus brought definitely to expression the attitude of neighborliness to which anyone could appeal and provided the soil out of which could arise a universal religion. That which is fine and admirable is universal—although it may be true that the actual society in which the universality can get its expression has not arisen.

Politically, America has, in a certain sense, given universality to what we term "self-government." The social organization of

4   Plato held that the city-state was the best—if not, indeed, the only practicable or feasible—type of state or social organization; and Aristotle agreed. According to Plato, moreover, the complete social isolation of any one city-state from the rest of the world was desirable. Aristotle, on the other hand, did recognize the necessity for social interrelations among different city-states or between any one city-state and the rest of the civilized world, but he could not discover a general principle in terms of which those interrelations could be determined without disastrously damaging or vitiating the political and social structure of the city-state itself; and this structure he wished, as did Plato, to preserve. That is to say, he was unable to get hold of a fundamental principle in terms of which the social and political organization of the Greek city-state could be generalized to apply to the interrelations between several such states within a single social whole, like the Alexandrian empire, in which they were all included as units, or to apply to that social whole or empire itself; and especially to apply to such a social whole or empire even if it did not contain city-states as its units. If we are right, this fundamental principle which he was unable to discover was simply the principle of social integration and organization in terms of rational selves, and of their reflection, in their respective organized structures, of the patterns of organized social behavior in which they are involved and to which they owe their existence.

the Middle Ages existed under feudalism and craft guilds. The immediate social organizations in which there was self-government were all particular provisional guilds or particular communities. What has happened in America is that we have generalized the principle of self-government so that it is the essential agency of political control of the whole community. If that type of control is made possible, there is theoretically no limit to the size of the community. In that sense alone would political bigness become an expression of the achievement of the community itself.

Democracy and Universality in Society

There is in human society a universality that expresses itself very early in two different ways—one on the religious side and the other on the economic side. These processes as social processes are universal. They provide ends which any form that makes use of the same medium of communication can enter upon. If a gorilla could bring coconuts and exchange them in some sort of market for something he might conceivably want, he would enter into the economic social organization in its widest phase. All that is necessary is that the animal should be able to utilize that method of communication which involves, as we have seen, the existence of a self. On the other hand, any individual that can regard himself as a member of a society in which he is—to use a familiar phrase—a neighbor of the other, also belongs to such a universal group. These religious and economic expressions of universality we find developing in one form or another in the Roman Empire, in India, and in China. In the outgrowth of the Empire into Christianity we find a form of propaganda issuing in the deliberate attempt to organize this sort of universal society.

If evolution is to take place in such a society, it would take place between the different organizations, so to speak, within this larger organism. There would not simply be a competition of different societies with each other, but competition would lie in the relationship of this or that society to the organization of a universal society. In the case of the universal religions we have such forms as that of the Mohammedan, which undertook by the force of the sword to wipe out all other forms of society and so found itself in opposition to other communities which it undertook either to annihilate or to subordinate to itself. On the other hand, we have the propaganda represented by Christianity and Buddhism, which merely undertook to bring the various individuals into a certain spiritual group in which they would recognize themselves as members of one society. This undertaking inevitably bound itself up with the political structure, especially in the case of Christianity; and back of that lies the assumption, which found its expression in missionary undertakings, that this social principle, this recognition of the brotherhood of men, is the basis for a universal society.

When we look at the economic proceedings, there is no such propaganda as this, no assumption of a single economic society that is undertaking to establish itself. An economic society defines itself insofar as one individual may trade with others; and then the very processes themselves go on integrating, bringing a closer and closer relationship between communities which may be definitely opposed to each other politically. The more complete economic texture appears in the development of trading itself and the development of a financial medium by means of which such trading is carried on, and there is an inevitable adjustment of the production in one community to the needs of the international economic community. There is a development which starts with the lowest sort of universal society and in which the original abstractness gives way to a more and more concrete social organization. From both of these standpoints, there is a universal society that includes the whole human race, and into which all can enter into relationship with others through the medium of communication. They can recognize others as members, and as brothers.

Such communities are inevitably universal in their character. The processes expressed in the universal religion inevitably carry with them that of the logical community represented by the universe of discourse, a community based simply on the ability of all individuals to converse with each other through use of the same significant symbols. Language provides a universal community which is something like the economic community. It is there, insofar as there are common symbols that can be utilized. We see such symbols in the bare signs by means of which savage tribes who do not speak the same language can communicate. They find some common language in the use of the fingers or in symbolic drawings. They attain some sort of ability to communicate, and such a process of communication has the tendency to bring the different individuals into closer relationship with each other. The linguistic process is in one sense more abstract than the economic process. The economic process, starting off with bare exchange, turns over the surplus of one individual in return for the surplus of another individual. Such processes reflect back at once to the process of production and more or less inevitably stimulate that sort of production which leads to profitable exchange. When we come to bare intercourse on the basis of significant symbols, the process by itself perhaps does not tend to such an integration, but this process of communication will carry or tend to carry with it the very processes in which it has served as a medium.

A person learns a new language and, as we say, gets a new soul. He puts himself into the attitude of those that make use of that language. He cannot read its literature, cannot converse with those that belong to that community, without taking on its peculiar attitudes. He becomes in that sense a different individual. You cannot convey a language as a pure abstraction; you inevitably in some degree convey also the life that lies behind it. And this result builds itself into relationship with the organized attitudes of the individual who gets this language and inevitably brings about a readjustment of views. A community of the Western world with its different nationalities and different languages is a community in which there will be a continued interplay of these different groups with each other. One nation cannot be taken simply by itself but only in its relationship to the other groups which belong to the larger whole.

The universe of discourse which deals simply with the highest abstractions opens the door for the interrelationship of the different groups in their different characters. The universe of discourse within which people can express themselves makes possible the bringing-together of those organized attitudes which represent the life of these different communities into such relationship that they can lead to a higher organization. The very universality of the processes which belong to human society, whether looked at from the point of view of religion or trading or logical thinking, at least opens the door to a universal society; and, in fact, these tendencies all express themselves where the social development has gone far enough to make it possible.

The political expression of this growth of universality in society is signalized in the dominance of one group over other groups. The earliest expression of this is in the empires of the valleys of the Nile, the Tigris, and the Euphrates. Different communities came in competition with each other, and in such competition is found a condition for the development of the empire. There is not simply the conflict of one tribe with another which undertakes to wipe out the other but rather that sort of conflict which leads to the dominance of one group over another by the maintenance of the other group. It is of importance to notice this difference when it signalizes the expression of self-consciousness reached through a realization of one's self in others. In a moment of hostility or fierce anger the individual or the community may seek simply to wipe out its enemies. But the dominant expression in terms of the self has been, even on the part of a militaristic society, rather that of subjection, of a realization of the self in its superiority to and exploitation of the other. This attitude of mind is an entirely different attitude from that of the mere wiping-out of one's enemies. There is, from this point of view at least, a definite achievement on the part of the individual of a higher self in his overcoming of the other and holding the other in subjection.

The sense of national prestige is an expression of that self-respect which we tend to preserve in the maintenance of superiority over other people. One does get the sense of one's self by a certain feeling of superiority to others, and that this is fundamental in the development of the self was recognized by Wundt. It is an attitude which passes over, under what we consider high conditions, into the just recognition of the capacity of the individual in his own fields. The superiority which the person now has is not a superiority over the other but is grounded in that which he can do in relation to the functions and capacity of others. The development of the expert who is superior in the performance of his functions is of a quite different character from the superiority of the bully who simply realizes himself in his ability to subordinate somebody to himself. The person who is competent in any particular field has a superiority which belongs to that which he himself can do and which perhaps someone else cannot do. It gives him a definite position in which he can realize himself in the community. He does not realize himself in his simple superiority to someone else but in the function which he can carry out; and insofar as he can carry it out better than anyone else, he gets a sense of prestige which we recognize as legitimate, as opposed to the other form of self-assertion which from the standpoint of our highest sense of social standards is felt to be illegitimate.

Communities may stand in this same kind of relation to each other. There is the sense of pride of the Roman in his administrative capacity as well as in his martial power, in his capacity to subjugate all the people around the Mediterranean world and to administer them. The first attitude was that of subjugation, and then came the administrative attitude which was more of the type to which I have already referred as that of functional superiority. It was that which Virgil expressed in his demand that the Roman should realize that in his ruling he was possessed with the capacity for administration. This capacity made the Roman Empire entirely different from the earlier empires, which used nothing but brute strength. The passage in that case is from a sense of political superiority and prestige expressed in a power to crush, over into a power to direct a social undertaking in which there is a larger co-operative activity. The political expression starts off with a bare self-assertion, coupled with a military attitude, which leads to the wiping-out of the other, but which leads on, or may lead on, to the development of higher community, where dominance takes the form of administration. Conceivably, there may appear a larger international community than the empire, organized in terms of function rather than of force.

The bringing-together of the attitude of universal religion on the one hand and the widening political development on the other has been given its widest expression in democracy. There is, of course, a democracy such as that of the Greek cities in which the control is simply the control of the masses in their opposition to certain economically and politically powerful classes. There are, in fact, various forms of democratic government; but democracy, in the sense here relevant, is an attitude which depends upon the type of self which goes with the universal relations of brotherhood, however that be reached. It received its expression in the French Revolution in the conception of fraternity and union. Every individual was to stand on the same level with every other. This conception is one which received its first expression in the universal religions. When carried over into the field of politics, it can get its expression only in such a form as that of democracy; and the doctrine that lies behind it is very largely Rousseau's conception, as found in the *Social Contract*.

The assumption there is of a society in which the individual maintains himself as a citizen only to the degree that he recognizes the rights of everyone else to belong to the same community. With such a universality, such a uniformity of interests, it would be possible for the masses of the community to take the attitude of the sovereign while he also took the attitude of the subjects. If the will of each one was the will of all, then the relationship of subject and sovereign could be embodied in all the different individuals. We get what Rousseau referred to as the "general will of the community" only when a man is able to realize himself by recognizing others as belonging to the same political organization as himself.[5]

That conception of democracy is in itself as universal as religion, and the appearance of this political movement was essentially religious insofar as it had the gospel of Rousseau be-

[5]   If you can make your demand universal, if your right is one that carries with it a corresponding obligation, then you recognize the same right in everyone else and you can give a law, so to speak, in the terms of all the community. So there can be a general will in terms of the individual because everyone else is expressing the same thing. There then arises a community in which everyone can be both sovereign and subject, sovereign insofar as he asserts his own rights and recognizes them in others, and subject in that he obeys the laws which he himself makes (1927).

hind it. It proceeded also with a sense of propaganda. It undertook to overthrow the old organization of society and substitute its own form of society in its place. In that sense these two factors—one the dominance of the individual or group over other groups, the other the sense of brotherhood and identity of different individuals in the same group—came together in the democratic movement; and together they inevitably imply a universal society, not only in a religious sense, but ultimately in a political sense as well. This receives expression in the League of Nations, where every community recognizes every other community in the very process of asserting itself. The smallest community is in a position to express itself just because it recognizes the right of every other nation to do the same.

What is involved in the development of a universal society is just such a functional organization as we find in economic development. The economic development is one which starts off on the basis of the exchange. You offer what you do not want in exchange for something which another does not want. That is abstract. But after you find you can produce something you do not want and exchange it for something you want, you stimulate by that action a functional development. You are stimulating one group to produce this and another to produce that; and you are also controlling the economic process, because one will not continue to produce more than can be offered in exchange on the market. The sort of thing ultimately produced will be that which answers to the demand of the customer. In the resulting functional organization, one develops an economic personality of a certain sort which has its own sense of superiority but which is used in the carrying-out of its particular function in relation to the others in the group. There can be a self-consciousness based on the ability to manufacture something better than anybody else; but it can maintain its sense of superiority only when it adjusts itself to the community that needs the products in this process of interchange. In such a situation, there is a tendency toward functional development, a functional development which may take place even in the political domain.

It might seem that the functional aspect is contradictory to the ends of democracy insofar as it considers the individual in relation to a whole and in that way ignores the individual; and that, accordingly, real democracy must express itself more in the tone of the religious attitude and in making secondary the functional aspect. If we go back to the ideal of democracy as presented in the French Revolution, we do reach just such a sort of conflict. There you have recognition of quality; you demand in yourself what you recognize in others, and that does provide the basis for a social structure. But when you consider the functional expression of that time, there is not the same sort of equality. However, equality in a functional sense is possible, and I do not see any reason why it should not carry with it as deep a sense of the realization of the other in one's self as the religious attitude. A physician who through his superior skill can save the life of an individual can realize himself in regard to the person he has benefited. I see no reason why this functional attitude should not express itself in the realization of one's self in the other. The basis of spiritual expression is the ability to realize one's self in the many, and that certainly is reached in the social organization. It seems to me that the apparent conflict under consideration refers to the abstract and preliminary development of the functional organization. Until that functional organization is fully carried out, there is the opportunity for exploitation of the individual; but with the full development of such organization we should get a higher spiritual expression in which the individual realizes himself in others through that which he does as peculiar to himself.[6]

Conflict and Integration

I have been emphasizing the continued integration of the social process and the psychology of the self which underlies

[6] For a discussion of pragmatism in relation to the American scene see "The Philosophies of Royce, James, and Dewey in their American Setting," *International Journal of Ethics*, XL (1930), 211 ff.; for historical genesis of pragmatism see *Movements of Thought in the Nineteenth Century*.

and makes possible this process. A word now as to the factors of conflict and disintegration. In the baseball game there are competing individuals who want to get into the limelight, but this can only be attained by playing the game. Those conditions do make a certain sort of action necessary, but inside of them there can be all sorts of jealously competing individuals who may wreck the team. There seems to be abundant opportunity for disorganization in the organization essential to the team. This is so to a much larger degree in the economic process. There has to be distribution, markets, mediums of exchange; but within that field all kinds of competition and disorganizations are possible, since there is an "I" as well as a "me" in every case.

Historical conflicts start, as a rule, with a community which is socially pretty highly organized. Such conflicts have to arise between different groups where there is an attitude of hostility to others involved. But even here a wider social organization is usually the result; there is, for instance, an appearance of the tribe over against the clan. It is a larger, vaguer organization, but still it is there. This is the sort of situation we have at the present time; over against the potential hostility of nations to each other, they recognize themselves as forming some sort of community, as in the League of Nations.

The fundamental socio-physiological impulses or behavior tendencies which are common to all human individuals, which lead those individuals collectively to enter or form themselves into organized societies or social communities, and which constitute the ultimate basis of those societies or social communities, fall, from the social point of view, into two main classes: those which lead to social co-operation and those which lead to social antagonism among individuals. They can be described as those which give rise to friendly attitudes and relations and those which give rise to hostile attitudes and relations among the human individuals implicated in the social situations. We have used the term "social" in its broadest and strictest sense; but in that quite common narrower sense, in which it bears an ethical connotation, only the fundamental physiological human impulses or behavior tendencies of the former class (those which are friendly, or which make for friendliness and co-operation among the individuals motivated by them) are "social" or lead to "social" conduct. Whereas those impulses or behavior tendencies of the latter class (those which are hostile or which make for hostility and antagonism among the individuals motivated by them) are "anti-social" or lead to "anti-social" conduct. Now it is true that the latter class of fundamental impulses or behavior tendencies in human beings are "anti-social" insofar as they would, by themselves, be destructive of all human social organization or could not, alone, constitute the basis of any organized human society; yet in the broadest and strictest non-ethical sense, they are obviously no less social than are the former class of such impulses of behavior tendencies. They are equally common to, or universal among, all human individuals, and, if anything, are more easily and immediately aroused by the appropriate social stimuli; and as combined or fused with, and in a sense controlled by, the former impulses or behavior tendencies, they are just as basic to all human social organization as are the former and play a hardly less necessary and significant part in that social organization itself and in the determination of its general character. Consider, for example, from among these "hostile" human impulses or attitudes, the functioning or expression or operation of those of self-protection and self-preservation in the organization and organized activities of any given human society or social community, let us say, of a modern state or nation. Human individuals realize or become aware of themselves as such, almost more easily and readily in terms of the social attitudes connected or associated with these two "hostile" impulses (or in terms of these two impulses as expressed in these attitudes) than they do in terms of any other social attitudes or behavior tendencies as expressed by those attitudes. Within the social organization of a state or nation the "anti-social" effects of these two impulses are curbed and kept under control by the legal system which is one aspect of that organization; these two impulses are made to constitute the fundamental principles in terms of which the economic system, which is another aspect of that organization, operates; as combined and fused with, and organized by means of the "friendly" human impulses—the impulses leading to social co-operation among the individuals involved in that organization—they are prevented from giving rise to the friction and enmity among those individuals which would otherwise be their natural consequence and which would be fatally detrimental to the existence and well-being of that organization; and having thus been made to enter as integral elements into the foundations of that organization, they are utilized by that organization as fundamental impulsive forces in its own further development, or they serve as a basis for social progress within its relational framework. Ordinarily, their most obvious and concrete expression or manifestation in that organization lies in the attitudes of rivalry and competition which they generate inside the state or nation as a whole among different socially functional subgroups of individuals—subgroups determined (and especially economically determined) by that organization; and these attitudes serve definite social ends or purposes presupposed by that organization and constitute the motives of functionally necessary social activities within that organization. But self-protective and self-preservational human impulses also express or manifest themselves indirectly in that organization by giving rise through their association in that organization with the "friendly" human impulses to one of the primary constitutive ideals or principles or motives of that organization—namely, the affording of social protection and the lending of social assistance to the individual by the state in the conduct of his life; and by enhancing the efficacy, for the purposes of that organization, of the "friendly" human impulses with a sense or realization of the possibility and desirability of such organized social protection and assistance to the individual. Moreover, in any special circumstances in which the state or nation is, as a whole, confronted by some danger common to all its individual members, they become fused with the "friendly" human impulses in those individuals, in such a way as to strengthen and intensify in those individuals the sense of organized social union and co-operative social interrelationship among them in terms of the state; in such circumstances, so far from constituting forces of disintegration or destruction within the social organization of the state or nation, they become, indirectly, the principles of increased social unity, coherence, and co-ordination within that organization. In time of war, for example, the self-protective impulse in all the individual members of the state, is unitedly directed against their common enemy and ceases, for the time being, to be directed among themselves; the attitudes of rivalry and competition which that impulse ordinarily generates between the different, smaller, socially functional groups of those individuals within the state are temporarily broken down; the usual social barriers between these groups are likewise removed; and the state presents a united front to the given common danger or is fused into a single unity in terms of the common end shared by, or reflected in, the respective consciousnesses of all its individual members. It is upon these wartime expressions of the self-protective impulse in all the individual members of the state or nation that the general efficacy of national appeals to patriotism are chiefly based.

Further, in those social situations in which the individual self feels dependent for his continuation or continued existence upon the rest of the members of the given social group to which he belongs, it is true that no feeling of superiority on his part toward those other members of that group is necessary to his continuation or continued existence. But in those social situations in which he cannot, for the time being, integrate his social relations with other individual selves into a common, unitary pattern (into the behavior pattern of the organized society or social community to which he belongs, the social behavior pattern that he reflects in his self-structure and that constitutes this structure), there ensues, temporarily (until he can so integrate his social relations with other individual selves), an attitude of hostility, of "latent opposition," on his part toward the organized society or social community of which he is a member; and during that time, the given individual self must "call in" or rely upon the feeling of superiority toward that society or social community or toward its other individual members in order to buoy himself up and "keep himself going" as such. We always present ourselves to ourselves in the most favorable light possible; but since we all have the job of keeping ourselves going, it is quite necessary that if we are to keep ourselves going, we should thus present ourselves to ourselves.

A highly developed and organized human society is one in which the individual members are interrelated in a multiplicity of different intricate and complicated ways whereby they all share a number of common social interests—interests in, or for the betterment of, the society—and yet, on the other hand, are more or less in conflict relative to numerous other interests which they possess only individually or else share with one another only in small and limited groups. Conflicts among individuals in a highly developed and organized human society are not mere conflicts among their respective primitive impulses but are conflicts among their respective selves or personalities, each with its definite social structure—highly complex and organized and unified—and each with a number of different social facets or aspects, a number of different sets of social attitudes constituting it. Thus, within such a society, conflicts arise between different aspects or phases of the same individual self (conflicts leading to cases of split personality when they are extreme or violent enough to be psychopathological), as well as between different individual selves. And both these types of individual conflict are settled or terminated by reconstructions of the particular social situations and modifications of the given framework of social relationships wherein they arise or occur in the general human social life-process. These reconstructions and modifications are performed, as we have said, by the minds of the individuals in whose experience or between whose selves these conflicts take place.

Mind, as constructive or reflective or problem-solving thinking, is the socially acquired means or mechanism or apparatus whereby the human individual solves the various problems of environmental adjustment which arise to confront him in the course of his experience and which prevent his conduct from proceeding harmoniously on its way until they have thus been dealt with. And mind or thinking is also—as possessed by the individual members of human society—the means or mechanism or apparatus whereby social reconstruction is effected or accomplished by these individuals. For it is their possession of minds or powers of thinking which enables individuals to turn back critically, as it were, upon the organized social structure of the society to which they belong (and from their relations to which their minds are in the first instance derived), and to reorganize or reconstruct or modify that social structure to a greater or less degree, as the exigencies of social evolution from time to time require. Any such social reconstruction, if it is to be at all far-reaching, presupposes a basis of common social interests shared by all the individual members of the given human society in which that reconstruction occurs, and it is shared by all the individuals whose minds must participate in, or whose minds bring about, that construction. And the way in which any such social reconstruction is actually effected by the minds of the individuals involved is by a more or less abstract intellectual extension of the boundaries of the given society to which these individuals all belong and which is undergoing the reconstruction— an extension resulting in a larger social whole in terms of which the social conflicts that necessitate the reconstruction of the given society are harmonized or reconciled, and by reference to which, accordingly, these conflicts can be solved or eliminated.[7]

The changes that we make in the social order in which we are implicated necessarily involve our also making changes in ourselves. The social conflicts among the individual members of a

[7]   The reflexive character of self-consciousness enables the individual to contemplate himself as a whole; his ability to take the social attitudes of other individuals and also of the generalized other toward himself, within the given organized society of which he is a member, makes possible his bringing himself, as an objective whole, within his own experiential purview; and thus he can consciously integrate and unify the various aspects of his self, to form a single consistent and coherent and organized personality. Moreover, by the same means, he can undertake and effect intelligent reconstructions of that self or personality in terms of its relations to the given social order, whenever the exigencies of adaptation to his social environment demand such reconstructions.

given organized human society, which, for their removal, necessitate conscious or intelligent reconstructions and modifications of that society by those individuals, also and equally necessitate such reconstructions or modifications by those individuals of their own selves or personalities. Thus the relations between social reconstruction and self or personality reconstruction are reciprocal and internal or organic; social reconstruction by the individual members of any organized human society entails self or personality reconstruction in some degree or other by each of these individuals, and vice versa; for, since their selves or personalities are constituted by their organized social relations to one another, they cannot reconstruct those selves or personalities without also reconstructing, to some extent, the given social order, which is, of course, likewise constituted by their organized social relations to one another. In both types of reconstruction the same fundamental material of organized social relations among human individuals is involved and is simply treated in different ways, or from different angles or points of view, in the two cases, respectively; or in short, social reconstruction and self or personality reconstruction are the two sides of a single process—the process of human social evolution. Human social progress involves the use by human individuals of their socially derived mechanism of self-consciousness, both in the effecting of such progressive social changes, and also in the development of their individual selves or personalities in such a way as adaptively to keep pace with such social reconstruction.

Ultimately and fundamentally societies develop in complexity of organization only by means of the progressive achievement of greater and greater degrees of functional, behavioristic differentiation among the individuals who constitute them; these functional, behavioristic differentiations among the individual members implying or presupposing initial oppositions among them of individual needs and ends, oppositions which in terms of social organization, however, are or have been transformed into these differentiations or into mere specializations of socially functional individual behavior.

The human social ideal—the ideal or ultimate goal of human

social progress—is the attainment of a universal human society in which all human individuals would possess a perfected social intelligence, such that all social meanings would each be similarly reflected in their respective individual consciousness—such that the meanings of any one individual's acts or gestures (as realized by him and expressed in the structure of his self, through his ability to take the social attitudes of other individuals toward himself and toward their common social ends or purposes) would be the same whatever for any other individual who responded to them.

The interlocking interdependence of human individuals upon one another within the given organized social life-process in which they are all involved is becoming more and more intricate and closely knit and highly organized as human social evolution proceeds on its course. The wide difference, for example, between the feudal civilization of medieval times, with its relatively loose and disintegrated social organization, and the national civilization of modern times, with its relatively tight and integrated social organization (together with its trend of development toward some form of international civilization), exhibits the constant evolution of human social organization in the direction of greater and greater relational unity and complexity, also more and more closely knit interlocking and integrated unification of all the social relations of interdependence which constitute it and which hold among the individuals involved in it.

Obstacles and Promises in the Development of the Ideal Society

We have presented the self from the side of experience; it arises through co-operative activity; it is made possible through the identical reactions of the self and others. Insofar as the individual can call out in his own nature these organized responses and so take the attitude of the other toward himself, he can develop self-consciousness, a reaction of the organism to itself. On the other hand, we have seen that an essential moment in this process is the response of the individual to this reaction which does contain the organized group, that which is common to all, that which is called the "me." If individuals are so distinguished from each other that they cannot identify themselves with each other, if there is not a common basis, there cannot be a whole self present on either side.

Such a distinction, for example, does lie between the infant and the human society in which he enters. He cannot have the whole self-consciousness of the adult; and the adult finds it difficult, to say the least, to put himself into the attitude of the child. That is not, however, an impossible thing, and our development of modern education rests on this possibility of the adult finding a common basis between himself and the child. Go back into the literature to which children were introduced in the sixteenth, seventeenth, and even eighteenth centuries, and you find children treated as little adults; the whole attitude toward them from the point of view of morals, as well as training, was that they were adults who were somewhat deficient and needed to be disciplined in order to get them into the proper attitude. That which they were to learn was to be brought to them in the form in which an adult makes use of the knowledge. It was not until the last century that there was a definite undertaking on the part of those interested in the education of children to enter into the experience of the child and to regard it with any respect.

Even in the society erected on the basis of castes there are some common attitudes, but they are very restricted in number, and as they are restricted they cut down the possibility of the full development of the self. What is necessary under those circumstances to get such a self is a withdrawal from that caste order. The medieval period in which there was a definite caste organization of society, with serfs, overlords, and ecclesiastical distinctions, presents a situation in which the attainment of membership in the spiritual community required the withdrawal of the individual from the society as ordered in the caste fashion. Such is at least a partial explanation of the cloistered life and of asceticism. The same thing is revealed in other communities in the development of saints who withdraw from the social order and get back to some sort of a society in which these castes as such are mediated or absent. The development of the democratic community implies the removal of castes as essential to the personality of the individual; the individual is not to be what he is in his specific caste or group as against other groups, but his distinctions are to be distinctions of functional difference which put him in relationship with others instead of separating him.[8]

The caste distinction of the early warrior class was one which separated its members from the community. Their characters as soldiers differentiated them from the other members of the community; they were what they were because they were essentially different from others. Their activity separated them from the community. They even preyed upon the community which they were supposed to be defending and would do so inevitably because their activity was essentially a fighting activity. With the development of the national army which took place at the beginning of the nineteenth century, there was the possibility of everyone's being a warrior, so that the man who was a fighting man was still a person who could identify himself with the other members of the community; he had their attitudes, and they had the attitude of the fighting man. Thus the normal relationship between the fighting man and the rest of the community was one which bound people together, integrated the army and the body of the state, instead of separating them. The same pro-

[8]   Insofar as specialization is normal and helpful, it increases concrete social relations. Differences in occupation do not themselves build up castes. The caste has arisen through the importation of the outsider into the group, just as the animal is brought in, when through the conception of property he can be made useful. The element of hostility toward the person outside the group is essential to the development of the caste. Caste in India arose out of conquest. It always involves the group enemy, when that has been imported into the group; so that I should not myself agree with Cooley that hereditary transmission of differentiated occupation produces castes.

The caste system breaks down as the human relations become more concrete. . . . Slaves pass over into serfs, peasants, artisans, citizens. In all these stages you have an increase of relations. In the ideal condition separation from the point of view of caste will become social function from the point of view of the group. . . . Democratic consciousness is generated by differences of functions (1912).

gression is found in the other castes, such as the governing as against the governed, an essential difference which made it impossible for the individual of that particular group to identify himself with the others, or the others to identify themselves with him. The democratic order undertakes to wipe that difference out and to make everyone a sovereign and everyone a subject. One is to be a subject to the degree that he is a sovereign. He is to undertake to administer rights and maintain them only insofar as he recognizes those rights in others. And so one might go on through other caste divisions.

Ethical ideas, within any given human society, arise in the consciousness of the individual members of that society from the fact of the common social dependence of all these individuals upon one another (or from the fact of the common social dependence of each one of them upon that society as a whole or upon all the rest of them) and from their awareness or sensing or conscious realization of this fact. But ethical problems arise for individual members of any given human society whenever they are individually confronted with a social situation to which they cannot readily adjust and adapt themselves, or in which they cannot easily realize themselves, or with which they cannot immediately integrate their own behavior; and the feeling in them which is concomitant with their facing and solution of such problems (which are essentially problems of social adjustment and adaptation to the interests and conduct of other individuals) is that of self-superiority and temporary opposition to other individuals. In the case of ethical problems, our social relationships with other individual members of the given human society to which we belong depend upon our opposition to them, rather than, as in the case of the development or formulation of ethical ideals, upon our unity, co-operation, and identification with them. Every individual must, to behave ethically, integrate himself with the pattern of organized social behavior which, as reflected or prehended in the structure of his self, makes him a self-conscious personality. Wrong, evil, or sinful conduct on the part of the individual runs counter to this pattern of organized social behavior which makes him, as a self, what he is, just as right, good, or virtuous behavior accords with this pattern; and this fact is the basis of the profound ethical feeling of conscience—of "ought" and "ought not"—which we all have, in varying degrees, respecting our conduct in given social situations. The sense which the individual self has of his dependence upon the organized society or social community to which he belongs is the basis and origin, in short, of his sense of duty (and in general of his ethical consciousness); and ethical and unethical behavior can be defined essentially in social terms: the former as behavior which is socially beneficial or conducive to the well-being of society, the latter as behavior which is socially harmful or conducive to the disruption of society. From another point of view, ethical ideals and ethical problems may be considered in terms of the conflict between the social and the asocial (the impersonal and the personal) sides or aspects of the individual self. The social or impersonal aspect of the self integrates it with the social group to which it belongs and to which it owes its existence; and this side of the self is characterized by the individual's feeling of co-operation and equality with the other members of that social group. The asocial or personal aspect of the self (which, nevertheless, is also equally social, fundamentally in the sense of being socially derived or originated and of existentially involving social relations with other individuals, as much as the impersonal aspect of the self is and does), on the other hand, differentiates it from, or sets it in distinctive and unique opposition to, the other members of the social group to which it belongs; and this side of the self is characterized by the individual's feeling of superiority toward the other members of that group. The "social" aspect of human society—which is simply the social aspect of the selves of all individual members taken collectively—with its concomitant feelings on the parts of all these individuals of co-operation and social interdependence, is the basis for the development and existence of ethical ideals in that society; whereas the "asocial" aspect of human society—which is simply the asocial aspect of the selves of all individual members taken collectively—with its concomitant feelings on the parts of all these individuals of individuality, self-superiority to other individual selves, and social independence, is responsible for the rise of ethical problems in that society. These two basic aspects of each single individual self are, of course, responsible in the same way or at the same time for the development of ethical ideals and the rise of ethical problems in the individual's own experience as opposed to the experience of human society as a whole, which is obviously nothing but the sum total of the social experiences of all its individual members.

Those social situations in which the individual finds it easiest to integrate his own behavior with the behavior of the other individual selves are those in which all the individual participants are members of some one of the numerous socially functional groups of individuals (groups organized, respectively, for various special social ends and purposes) within the given human society as a whole, and in which he and they are acting in their respective capacities as members of this particular group. (Every individual member of any given human society, of course, belongs to a large number of such different functional groups.) On the other hand, those social situations in which the individual finds it most difficult to integrate his own behavior with the behavior of others are those in which he and they are acting as members, respectively, of two or more different socially functional groups: groups whose respective social purposes or interests are antagonistic or conflicting or widely separated. In social situations of the former general type, each individual's attitude toward the other individuals is essentially social; and the combination of all these social attitudes toward one another of the individuals represents, or tends to realize more or less completely, the ideal of any social situation respecting organization, unification, co-operation, and integration of the behavior of the several individuals involved. In any social situation of this general type, the individual realizes himself as such in his relation to all the other members of the given socially functional group and realizes his own particular social function in its relations to the respective functions of all other individuals. He takes or assumes the social attitudes of all these other individuals toward himself and toward one another and integrates himself with that situation or group by controlling his own behavior or conduct accordingly, so that there is nothing in the least competitive or hostile in his relations with these other individuals. In social situations of the latter general type, on the other hand, each individual's attitude toward the other individuals is essentially asocial or hostile (though these attitudes are of course social in the fundamental non-ethical sense, and are socially derived); such situations are so complex that the various individuals involved in any one of them either cannot be brought into common social relations with one another at all or else can be brought into such relations only with great difficulty, after long and tortuous processes of mutual social adjustment. Any such situation lacks a common group or social interest shared by all the individuals. It has no single, common social end or purpose characterizing it and serving to unite and co-ordinate and harmoniously interrelate the actions of all those individuals; instead, those individuals are motivated, in that situation, by several different and more or less conflicting social interests or purposes. Examples of social situations of this general type are those involving interactions or relations between capital and labor, that is, those in which some of the individuals are acting in their socially functional capacity as members of the capitalistic class, which is one economic aspect of modern human social organization; whereas the other individuals are acting in their socially functional capacity as members of the laboring class, which is another (and in social interests directly opposed) economic aspect of that social organization. Other examples of social situations of this general type are those in which the individuals involved stand in the economic relations to each other as producers and consumers or as buyers and sellers and are acting in their respective socially functional capacities as such. But even the social situations of this general type (involving complex social antagonisms and diversities of social interests among the individuals implicated in any one of them, and respectively lacking the co-ordinating, integrating, unifying influence of common social ends and motives shared by those individuals), even these social situations, as occurring within the general human social process of experience and behavior, are definite aspects of or ingredients in the general relational pattern of that process as a whole.

What is essential to the order of society in its fullest expression on the basis of the theory of the self that we have been discussing is, then, an organization of common attitudes which shall be found in all individuals. It might be supposed that such an organization of attitudes would refer only to that abstract human being which could be found as identical in all members of society, and that that which is peculiar to the personality of the individual would disappear. The term "personality" implies that the individual has certain common rights and values obtained in him and through him; but over and above that sort of social endowment of the individual, there is that which distinguishes him from anybody else, makes him what he is. It is the most precious part of the individual. The question is whether that can be carried over into the social self or whether the social self shall simply embody those reactions which can be common to him in a great community. From the discussion we have given, we are not forced to accept the latter alternative.

When one realizes himself, in that he distinguishes himself, he asserts himself over others in some peculiar situation which justifies him in maintaining himself against them. If he could not bring that peculiarity of himself into the common community, if it could not be recognized, if others could not take his attitude in some sense, he could not have appreciation in emotional terms, he could not be the very self he is trying to be. The author, the artist, must have his audience; it may be an audience that belongs to posterity, but there must be an audience. One has to find one's self in his own individual creation as appreciated by others; what the individual accomplishes must be something that is in itself social. So far as he is a self, he must be an organic part of the life of the community, and his contribution has to be something that is social. It may be an ideal which he has discovered, but it has its value in the fact that it belongs to society. One may be somewhat ahead of his time, but that which he brings forward must belong to the life of the community to which he belongs. There is, then, a functional difference, but it must be a functional difference which can be entered into in some real sense by the rest of the community. Of course, there are contributions which some make that others cannot make, and there may be contributions which people cannot enter into; but those that go to make up the self are only those which can be shared. To do justice to the recognition of the uniqueness of an individual in social terms, there must be not only the differentiation which we do have in a highly organized society but a differentiation in which the attitudes involved can be taken by other members of the group.

Take, for example, the labor movement. It is essential that the other members of the community shall be able to enter into the attitude of the laborer in his functions. It is the caste organization, of course, which makes it impossible; and the development of the modern labor movement not only brought the situation actually involved before the community but inevitably helped to break down the caste organization itself. The caste organization tended to separate in the selves the essential functions of the individuals so that one could not enter into the other. This does not, of course, shut out the possibility of some sort of social relationship; but any such relationship involves the possibility of the individual's taking the attitude of the other individuals, and functional differentiation does not make that impossible. A member of the community is not necessarily like other individuals because he is able to identify himself with them. He may be different. There can be a common content, common experience, without there being an identity of function. A difference of functions does not preclude a common experience; it is possible for the individual to put himself in the place of the other although his function is different from the other. It is that sort of functionally differentiated personality that I wanted to refer to as opposed to that which is simply common to all members of a community.

There is, of course, a certain common set of reactions which belong to all, which are not differentiated on the social side but which get their expression in rights, uniformities, the common methods of action which characterize members of different communities, manners of speech, and so on. Distinguishable from those is the identity which is compatible with the difference of social functions of the individuals, illustrated by the capacity of the individual to take the part of the others whom he is affecting, the warrior putting himself in the place of those whom he is proceeding against, the teacher putting himself in the position of the child whom he is undertaking to instruct. That capacity allows for exhibiting one's own peculiarities and at the same time taking the attitude of the others whom he is himself affecting. It is possible for the individual to develop his own peculiarities, that which individualizes him, and still be a member of a community, provided that he is able to take the attitude of those whom he affects. Of course, the degree to which that takes place varies tremendously, but a certain amount of it is essential to citizenship in the community.

One can say that the attainment of that functional differentia-ation and social participation in the full degree is a sort of ideal which lies before the human community. The present stage of it is presented in the ideal of democracy. It is often assumed that democracy is an order of society in which those personalities which are sharply differentiated will be eliminated, that every-thing will be ironed down to a situation where everyone will be, as far as possible, like everyone else. But of course that is not the implication of democracy: the implication of democracy is rather that the individual can be as highly developed as lies with-in the possibilities of his own inheritance and still can enter into the attitudes of the others whom he affects. There can still be leaders, and the community can rejoice in their attitudes just in-sofar as these superior individuals can themselves enter into the attitudes of the community which they undertake to lead.

How far individuals can take the roles of other individuals in the community is dependent upon a number of factors. The community may in its size transcend the social organization, may go beyond the social organization which makes such identifica-tion possible. The most striking illustration of that is the eco-nomic community. This includes everybody with whom one can trade in any circumstances, but it represents a whole in which it would be next to impossible for all to enter into the attitudes of the others. The ideal communities of the universal religions are communities which to some extent may be said to exist, but they imply a degree of identification which the actual organization of the community cannot realize. We often find the existence of castes in a community which make it impossible for persons to enter into the attitude of other people although they are actually affecting and are affected by these other people. The ideal of human society is one which does bring people so closely together in their interrelationships, so fully develops the necessary system of communication, that the individuals who exercise their own peculiar functions can take the attitude of those whom they affect. The development of communication is not simply a matter of abstract ideas, but is a process of putting one's self in the place of the other person's attitude, communicating through significant symbols. Remember that what is essential to a significant symbol is that the gesture which affects others should affect the individual himself in the same way. It is only when the stimulus which one gives another arouses in himself the same or like response that the symbol is a significant symbol. Human communication takes place through such significant symbols, and the problem is one of organizing a community which makes this possible. If that system of communication could be made theoretically perfect, the individual would affect himself as he affects others in every way. That would be the ideal of communication, an ideal attained in logical discourse wherever it is understood. The meaning of that which is said is here the same to one as it is to everybody else. Universal discourse is then the formal ideal of communication. If communication can be carried through and made perfect, then there would exist the kind of democracy to which we have referred, in which each individual would carry just the response in himself that he knows he calls out in the community. That is what makes communication in the significant sense the organizing processes in the community. It is not simply a process of transferring abstract symbols; it is always a gesture in a social act which calls out in the individual himself the tendency to the same act that is called out in others.

What we call the ideal of a human society is approached in

some sense by the economic society on the one side and by the universal religions on the other side, but it is not by any means fully realized. Those abstractions can be put together in a single community of the democratic type. As democracy now exists, there is not this development of communication so that individuals can put themselves into the attitudes of those whom they affect. There are a consequent leveling-down and an undue recognition of that which is not only common but identical. The ideal of human society cannot exist as long as it is impossible for individuals to enter into the attitudes of those whom they are affecting in the performance of their own peculiar functions.

Part VIII

9

AUGUSTE COMTE

THE important characteristic of Comte's doctrine was its recognition of what we may term the "philosophical import" of scientific method. As I have indicated, the scientific method recognized the object of knowledge in the experience of the individual, in that which is ordinarily termed the "fact." If one is to identify the fact, he must do it in terms of his experience. It is, of course, true that the observer states his observation in such terms that it can also be made an object by others and so be tested by them. He tries to give it a universal form, but still he comes back eventually to the account which he gives of his observation as such.

What is not recognized in the positivistic doctrine is that the observation is always one that has an element of novelty in it. That is, it is in some sense unusual. It is observed because it is distinct in some way from the expected experience. One does not observe that which is to be expected. One notes it; one recognizes it. We recognize what we expect, and give attention only to that which differs from that which is expected. If one reaches for a tool that he is after and it is in its expected place, or for a book in its place on the shelf, all he gives attention to is that

First published in *Movements of Thought in the Nineteenth Century,* ed. Merritt H. Moore (Chicago: University of Chicago Press, 1936), pp. 456–66).

the object is of the type that he expects to find. He gives as little attention as is necessary in order to identify it. More than this would mean loss of effort and time. One does not stop to examine the expression of his friend unless there is something unusual about it. He sees only enough to identify him. Ordinarily, then, we would not speak of an observer as one who merely recognizes. Observation implies careful noting of all the details of the object. It is true that you do not observe everything about anything. What one does is to observe all that enables one to assure himself that the object is not exactly what one expects. One reaches for a tool, thinking he is going to pick up a hammer, and finds it is a chisel; and he pays attention to find why it was that he made the mistake. He observes the character of a plant that misled him. His observation is given to that which distinguishes it from the expected thing. These are the facts of science—those observations that enable us to determine characters that would not have been anticipated. One may also, of course, give attention to objects that seem quite familiar. That is what is implied. You are looking for something that will strike your attention as in some sense unusual.

The positivistic doctrine assumes that our objects are given in such observation, and that is the logical weakness of positivism. It assumes that the world is made up, so to speak, out of facts, is made up out of those objects that appear in the experience of the scientific observer. Most objects we regard simply as they identify themselves. The objects of scientific observation answer to a detailed analysis, which implies an interest of some sort. We can explain this position in terms of the method to which I refer, by saying that the objects of science do not always have behind them implicit or explicit problems. In other words, science is really research science. Research always implies a problem. Where there is nothing of this sort, we are not engaged in research. There is a type of thinking which is not problematical— that of carrying out a habitual act, of attending a machine with which you are familiar, for example. That sort of concentrated attention is given simply to those stimuli that will enable us to carry out a well-formed habit. There we have concentrated attention, but it is not occupied with the proceedings of our research science. It is occupied in a world where one is awake only to the next stimulus that is necessary to carry on an activity that more or less runs itself.

A further step which Comte did not recognize, because it belongs to a later period, is the evolutionary one which undertakes to see how these forms, these experiences, arise. Evolutionary doctrine started off with the life-process, and undertook to account for the appearance of species themselves. It carries us back to a world in which the nature of the object, the experience as such, arises. Neither Comte nor John Stuart Mill, who would be the corresponding figure in England, was influenced by evolutionary doctrine to any great degree. Mill was also, to all intents and purposes, a positivist. He, too, assumed that the analysis that the scientist makes of an object reveals the characters of things, reveals the elements of things, the parts of things; and if we want to know the world, we must discover these elements which the scientist finds. Mill, as you know, embodied this doctrine in his logic in which he undertook to state the logic of science. It is by no means an adequate account of scientific procedure; but his theory of induction and of the inductive process in science, his method of agreement and difference, are definitely attempts to state the scientist's procedure. They are really methods of distinguishing rather than of forming hypotheses.

What I am attempting to make clear is that the positivistic doctrine was one which undertook to give the philosophic implications the form of scientific method. But neither Comte nor Mill gave a competent account of the scientist's procedure. They did assume that science—what we would call "research science"—was the most efficient method of knowing. They did recognize that this type of science was one which was an advance over metaphysical science, while the metaphysical was a natural successor to theology. We have, then, in the French thought of this period, the reconstruction of science as presenting the form of the philosophic problem.

The step which positivism represents is that of stating a

problem so that it is put in the form of a method rather than of a result. Is the method of science the method of philosophy? Can one make the method of science the method of philosophy? One great, somewhat grandiose effort to solve this problem was made by the Romantic idealists. Hegel, who was most complete in his statement, undertook to show that the method of science and the method of human thought in all its endeavor and the method of the universe were all the same, the method which he represented by his dialectic process. His philosophy was in one sense a philosophy of evolution; but the same process, the same method, the same logic, lay back of physical nature, back of moral effort, back of human history, back of all that science presents. It was, as I said in other connections, a grandiose undertaking which was a failure. Particularly, it was unable to present the scientific procedure within each field. It could not successfully state the method of research science. This is the problem, then, that is presented in positivism. For positivism, metaphysics is past; it is gone. Just as metaphysics was supposed to have wiped out theology, so the positivists were presenting a method which could be immediately applied, and through which we could get rid of metaphysics.

Comte had as vivid an interest in the relation of his philosophy to society and its values as any others of the period. He looked for the forms of a society of the human race whose values should determine the conduct of the individual. But, as far as the process of knowing social values was concerned, it would be the same as in the physical and the biological sciences. He assumed that there could be a study of society which could be undertaken in the same way as the study of the physical sciences. That was the most striking character of his doctrine in its immediate impact. The church had a metaphysical doctrine behind it. And this is no less true in this period of what we may call "political science," the theory of law, of ethics, of education. That is, each of them had essential doctrines. The sovereignty of the state, in the attitude of an English community, is to be found in the individuals that form the republic. Sovereignty was a dogma. It was that in the state which exercised absolute power. And the state had to be conceived of in terms of such metaphysical entity as that. Similarly, the family was a certain definite entity, and the school was a certain definite entity. One argued from the nature of the sovereign, of the family, of the school, what the position of the individual under it must be. In each case the attitude was essentially metaphysical. What Comte presented was the demand for the use of positivistic method in the study of society. He presented sociology as a new field. What I want to emphasize is that we do not think of it as another science. We have economics, education, political science; and here comes sociology, another science covering the same field and yet claiming to be different. It has been, in very recent times, a great question as to whether there was any such thing as sociology. And I have seen theses presented in this university for the degree of Doctor of Philosophy in the field of sociology upon the problem of whether or not there is any such thing as sociology. What is characteristic of Comte's position is his demand that society and social events should be approached in the same fashion that the study of plants and animals and moving bodies are approached. He was breaking away from the metaphysical attitude and presenting another science, that of society. As he conceived of society, it inevitably includes the whole human race; and he thought there could be one science of it. Sociology, then, was the attempt to apply the method of positivism, the method of science, to the field of society, an attempt to displace what was, at that time, an essentially metaphysical approach, one which started off with the definition of the state, with a study of the processes of social changes going on in various institutions. Comte undertook to approach human affairs in the way of the scientist who simply analyzes things into their ultimate elements in a positivistic fashion and then from that finds the laws of their behavior. But there lay in the back of Comte's mind pictures of a medieval period, only he would have substituted society for the pope. He was not freed from that. This other side of Comte's doctrine is one that harks back to the medieval period.

I pointed out that early in the century, during the period of De Bonald and De Maistre, reactionary philosophers sought to go back to the church as the source of all authority, as that which must give an interpretation of life. Their statement, however, was different from the medieval statement. They were particularly impressed with the society of Europe in the twelfth and thirteenth centuries, the period which is best represented by Dante. It was a period in which the world realized itself as a single community, in which everything could be explained by the doctrine of the church. There was no difficulty in the explanation, because this world was so created that man can be moral; and, if he can be moral, it must also be possible for him to be immoral. It is a world in which sin has a legitimate place; and if man sins, the punishment of sin follows. The world at that period was entirely comprehensible from the point of view of the church theology. It included everyone. Anything that happened that was undesirable could be explained by the fact that God was using it to bring about the great good, including the good of man. The Western world was conceived of as a single society. It took in nearly the whole of the human race. It was organized through the church. The church took over the statement that St. Paul gives, you remember, of the church as the body of which Christ was the head. In his concept of a unified society everyone has his place and everything can be explained from the point of view of the theory of the church. It was to that conception of a society which was a world society, an organic society, and a society which answered to the immediate impulse of the individual that these philosophers, De Bonald and De Maistre, went back.

Comte was never influenced by this account. His positions freed him from the dogma of the church, but he still looked to such a picture of the whole society of man as representing the idea that should be realized. The curious thing from our standpoint is that he should have copied to such an extent the characters of the church. His idea, too, was that society should be an organic whole. It must then have some organized value. What Comte presents, instead of welfare by the church, is the welfare of the community as a whole. This community as a whole comes to take the place of the glory of God, which, as spoken of by the church, is the end of all existence. For the positivist it is not the glory of God but the good of mankind that is the supreme value. That is the supreme value in terms of which everything should be stated. This point of view is stated in less emotional form in the utilitarianism in England during the same period. Bentham and the Mills are, in a sense, companion figures to Comte. Their idea of the ideal society is one which achieves the greatest good of the greatest number. This welfare of the community transcends the good of any particular individual. This is something all should see, and man's attitude toward it should be a religious attitude. This should be recognized as the supreme value that determines all others. And Comte recognized that an emotional attitude was essential.

John Stuart Mill said that everyone finds himself and his conduct constantly influenced by others. Each can retain his own pleasure by recognizing others in the pursuit of their pleasure. The individual feels continually the presence of the community about him forcing him to recognize the interest of others. It seems a skeptical account which Mill gives of the origin of virtue. Comte would put up the good of the community itself through an emotional expression which should be essentially religious in its character. That is, men should actually worship the Supreme Being in the form of society. Society as an organized whole, as that which is responsible for the individual, should be worshiped; and on this basis Comte undertook to set up a positivistic religion. Now, this religion of positivism had some vogue among the followers of Comte. There was a devoted group of this sort to be found in England. It never attained any size. A wag, referring to a dissension among them, said of the sessions, "They came to church in one cab and left in two." It never became a widespread religious movement, but the undertaking to set up such a religion which should find the highest value in society and fuse that into a unity which could be worshiped was characteristic of Comte. He thought and looked for a society that could be organized in the same fashion as medieval society had been by the church. And he attempted to work out in some detail how this sort of ordering of society would take place. He did not try to substitute the value of society itself for the Deity, but tried to take over the religious attitude toward the Deity into the religious attitude of members of the community toward society itself.

This phase of Comte's sociology was not a lasting one. What was of importance was his emphasis on the dependence of the individual on society, his sense of the organic character of society as responsible for the nature of the individual. This is what Comte put into a scientific form. It had already found its theological statement, as I have said, in Paul's account of the relation of men in the church to parts of the body and to the church as the whole. That is, he conceived of the individual as determined by society as an organism, just as there are different organs which must be conceived of as dependent on the organism as a whole. You cannot take the eye as a separate reality by itself. It has meaning only in its relationship to the whole organism of which it is a part. So you must understand an individual in a society. Instead of thinking of society made up of different entities, Comte thought of it in terms of a union of all which was an expression of a certain social nature which determined the character of the individual. There are two characteristics of Comte: first, his recognition that society as such is a subject for study; and second, his conviction that we must advance from the study of society to the individual rather than from the individual to society.

10

COOLEY'S CONTRIBUTION TO

AMERICAN SOCIAL THOUGHT

"I HAVE often thought that, in endowment, Goethe was almost the ideal sociologist, and that one who added to the more common traits his comprehension, his disinterestedness and his sense for organic unity and movement might accomplish almost anything." Cooley wrote this at almost the end of his third book, that on *Social Process*. It is indicative in a fundamental way of Cooley's conception of sociology and of the sort of mind which Cooley brought to his writings within this field. The men from whom he loves to quote are Thoreau, Emerson, Luther, Thomas à Kempis, and Charles Darwin. The style of his writing is that of Emerson, that is, the organization of his thought belonged rather to the felt unity of the structure that his thinking illuminated than to any closely knit concatenation of elements which analysis presented to thought. And Emersonian sentences stand out from his pages. For example, "The severely necessary can never be vulgar, while only nobleness can prevent the superfluous from being so."

It becomes then of peculiar importance to identify the living social reality which Cooley felt and upon which his thought throws

First published in the *American Journal of Sociology*, XXXV, No. 5, 693–706.

light. It was, indeed, the society of which he was a part and which he could enter by way of his own human nature. No one could be less self-centered than Cooley, but it was by way of the discovery of what went on in his own living with other people that he discovered the community with which the sociologist is concerned. His approach was that of objective introspection. The community that he discovered, so to speak from the inside, was a democracy, and inevitably an American democracy. I call it a discovery, for what anyone finds for himself and by his own way of search must be a discovery. Finding it in living, it was a process. Its organization was a manner of living. Its institutions were the habits of individuals. In a sense Cooley says the same thing in his three books, that is, he illuminates the same reality in different ways.

Society, then [says Cooley] in its immediate aspect, is a relation among personal ideas. In order to have a society it is evidently necessary that persons should get together somewhere, and they get together only as personal ideas in the mind. Where else? What other possible *locus* can be assigned for the real contacts of persons, or in what other form can they come in contact except as impressions or ideas formed in this common *locus?* Society exists in my mind as the contact and reciprocal influence of certain ideas named "I," Thomas, Henry, Susan, Bridget, and so on. It exists in your mind as a similar group, and so in every mind.[1]

I do not see how any one can hold that we know persons directly except as imaginative ideas in the mind.[2]

I conclude, therefore, that the imaginations wihch people have of one another are the *solid facts* of society, and that to observe and interpret these must be a chief aim of sociology.[3]

In saying this I hope I do not seem to question the independent reality of persons or to confuse it with personal ideas. The man is one thing and the various ideas entertained about him are another; but the latter, the personal idea, is the immediate social reality, the thing in which men exist for one another and work directly upon one another's lives.[4]

1   *Human Nature and the Social Order* (New York: Charles Scribner's Sons, 1902), p. 119.

2   *Ibid.*, p. 120.

3   *Ibid.*, p. 121.   4   *Ibid.*, p. 123.

We may view social consciousness either in a particular mind or as a co-operative activity of many minds. The social ideas that I have are closely connected with those that other people have, and act and react upon them to form a whole. This gives us public consciousness, or to use a more familiar term, public opinion, in the broad sense of a group state of mind which is more or less distinctly *aware of itself*. By this last phrase I mean such a mutual understanding of one another's points of view on the part of the individuals or groups concerned as naturally results from discussion. . . .

In a congenial family life, for example, there may be a public consciousness which brings all the important thoughts and feelings of members into such a living and co-operative whole. In the mind of each member, also, this same thing exists as a social consciousness embracing a vivid sense of the personal traits and modes of thought and feeling of the other members. And finally quite inseparable from all this, is one's consciousness of himself, which is directly a reflection of the ideas about himself he attributes to the others, and is directly or indirectly altogether a product of social life. . . .

There are, then, at least three aspects of consciousness which we may usefully distinguish; self-consciousness, or what I think of myself; social consciousness(in its individual aspect), or what I think of other people; and public conciousness or a collective view of the foregoing as organized in a communicative group. And all three are phases of a single whole.[5]

From these passages I think we may form a definite conception of Cooley's doctrine of society. It is an affair of consciousness, and a consciousness that is necessarily social. One's consciousness of himself is directly a reflection of the ideas about himself which he attributes to the others. Others exist in his imagination of them, and only there do they affect him, and only in the imaginations which others have of him does he affect them. These ideas differ from each other as they exist in the conscious experience of different people, but they also have cores of identical content, which in public consciousness act uniformly. This identity Cooley insists upon. It is as real as the differences. But its *locus* is found in the experience of the individuals. Furthermore its organization

[5]   *Social Organization* (New York: Charles Scribner's Sons, 1909), p. 10.

is that of the functional relations of the different members of the society, and its unity is that of organization, not that of a common stuff. As stuff it is psychical and as such the experience of different individuals. The advantage of this approach has been very considerable in the development of Cooley's social doctrine. The "other" lies in the same field as that of the "self." It can be recognized as quite as immediate as the self. The stream of consciousness is the carrier of both—the self and its society— and each can be seen to be dependent upon the other for its evolution in experience. The semimetaphysical problems of the individual and society, of egotism and altruism, of freedom and determinism, either disappear or remain in the form of different phases in the organization of a consciousness that is fundamentally social.

The self is no longer a Cartesian presupposition of consciousness. In conduct it is a precipitate about a fundamental impulse or instinct of appropriation and power, while the primary content appears as a feeling or sentiment, the self-feeling which defies further analysis. Here Cooley follows James very closely. Its development is wholly dependent upon another or others who are necessarily as immediate as the self. Being a resultant in experience, those objects, through relationship to which it emerges, cannot be dependent upon it for their existence in experience. The other cannot appear first as an experience of my own self, if my own self appears through the reaction of the individual to others. "A self-idea of this sort seems to have three principal elements: the imagination of our appearance to the other person; the imagination of his judgment of that appearance, and some sort of self-feeling, such as pride or mortification."[6] But the imagination cannot exist in experience as the imagination of a self, but must exist as an imagination within which both self and the other have their origin and development. Cooley thus leaves the "person" or the "man" as metaphysically antecedent to the self and the others. This problem is not, however, Cooley's problem. He is undertaking to locate and define the "solid facts of society," to observe and interpret which must be the chief aim of sociology.

6   *Human Nature and the Social Order*, p. 184.

Ignoring the philosophical problem does give him elbowroom. On the one hand, the organic nature of society Cooley recognizes and emphasizes, and he can present it as the physical outside, so to speak, of the social consciousness which he regards as psychical, as the organization of personal ideas, which can get together only in the mind, it should be said in the *minds* of persons or men. If one were to push the analogy, there should be a public consciousness which is the psychical counterpart of the social organism.

But Cooley draws back from such a departure from direct experience. Public consciousness is the expression of communication, discussion, and resides in the common ideas of persons, and in their organization. On the other hand, Cooley can regard the relations of selves and others in this society in terms of mental processes. Ideas have definition and reality only in their relationship to other ideas. If selves and others are ideas in people's minds, then the relation of the individual to society is as little a problem as is the relation of any idea to the group of ideas that define it. Furthermore, the goods or values that attach to any idea can only be defined in terms of the values that belong to the whole ideal structure to which the idea belongs. The beauty that belongs to your presentation of an arm of a statue could not possibly be stated apart from that of the beauty of the whole figure. The values that are the expression of an economist's theory of production cannot be presented except in terms of consumption. In the same fashion, if an individual consists of the ideas in his mind which he imagines that others entertain of him, and if the others exist as members of society as the ideas which he entertains in his imagination, it is evident that they will have common goods insofar as they are organized in his imagination into some social whole, such as a family.

That which distinguishes Luther from the vulgarly ambitious and aggressive people we know is not the quality of his self-feeling, but the fact that it was identified in his imagination and endeavors with sentiments and purposes that we look upon as noble, progressive, and right. No one could be more ambitious than he was, or more determined to secure the social aggrandizement of his self; but in his case the self for which he was ambitious and resentful consisted largely of certain convictions regarding justification by faith, the sacrilege of the sale of indulgences, and, more generally, of an enfranchising spirit and mode of thought fit to awaken and lead the aspirations of the time.[7]

In the mind this identification of the values of the individual and of the society he imagines is complete. In defining the selfish man Cooley says, "There is some essential narrowing or vulgarity of imagination which prevents him from grasping what we feel to be the true social situation, and having the sentiments which should respond to it."[8]

If you fix your attention on the individual phase of things and see life as a theatre of personal action, then the corresponding ideas of private will, responsibility, praise and blame rise before you; if you regard its total aspect you see tendency, evolution, law, and impersonal grandeur. Each of these is a half truth needed to be completed by the other; the larger truth, including both, being that life is an organic whole, presenting itself with equal reality in individual and general aspects.[9]

The fact for Cooley is that these social ideas and their organization are not presentations of a reality lying outside but the "solid facts of society." The metaphysical question as to the freedom of will of the individual apart from the social situation that exists in his imagination has no sociological meaning. So the data of the scientist's problem as they lie in his mind cannot *compel* him to present the hypothesis which his imagination evolves. He is free over against the problem. Whether his mind, dependent upon a nervous system, is compelled to think as it does in forming his hypothesis by physical and chemical causes has no bearing upon the absence of compulsion in his statement of the problem.

Mind is an organic whole made up of co-operating individualities, in somewhat the same way that the music of an orchestra is made up of divergent but related sounds. . . . When we study the social

7   *Ibid.*, p. 212.

8   *Ibid.*, p. 214.

9   *Social Organization*, p. 20.

mind, we merely fix our attention on larger aspects and relations rather than on the narrower ones of ordinary psychology.[10]

By communication is here meant the mechanism through which human relations exist and develop—all the symbols of mind, together with the means of conveying them through space and preserving them in time. . . . All these taken together, in the intricacy of their actual combination, make up an organic whole corresponding to the organic whole of human thought; and everything in the way of mental growth has an external existence therein. The more closely we consider this mechanism the more intimate will appear its relation to the inner life of mankind, and nothing will more help us to understand the latter than such consideration. . . . Without communication the mind does not develop a true human nature, but remains in an abnormal and nondescript state neither human nor properly brutal.[11]

In these passages is presented Cooley's conception of the relation of social mind to the organic structure and process of society. It is a structure and process which is particularly found in the vehicles of communication, that is, everything that interrelates the conduct of members of society, and which become therefore symbols in their minds. The structure and process are external, but they are the structure and process of a living reality, where interrelationships make possible the social mind in the individuals. Just as the conscious processes of the mind of "ordinary psychology" correspond to the living processes of the physiological individual, so the social processes of the mind answer to the living processes of society. However, there is an essential difference between the two. Our physical and biological observation presents us with the objects that make up society and its mechanisms, which can be stated and defined without recourse to a living social process. It is in fact necessary to endue these physiological and physical objects with the meanings which, for Cooley, reside in the mind before life can be breathed into the social organism. I will recur to this later, but it is of first importance to recognize the value for social psychology which flows from Cooley's finding of the solid facts of sociology in the mind.

It can be most sharply stated in Cooley's recognition that the

10   *Ibid.*, p. 7.   11   *Ibid.*, pp. 61–62.

self is not an immediate character of the mind but arises through the imagination of the ideas which others entertain of the individual, which has as its counterpart the organization of our ideas of others into their selves. It is out of this bi-polar process that social individuals appear. We do not discover others as individuals like ourselves. The mind is not first individual and then social. The mind itself in the individual arises through communication. This places Cooley's doctrine in advance of Baldwin's and Tarde's and even of James's. Tarde looked for a psychological mechanism which determined the individual through the attitudes and manners of the community, and found this in imitation. As a mechanism, imitation proves hopelessly inadequate. It becomes simply a covering term for the likeness of the characters of the individual and of the group. Baldwin sought to work out, in a so-called circular reaction that reinstated the favored impulse, a possible psychological mechanism, but without success. While James recognized early the influence of the social environment upon the individual in the formation of the personality, his psychological contribution to the social character of the self was rather in showing the spread of the self over its social environment than in the structure of the self through social interactions. The superiority of Cooley's position lies in his freedom to find in consciousness a social process going on, within which the self and the others arise. By placing both phases of this social process in the same consciousness, by regarding the self as the ideas entertained by others of the self, and the other as the ideas entertained of him by the self, the action of the others upon the self and of the self upon the others becomes simply the interaction of ideas upon each other within mind. In this process the oppositions as well as the accords can be recognized and both can be placed upon the same plane.

It is then to a process of social growth and integration, exhibited both in the individual consciousness and in society, that Cooley directs attention. The forming influence of the group takes place through the ideas which are aroused in mind, and these ideas are not primarily ideas that belong to a self. This study of the social growth of the self and the others Cooley carried out in the observation of his own children, and it was the same process which he could trace in the relation of the individual and society. It was the same social process that was going on, looked at now from the inside and now from the outside. Rivalries and conformity operating on the same level could be stated in terms of the interaction of ideas and in terms of social forces. It was Cooley's firm belief that the process was the same—the growth or decay of the social organism. He was peculiarly successful in analyzing the phase of social degeneration. He could show that unheathful social conditions reflected themselves in degenerate selves, and he could indicate the responsibility of the environment for the degeneration, at the same time recognizing the responsibility that belong to the self. He could study traits of character as they appeared in the personality and as they appeared in the social forces which these personalities embodied. He could exhibit the social habits within consciousness and in the institutions of the community. He could present the culture of the community as it informed and refined the mind of the individual and as it existed in the literature, art, and history of the nations. In general, just as Cooley, following a psychophysical psychology, recognized the same life-process exhibiting itself in the sensitivity and motor process of the organism and in the consciousness of the organism, so he could relate the social consicousness of the same individual to the social organism to which it belonged. The social process was the same. It was viewed simply from two different standpoints, from without and from within. Such a view would have been impossible if all experience is lodged in a pre-existent self that must reach other selves through conscious or subconscious inference, and if the influence which selves exercise upon each other must take place through mechanisms which operate through the physiological and psychological apparatus of "ordinary psychology." These presupposed an individual that is in its experience pre-existent, and attains acquaintance with other objects through its inner experience. Tarde and Baldwin were after all operating with such psychological mechanisms. A self that can reach other selves only through the interpretation of states of consciousness that are primarily states of itself, can never be primarily a social self, no matter how social the group may be within which as a living organism it has its being. The question then arises whether the consciousness that belongs to Cooley's "person" or "man" within which the self and the other arise can serve as the inside of the social process of which the life of society is the outside. I am not raising a metaphysical question. The question is whether the "solid facts of society" can be found in such a consciousness. I think that Cooley was Emersonian in finding the individual self in an overself, but he does not depend upon such a doctrine for his sociology. He comes back to what he calls "ordinary psychology" for his interpretation of what goes on in the mind.

I have already indicated a serious difficulty that arises if we carry over the method of psychophysical parallelism into social psychology, accepting Cooley's interpretation of psychophysical parallelism. His interpretation is that consciousness is an inside experience of the life of the external organism. In ordinary psychology this sets up a parallelism between sensations, percepts, emotions, volitions, and so forth, and physiological processes; and Cooley seems to be committed to this ordinary psychology. This implies that we can give a scientific account of the physiological process without introducing the parallel states of consciousness. But for Cooley selves and others lie inside of the consciousness of ordinary psychology, and yet they also are the "solid facts" of sociology, that is, they are the field of the external social organism. Now, I have no interest in pressing a point of logical or terminological conflict. Cooley has in a sense met such a criticism by his assurance that his parallelism connotes an outside and an inside view of the same reality, not a parallelism between states or processes in two different realms of metaphysical being. The only pertinent question is whether he succeeds in presenting adequately the "solid facts of society" by means of his apparatus of social psychology.

In the first place it follows from Cooley's lodging of the self and the others in consciousness, while he accepts the parallelism of ordinary psychology, that he cannot and does not wish to identify the self with the physical organism. Now, while Cooley

Cooley's Contribution   303

slips out of this segregation of the animal organism from social and so moral experience by merging the life-process and the social process in a universal onward evolution in which he had a profound faith, the actual effect was to take the mental organization of society as it lay in his own liberal and wholesome view as the standard by which primitive impulses must be tested. What impresses one in reading his chapter "The Social Aspects of Conscience," in *Human Nature and the Social Order*, is that it is an admirable ethical treatise rather than a scientific analysis of the situation within which lie moral judgments and the whole apparatus of impulses. The healthful social order is mental, not in the sense that there have appeared there the intellectual processes of reflection, but in the sense of a developing culture which carries all the values of society which are the standards and tests of social theory and conduct. Such a culture has a *locus* in minds. It is not true that Cooley conceived of the best culture of his time as the final culture of mankind. He recognized that it is in a constant process of evolution, but it was true that Cooley was prescribing for society insofar as it was sick in terms of processes and standards that were for the time being established in minds, which could be distinguished from what was merely physical, animal, and brutal. He did not feel it to be his primary task to state the whole of human behavior in scientific terms which would be equally applicable to primitive impulses and to the so-called higher processes and cultural expressions. It followed that the beginnings of behavioristic and Freudian psychology did not attract him or suggest new avenues of approach.

In the second place, the problem of the application of scientific method to the study of society did not interest him. The importance of statistical methods he recognized, and those of community surveys, but the question as to the form in which experience could be stated so as to be amenable to exact definition and formulation seemed to him unimportant. He rejected the economic interpretation of history, and presented his organic view of history in which all factors must be recognized as phases of a unitary life-process whose primary category was that of growth. In this sense, evolution was for Cooley the conception that brought society within the realm of science, but evolution was for him a philosophy and a faith rather than a method. He made use of primitive society to illustrate his striking conception of primary groups and their face-to-face association and cooperation, but he made no attempt after the fashion of the French school to analyze primitive mind, nor did he undertake to understand human society through its development from its earlier forms. His method was that of an introspection which recognized the mind as the *locus* of the selves that act upon each other, but the methodological problem of the objectification of this mind he pushed aside as metaphysical. His method was therefore psychological. For him society was a psychical whole.[12]

The question that this method presents is this: Does Cooley's psychological account of the self lying in the mind serve as an adequate account of the social individual in the objective life of society? The crucial point, I think, is found in Cooley's assumption that the form which the self takes in the experience of the individual is that of the imaginative ideas which he finds in his mind that others have of him. And the others are the imaginative ideas which he entertains of them. Now we do make a distinction between selves—our own and those of others—and our ideas of ourselves and of others, and we assume that these selves and our ideas of them exist in our experience. Our ideas of others and of our own selves are frequently mistaken, while we assume that the real selves were there in experience. We correct our errors and reach the genuine personalities which were there all the time. The stuff of these selves social psychologists have found in impulses, fundamental wishes, and the like, especially as these appear in crises in social experience. The question which Cooley's approach raises is whether the form of a self belongs to this level of human experience, or whether this is reached only in the imagination or idea of the other and of the self. Are selves psychical, or do they belong to an objective phase of experience which we set off against a psychical phase? I think it can be shown that selves do belong to that objective experience, which, for example, we use to test all scientific hypotheses, and which we distinguish

12   *Ibid.*, p. 31.

from our imaginations and our ideas, that is, from what we term psychical. The evidence for this is found in the fact that the human organism, in advance of the psychical experiences to which Cooley refers, assumes the attitude of another which it addresses by vocal gesture, and in this attitude addresses itself, thus giving rise to its own self and to the other.[13] In the process of communication there appears a social world of selves standing on the same level of immediate reality as that of the physical world that surrounds us. It is out of this social world that the inner experiences arise which we term psychical, and they serve largely in interpretation of this social world as psychical sensations and percepts serve to interpret the physical objects of our environment. If this is true, social groups are not psychical but are immediately given, though inner experiences are essential for their interpretation. The *locus* of society is not in the mind, in the sense in which Cooley uses the term, and the approach to it is not by introspection, though what goes on in the inner forum of our experience is essential to meaningful communication.

Whether this account of the appearance of selves be correct or not, it is evident that the acceptance by the sociologist of a society of selves in advance of inner experiences opens the door to an analysis which is behavioristic. I refer to such analyses as those of W. I. Thomas, Park and Burgess, and Faris. In many respects Cooley's analyses are of this type, but they always presuppose a certain normal social order and process as given. It is the organization and process which his introspection revealed. One misses perhaps the neutral attitude of the scientist, and one feels that the door is closed to a more profound analysis. In other words, Cooley did not find selves and society arising in primitive processes of communication, so that he could grasp their reality in early human behavior. He felt that he grasped this reality when he found them within what was for him the normal social process. His sociology was in a sense an account of the American community to which he belonged, and pre-supposed its normal healthful process. This process was that of the primary group

[13]   G. H. Mead, "The Genesis of Self and Social Control," *International Journal of Ethics*, Vol. XXXV, No. 3 (1925).

with its face-to-face organization and co-operation. Given the process, its healthful growth and its degenerations could be identified and described. Institutions and valuations were implicit within it. The gospel of Jesus and democracy were of the essence of it, and more fundamentally still it was the life of the spirit. Cooley never sought for the reality of this in the dim beginnings of human behavior.

If we can carry back the social behavior within which selves and others arise to a situation that antedates the appearance of the psychical as distinguished from an outer world, it will be to this primitive behavior that we can trace back the origins of the social patterns which are responsible not only for the structure of society but also for the criticism of that structure and for its evolution. The social pattern is always larger than the group that it makes possible. It includes the enemy and the guest and the morale of behavior toward him. Its mechanism of communication carries with it the possibility of conversation with others who are not members of the group. It has in it the implication of the logical universe of discourse. If symbolization can be stated in terms of the behavior of primitive communication, then every distinctively human being belongs to a possibly larger society than that within which he actually finds himself. It is this, indeed, which is implied in the rational character of the human animal. And these larger patterns afford a basis for the criticism of existing conditions and in an even unconscious way tend to realize themselves in social conduct. For social theory a great deal hinges upon the answer to the question whether society is itself psychical or whether the form of the psychical is a sort of communication which arises within primitive human behavior. Do the self and others lie within mind, or is mind itself, as psychical, a phase of experience that is an outgrowth of primitive human communication? Whether the question is stated in this form or not, it is evident that a great deal of recent social psychology has been occupied with an analysis of selves and their minds into more primitive forms of behavior. To this type of analysis Cooley's assumption of the psychical nature of society closes the door. And it commits him to a conception of society which is mental rather than scientific.

But I am unwilling to conclude a discussion of Cooley's social psychology upon a note of criticism. His successful establishment of the self and the others upon the same plane of reality in experience and his impressive study of society as the outgrowth of the association and co-operation of the primary group in its face-to-face organization are positive accomplishments for which we are profoundly indebted to his insight and constructive thought.

11

HENRI BERGSON

IN DISCUSSING the relationship of mind and body in Bergson's doctrine we have seen that the center of reality is to be found in the psychical experience, as he indicates in the use of the term "image." These images answer in one sense to the impressions and ideas of the empirical school. For Bergson the center of reality is the psychical experience which is revealed in intuition, as distinct from conceptual knowledge and also as distinct from the organism of the spatial world. For Bergson the category of time, as he conceives time, is closer to reality than that of space. The time to which he refers is duration, *duré*, that which appears in the inner experience, that within which there can be different types of interpenetration. This he puts in sharp contrast with the spatial world, which is external, which is the state of quantity, while the inner experience is the state of quality, which is a matter of extensive magnitude against intensive magnitude. He refuses to recognize that this intensive magnitude can be dealt with from the point of view of extensive magnitude. In Bergson's mind, concepts involve the same sort of externality which he criticized in the attempts to state our inner experience in terms of external stimulation. When we think of things in terms

---

First published in *Movements of Thought in the Nineteenth Century*, ed. Merritt H. Moore (Chicago: University of Chicago Press, 1936), pp. 503–10.

of concepts with the sharp differences of which they are capable, separating one from another, we are doing the same sort of injustice to reality as that to which I just referred in the relation of an extensive stimulation or an extensive physiological response in its relationship to the inner experience. Bergson does not say that a concept is a spatial event, but he says that it has just the same character of externality. Concepts are exclusive of each other, and that exclusiveness is almost externality. What Bergson finds in the world, especially in the biological world, is a creative process which grows out of that which has taken place but which is not itself given in that which has come before. Duration is always the happening of that which is novel. If you get a spatial statement of time, you get that which has no succession in it, at least no duration in it. Duration involves the appearance of something that was not present before.

The account which Bergson gives of this world, as against what he speaks of as a "distortion of reality," is in terms of the characters in which the organism, the mind, puts its experience. He assumes that the nature of the individual fixes the world, and fixes it in terms of the uniformities of an individual's past experience in order that he may utilize it. The mind selects out certain characters of experience on which it can depend, on which its past experience indicates it can depend, and states a world in these fixed forms. It is a pragmatic sort of procedure, a selection of characters which are relatively permanent and a statement of these in the interest of the solution of problems. The externalized world is, therefore, a fixing, a freezing, of reality in terms of certain uniformities that are applied to the world as if they dominated and expressed that reality. The mind, then, is that which within itself is psychical, and which fixes its own universe and its own organism for the purposes of conduct. The great instrument for this purpose is the central nervous system.

Bergson passes on from this sort of a statement which is in psychical terms over to a statement in biological terms in the notion of a creative evolution. Reality, insofar as it is living, is that which advances, that which changes in its own nature, that whose nature it is to change. In Bergson's sense, motion is something that goes on in the nature of the thing that is moving. It is not a mere change of position. It does not change that which is itself moving. Life is a change in the very nature of that which lives. Insofar as we are living beings, we are not at any second what we were the second before. If we undertake to state life in terms of a permanent content, we have taken the whole meaning out of life as life. There is a physical, chemical statement available, but it is applied to inanimate things. It cannot be made into a statement of life, for our conduct is from one reality to another in which that reality is always changing. That, Bergson says, identifies life with this inner nature which our intuition reveals to us. Life is in that sense a sort of mind. It has the same relationship to its environment as mind has to its world and physical organism. It is selecting, it is petrifying its world in spatial terms in the same fashion that mind does. In an account of the process of evolution he gives this statement of an onward move that is creation, that is constantly changing, producing that which was not there before, changing itself but doing it by means of the physical world. This picture we must get from the outside, from what biology presents. But we interpret the form from within, for reality lies in our own experience. In our own experience we are cutting things up into homogeneous elements. That is, we want to have the same science for tomorrow that we have today. We do not wish to have to remember in detail. Therefore, we fix our world and become familiar with it.

Evolution is a process of constructing a world that is exactly parallel, in Bergson's sense, to our perception of it. Selection is going on. Processes are continued; and in this selection that which is novel is happening, making duration possible. That takes place in our conduct too. Now, Bergson brings this over into a grand evolution in the development of life-processes. Life-forms in this fashion do just what we do in sense perception. They mobilize themselves. They maintain themselves by means of skeletons they develop, by sense organs which are produced by their environment, which bound it and analyze it into elements which can be regarded as relatively permanent. The organism does this sort of thing just as our perception builds up its field of perception and its objects. But this very world impresses life in just the way that habit impresses our own action. Man becomes the slave of his habits, of the exoskeletons which cover us. We can only see what we have habituated ourselves to see. We live in the world which is cut out by our past habits. This situation is presented from the Bergsonian standpoint on the side of evolution in its relation to an environment of organisms which have picked out that which they can eat, that which they can reach by their method of procreation, that by means of which they can avoid this danger and that. The organism has fixed itself, and it cannot go ahead. The man who is getting on in years loses the vital spark. Health is gone; he has nothing left but the fixed habits of life; he can see nothing but that which he has selected in his conduct; he has impressed himself, and there is no further advance for him; he can no longer be in a field of creation.

What I want to leave with you is a clue for the comprehension of Bergson's conception of the world—the parallelism of the perceptual process and the living process with this metaphysical assumption of process which he never fully worked out. He does not show us in any detail how the method does actually get stereotyped, nor does he show how life stereotypes its world. He appeals to the process of perception and refers us to that sort of intuition which is so difficult to get, and assumes that the same thing is taking place in the external world that is taking place from the standpoint of our inner perception. It is that to which he refers, as I have said.

Here, then, we have Bergson's solution of the problem he took over from Boutroux and Renouvier—the problem of freedom. If one accepts his statement, he has more than solved it. The only reality is this duration in which that which is novel is continually coming into being. Bergson's problem can be presented in this way. It is true that you can never previse what is going to happen. There is always a difference in what takes place and what has existed in the past. You cannot determine what you are going to be later. But the question is now: What is the relationship of means to ends? We are constantly stating the means. Bergson is correct in his position that, if we state an end in the form in which it is going to be realized, or if we state it in such form that we must stick to the account that we give of it, then we distort the thing. There is a story of James and Royce, who were out sight-seeing in a city. Royce had information of where they were going and told James what car they would take so that in the end they would get to such and such a place. They got to a junction where they had to change cars. James got on the wrong car. Royce corrected him, telling him he was on the wrong car, that the car he was on went to another point. "Yes," said James, "that is where I wanted to go." There he puts in acute form the present problem. Can we state the end of our own conduct and the end of creation; can it be stated in exact, definite form if the world is something that is moving on from that which is to that which is not? If that is the nature of reality, can the end toward which movement is to take place be stated in a conceptual form? Certainly we can say that it cannot be stated at any given time.

What Bergson overlooks in his treatment of science is that science does not undertake to make such a statement. It is continually presenting hypotheses of the world as it is, but science is a research affair and goes forward on the basis of the fact not only that the world will be intelligent but that it will always be different from any statement that science can give of it. That is, we are looking for an opportunity to restate any statement which we can give of the world. That is the implication of our research science. But that does not mean that we cannot think in conceptual terms. It means that we are always restating our restatement of the world. The same is true of our own ends and process in life. If a person could state to himself everything that is going to happen, his life would be unbearable. Life is a happening; things take place; the novel arises; and our intelligence shows itself in solving problems. But the solution of problems is by means of a definite conceptual procedure. The collapse of absolute idealism lies in the fact that everything is all accomplished in the Absolute. All that is to take place has already taken place in the Absolute. But our life is an adventure. And we can be intelligent in stating at every point the form which our conduct should take. We show our intelligence by giving as elaborate a statement of the world as we can. The realization of emergence in philosophy, the large acceptance of pluralism which you see, is involved in the assumption that the novel can appear by saying it is an enlarging of our finite imperfect experience. But there can be nothing novel in an Absolute. You can have a process of an infinite type, but it is one in which all the movements are determined. You can have contradictions, but they are always overcome. You have that which goes on; but it is going on in eternity, in an infinity in which the result is obtained already, but in which it does not appear.

It is this element that Bergson insists is involved in passage. That other statement is of a conception of the reality of the world in which everything is fixed in advance. It is its acceptance which Bergson is fighting. When you state reality in terms of a mechanism, it is an academic statement of nature. When you undertake to state your ends and problems, you fix and stereotype it. You stop advancing. Does that mean you cannot use the intelligence that enables you to get hold of means of stating the ends toward which you are moving? If this is true, Bergson's doctrine is correct, and we must draw away our intellectual control of life and give ourselves up to our impulses. But if you can state your end in terms of your means, with a definite recognition that that statement is one which you are going to change, that your life is a process of adaptation, you can have the full reign of intellectual life and the control that it gives and still not stereotype your experience.

That brings out the problem which Bergson presented in his philosophy. The problem is that involved in the opposition, if you like, the antimony, between a conceptualized statement of that which is going to take place, of that which we are going to do, and of that which does arise, that which we do do, that which takes place in nature. Is there any real duration?

If there is, there is that in which the novel is appearing. We are passing on constantly to that which is new, and our conceptual statement is in terms of the situation in which we find ourselves. How can we state that which is not? That is the Bergsonian problem in its simplest form. I have tried to present it as it appears in perception, as it appears in mechanical science, in evolution, and in terms of social progress. We are moving on, in the very nature of the case, in a process in which the past is moving into the present and into the future. Can we use our intellects to get hold of and direct this movement? Bergson says that we cannot, because in the nature of the case that toward which we are going is not here yet and, if you do not have knowledge of the end to which you are going, you cannot travel toward it intellectually. You must depend on the wind blowing behind you. You cannot reach it by conceptual means. But there is another statement which can be made over against this: that the man who is finding his way toward a goal which he cannot state can make a tentative plan as he goes along; and then he can make that better, more accurate, more complete. But he has got to be in the attitude of continually reconstructing it and restating it. We do not know what the end of society should be, but we are sure that disease and misery in its various forms should be gotten rid of. How we are going to get rid of disease we do not know. How the values that have rested in it in the past, the care for the sick, and so on, fit in with the conception of a place where there will be no suffering we do not know. But we are stating in our conceptual way what the end is to be, and then we test our steps and restate it. What Bergson denies is the possibility of advancing by a set of hypotheses which are being continually reconstructed if they do not hold—hypotheses which are confessedly hypothetical. We have only the statement which we can give at the time, hypotheses which are open to unexpected happenings and which are ready for reconstruction, hypotheses that belong to a world in which things are going on, in which there is duration. What Bergson says is that this sort of intelligent control of our conduct and intelligent control over our comprehension of and appreciation of nature in the direction of the movements in society is impossible. He refuses that because any statement that is made at this time would be an absurd statement of what is going to be later. If we had to conduct the world by the hypotheses of the seventeenth century, we would not get along. They undertook to state the world as they gave it in conceptual terms. But that did not interfere with a continued restatement of them. The scientist is always ready to reconstruct, and it is by means of such refined statement that he gets ahead. If, of course, science had undertaken to give infallibility to any statement that it had and refused to reconstruct that statement, it would have been in a prison. But a restatement at every point possible is what science wants. Thus, Bergson's attack upon science represents a misconception of its method and ideal. His flight to irrationalism is unnecessary.

Part IX

12

HISTORY AND THE

EXPERIMENTAL METHOD

HISTORY has enrolled itself among the sciences that make use of the experimental or observational method, that is, the historian professes to be ready to approach the solution of any problems that appear within his field in terms of scientific method. If he finds that some of his material belongs to the fields where the scientific method is not welcomed, he is likely to undertake to free his own problem of the reconstruction of past events from these other issues and attempt to keep within his own field a clean scientific conscience. That this has proved again and again an impossible program is abundantly shown in fields of higher criticism and evolution. In fact, it has been the history of dogmas that has brought more than one metaphysical problem into the range of scientific investigation. The scientific treatment of religious institutions, beliefs, and experiences has arisen in each case out of the history of these subjects. Given an orderly statement of the situations out of which these have arisen, it is impossible to avoid the hypothesis of the causal relation of these conditions to the appearance of the institutions and beliefs, and the testing of this hypothesis is found in the

First published in *The Philosophy of the Act*, ed. Charles W. Morris (Chicago: University of Chicago Press, 1938), pp. 92–100.

observation of the changes which it undergoes in the presence of like conditions.

Scientific method in history has a direct bearing on one question which I should like to discuss. Does the significance of the results of historical investigation and consequent reconstruction belong to the past where these events lie, or is it to be found in the present and future? Otherwise stated, do we know the past through the present, and the future insofar as the test of our hypotheses depends upon future observation and discovery, or is the knowledge we are gaining knowledge of the present and future through the past? A present fossil implies a past animal, a present document a past author. The knowledge of either waits upon future investigation and observation, perhaps even upon experiment. History as an observational science can get at its past only through the present and future. But scientific investigation does not end in its data; it begins with it. The outcome of science is a theory or working hypothesis, not so-called facts. It is not the recovery of the dream we seek but the interpretation thereof. Is the serious interest in history, which is not the meanest of the attainments of an educated mind, an interest that centers in the past, in the present, or in the future? Have we learned to understand the past through the present, or are we learning to understand the present and future through the past?

The first comment that will be made upon this question is, Why this disjunction? Why not both? Certainly history provides the candle to light our feet as we advance, but on the other hand, our very advance may be into a fuller, richer, and more significant past, where we may dwell contentedly, using the present only as the soil within which may be found the data for its reconstruction, and the vantage point for its interpretation and romantic enjoyment, and the field of interesting controversies with rival historians.

> Much have I travelled in the realms of gold,
> And many goodly states and kingdoms seen;
> Round many western islands have I been
> Which bards in fealty to Apollo hold.

Certainly the historical scholar and those who are privileged to see the resplendent past through the medium of trained vision and sympathetic imagination are not disjunctively bound either to the strategic use of its treasures in fighting society's advancing campaigns or to an irrevocable domicile in its pictured realms. Or shall we say of the historically minded, *vestigia nulla retrorsum?* The answer is in the negative. Not only do we find the historically minded dwelling comfortably on both horns of the spurious dilemma, but the forward impulse gathers momentum from the concreting past, while its very furniture, tapestries, and personae are created in the factories of ongoing experience. The histories that have most fastened upon men's minds have been political and cultural propaganda, and every great social movement has flashed back its light to discover a new past.

But the question I have asked is somewhat more hidden and technical than that which has just been answered. Is the actual object of knowledge, the significant content which historical research reveals, the past object as implied in the present, or is it a newly discovered present which can only be known and interpreted in the past which it involves? My own answer, which I do not expect to find sympathetically received, is the latter; still I would like to present it.

The answer turns, as I have indicated, more or less upon the identification of knowledge with scientific research. If knowledge is the mere presence of an object in experience, if these walls and windows, these chairs and lights, and the people in the room, are, by grace of their being perceptually related to us, objects of our knowledge, then the person whom you discover to have written the hitherto anonymous document is, where he was and when he was, the object of your knowledge. You have simply by means of scientific research extended your specious present so that this formerly unrecognizable individual has been drawn out of the shadows, and, in this novel temporal perspective, he becomes one more figure in the world. His being there in your perspective is your knowledge of him. This definition of knowledge, this identification of the object of knowledge with the so-called percept, whether a percept by virtue of the eye or the imagination, in company with various other pragmatists I reject—and for reasons with which I will not burden you, though I will point out that the rejection sweeps out a vast amount of philosophic riffraff known as epistemology, and relieves one of the hopeless task of bridge-building from a world of one's states of consciousness to an outside world that can never be reached.

Knowledge, I conceive, is the discovery through the implication of things and events of some thing or things which enable us to carry on when a problem had held us up. It is the fact that we can carry on that guarantees our knowledge.

I should like to adduce that this view is the only doctrine that justifies the feeling of assurance in knowledge. We cannot find justification in a permanent and irrefragable past. Each generation and often different minds within a generation have discovered different pasts. And these pasts are not only different because they have become more spacious and richer in detail. They have become essentially different in their fundamental significance. We speak of the past as final and irrevocable. There is nothing that is less so, when we consider it as the pictured extension which each generation has spread behind itself. One past displaces and abrogates another as inexorably as the rising generation buries the old. How many different Caesars have crossed the Rubicon since 1800? But, you say, there must be identical events in each, else the new past could not displace the old and occupy its field. Yes, there are coincidences of events that are relatively permanent and which make possible translation from one historic account to another. But coincidences of events are not the objects of our knowledge. Through centuries the Mesopotamian magicians recorded the dim eclipses that disastrous twilight shed on half the nations and, with fear of change, perplexed their monarchs. The clever Greeks took over their Great Saros but saw planetary bodies interposed through the revolution of heavenly spheres about the central stable earth. Copernicus, more successful than his Greek prototype Aristarchus, with the hand of Joshua stayed the sun in the heavens and dispatched the earth with her satellite in an orbit about the sun to cast the stellar shadows that are no longer ominous; and now it is a matter of indifference to the relativist whether earth or sun revolve to bring about these eclipses. The Mesopotamian recognized fantastic gods in hostile chase; the Greek, incorruptible spheres within spheres. Since the Renaissance the Western world has known inert masses moving through an indifferent space according to Newtonian laws. I am quite incompetent to paraphrase stellar history in an Einsteinian world, nor has eye seen or ear heard what new heavens and new earth will in another fifty or a hundred years displace ours in the history that that generation will write of its habitat. In all the histories, there were certain coincidences that ran through all and make a thread on which all can be strung in the history of histories. But, whatever else they may be, these coincidences are but abstractions from the objects of our knowledge. They are not the past that interprets our present.

No scientist secure in his experimental method would base that security upon the agreement of its results with the structure of any changeless past that is within his ken. Indeed, if the past were fixed, there could be no more progress in knowledge, for every discovery refashions that past *pari passu* with the present.

Otherwise stated, the past is a working hypothesis that has validity in the present within which it works but has no other validity. However, the question of validity does not arise at all, except in the presence of some problem. It is only then that we undertake to discover the solution to the problem and assure ourselves of its validity by experiment or observation in some crucial instance if possible. And then we say that we know. We act with reference to whatever fits into the world that is there (as we do with reference to the world that is there, so far as experience is concerned) until in conduct we find that it is not there; and then we have a problem on our hands and have to find out what is there—a problem of inference, of implication, and of knowledge.

That sort of knowledge belongs to the present and the future that tests the hypothetical present. It does not belong to the past, that is, it does not find its significance in the past. Here again we have to distinguish between significance for knowledge and the significance that belongs, for example, to a drama. There is significance in President Wilson's fight for the League of Nations that has a timeless significance like that of an Ibsen tragedy. The significance of the planetesimal hypothesis does not lie in the past aeons in which we assume its operation but in our present use of it in stating a going universe. With new data it will be modified or laid aside. At present it is presumably truer than any other hypothesis. The past that is there for us, as the present is there, stands on the same basis as the world that is there about us. The past that has to be found out, to be inferred, is appealing for its significance to our present undertaking of interpreting our world, so that it will be intelligible for present conduct and estimation.

The long and short of it is that the only reality of the past open to our reflective research is the implication of the present, that the only reason for research into the past is the present problem of understanding a problematic world, and the only test of the truth of what we have discovered is our ability to so state the past that we can continue the conduct whose inhibition has set the problem to us.

Now this assumption of the pragmatist that the individual only thinks in order that he may continue an interrupted action, that the criterion of the correctness of his thinking is found in his ability to carry on, and that the significant goal of his thinking or research is found not in the ordered presentation of the subject matter of his research but in the uses to which it may be put, is very offensive to many people, and, I am afraid, particularly so to the historian. Pragmatism is regarded as a pseudo-philosophic formulation of that most obnoxious American trait, the worship of success; as the endowment of the four-flusher with a faked philosophic passport; as the contemptuous swagger of a glib and restless upstart in the company of the mighty but reverent spirits worshiping at the shrine of subsistent entities and timeless truth; as a blackleg pacemaker introduced into the leisurely workshop of the spirit to speed up the processes of thinking *sub specie aeternitatis;* as a Ford efficiency engineer bent on the mass production of philosophical tin lizzies. These disparagements are all boomerangs, but I will not constitute this a clinic in which to demonstrate the contusions which those who have hurled them have suffered, but will address myself to the single charge that this philosophy would dispossess men of the leisured contemplation and enjoyment of the past.

First of all, pragmatism holds no brief against aesthetic experience. It is an activity to be acknowledged like all other human activities, and like these it faces its own problems, those of appreciation, and solves them by reflection. When by reflection have been reconstructed the landscapes of that mighty world of eye and ear, or of the confused pageants of the past, the spirit enters into its enjoyment with the sense

> Of something far more deeply interfused,
> Whose dwelling is the light of setting suns,
> And the round ocean and the living air,
> And the blue sky, and in the mind of man.

But beside the literary historian, whose works are as precious as are those of the great dramatists and architects, there is the dry-as-dust, or as he is called today, the scientific, historian. His criterion may not be aesthetic, at least not until he has satisfied his scientific conscience. His task is the scrupulous determination of facts, the formation of hypotheses and the testing of them by the data within the reach of his investigation. But facts are not there to be picked up. They have to be dissected out, and data are the most difficult of abstractions in any field. More particularly, their very form is dependent upon the problem within which they lie. There is, of course, a vast amount of machinery involved in the storing, cataloguing, and analyzing of unbound material, pertinent and impertinent, but the working of this machinery does not constitute the work of the historian. It is but his apparatus.

It is, after all, in the problem that he finds the definition of his data and in its solution the test of his sufficiency. Have those problems any other residence than in the need to better comprehend the society of which we are a part, and is the comprehension of that society anything but the considerate effort to face conduct in that society intelligently? I do not think so. I think we overlook the intricate organization of the republic of letters to which we belong. A man picks up a problem and calls it his, with perhaps slight appreciation that he is taking up a task which arises out of the conflict of insistent social processes, for the solution of which he has volunteered. He makes it his own, but he did not originate it. The academic attitude of creating problems for Doctor's theses is not favorable to the just realization of what problems are when they are genuine. And then the man who has taken up the assignment naturally magnifies his office. He looks at the results of his labors *sub specie aeternitatis* because he does not see just what part of the whole job his has been. It requires the detached attitude of a later day to see the fruit of his efforts combined with that of many others in a shift of the community's attitude toward the incompetency of its institutions.

Now the past that is thus constituted is a perspective, and what will be seen in that perspective, and what will be the relations between its elements, depends upon the point of reference. If we wish to regard it metaphysically, there are an infinite number of possible perspectives, each of which will give a different definition to the parts and reveal different relations among them. Which of these particular perspectives is the right one, metaphysically? There is no answer to the question, except a mystical engulfing of all the perspectives and ourselves with them in the Absolute. But the Absolute answers no queries. It provides emotional aspirations at the price of intellectual immolation.

This particular perspective is there, thanks to the particular problem of social reconstruction that is going on, and with the change in the situation all of its features will have suffered a transformation, and the landscape will melt into other contours as they do for the eye of him who ascends a mountain. Its significance is eternally fixed in the eternally passing and creative present. The most that we can do is to find the constants of coincident events, in themselves bloodless abstractions, by which to translate from one consentient set to another, to use the jargon of the relativist.

I do not think that this standpoint abrogates from the potency or impressiveness of the past or relaxes the sinews of the historian, unless it be from the standpoint of the lotus-eater for whom

> All things are taken from us and become portions and parcels
> of the dreadful past.
> Looking over wasted lands,
> Blight and famine, plague and earthquake, roaring deeps and
> fiery sands,
> Clanging fights and flaming towns, and sinking ships and
> praying hands.

The past is impressive as it emerges into that form and structure which gives solidity and significance to the hasting and evanescent present.

13

TIME

WHAT do we mean, now, by the statement that there has been some real past with all its events, in independence of any present, whose contents we are slowly and imperfectly deciphering? We come back of course to the very corrections which we make in our historical research, and to the higher degree of evidence of that which has been discovered over that which can be offered for the discarded account. Higher degrees of probability and added evidence imply that there is or has been some reality there which we are bringing to light. There is thus a palpable reference to the unquestioned past by means of whose evidence we investigate and solve the problems that arise. And the very fact to which I have referred, that any accepted account of the past, though not now in question, may be conceivably thrown into doubt, seems to imply some unquestionable past which would be the background for the solution of all conceivable problems. Let us admit this for the time being, and ask the further question whether this past independent of any present does enter at all into our investigations—I mean as a presupposition that plays any part in our thinking? If we should take away this presupposition, would our apparatus and the operation of it in histori-

First published in *The Philosophy of the Present,* ed. Arthur E. Murphy (LaSalle, Ill.: Open Court Publishing Co., 1932, 1959), pp. 6–177, except the last segment, reprinted from an article in The International Journal of Ethics (1925).

cal research be in any way affected? Certainly not, if we concern
ourselves only with the problems with which historians in social
or scientific history are concerned. Here the reference is always
and solely to the given past out of which a problem has arisen;
and the outlines of the problem and the tests to which presented
hypotheses are subjected, are found in the given past. As we have
seen, this given past may itself at a later date be affected with
doubt and brought under discussion. And yet the possible dubiety
of the given past in no way affects the undertaking. This is another way of saying that the dubiety of all possible pasts never
enters into the historian's thinking. The only approach to such
entrance is the demand that all past pasts should be accounted
for and taken up into the latest statement. And every past past,
insofar as it is reconstructed, is insofar shown to be incorrect.
In the implications of our method we seem to approach a limiting statement, even if at infinity, which would fill out all gaps
and correct all errors. But if we are making corrections there
must seemingly be some account that is correct, and even if we
contemplate an indefinite future of research science which will
be engaged in the undertaking, we never escape from this implication.

There is another way of saying this, and that is that our
research work is that of discovery, and we can only discover
what is there whether we discover it or not. I think however that
this last statement is in error, if it is supposed to imply that
there is or has been a past which is independent of all presents,
for there may be and beyond doubt is in any present with its
own past a vast deal which we do not discover, and yet this
which we do or do not discover will take on different meaning
and be different in its structure as an event when viewed from
some later standpoint. Is there a similar error in the conception
of correction of the past error and in the suggestion that it implies the absolutely correct, even if it never reaches it? I am
referring to the "in-itself" correctness of an account of events,
implied in a correction which a later historian makes. I think
that the absolute correctness which lies back in the historian's
mind would be found to be the complete presentation of the

given past, if all its implications were worked out. If we could know everything implied in our memories, our documents, and our monuments, and were able to control all this knowledge, the historian would assume that he had what was absolutely correct. But a historian of the time of Aristotle, extending thus his known past, would have reached a correct past which would be at utter variance with the known world of modern science, and there are only degrees of variance between such a comparison and those which changes due to research are bringing out in our pasts from year to year. If we are referring to any other "in-itself" correctness, it must be either to that of a reality which by definition could never get into our experience or to that of a goal at infinity in which the type of experience in which we find ourselves ceases. It is, of course, possible to assume that the experience within which we find ourselves is included in some world or experience that transcends it. My only point is that such an assumption plays no part in our judgments of the correctness of the past. We may have other reasons, theological or metaphysical, for assuming a real past that could be given in a presentation independent of any present, but that assumption does not enter into the postulations or technique of any sort of historical research.

While the conception of an "in-itself" irrevocable past is perhaps the common background of thinking, it is interesting to recur to the statement that I made earlier that the research scientist looks forward, not only with equanimity, but also with excited interest to the fundamental changes which later research will bring into the most exact determinations which we can make today. The picture which this offers is that of presents sliding into each other, each with a past which is referable to itself, each past taking up into itself those back of it, and in some degree reconstructing them from its own standpoint. The moment that we take these earlier presents as existences apart from the presentation of them as pasts, they cease to have meaning to us and lose any value they may have in interpreting our own present and determining our futures. They may be located in the geometry of Minkowski space-time, but even under that assumption, they can reach us only through our own frames of reference or perspectives; and the same would be true under the assumptions of any other metaphysics which located the reality of the past in pasts independent of any present.

It would probably be stated that the irrevocability of the past is located in such a metaphysical order, and that is the point which I wish to discuss. The historian does not doubt that something has happened. He is in doubt as to what has happened. He also proceeds upon the assumption that if he could have all the facts or data, he could determine what it was that happened. That is, his idea of irrevocability attaches, as I have already stated, to the "what" that has happened as well as to the passing of the event. But if there is emergence, the reflection of this into the past at once takes place. There is a new past, for from every new rise the landscape that stretches behind us becomes a different landscape. The analogy is faulty, because the heights are there, and the aspects of the landscapes which they reveal are also there and could be reconstructed from the present of the wayfarer if he had all the implications of his present before him; whereas the emergent is not there in advance, and by definition could not be brought within even the fullest presentation of the present. The metaphysical reality suggested by Eddington's phrase that our experience is an adventuring of the mind into the ordered Geometry of space-time[1] would, however, correspond to a pre-existent landscape.

* * *

If, in Bergson's phrase, "real duration" becomes time through the appearance of unique events which are distinguishable from each other through their qualitative nature, a something that is emergent in each event, then bare passage is a manner of arranging these events. But what is essential to this arrangement is that in each interval which is isolated, it must be possible that something should become, that something unique should arise. We are subject to a psychological illusion if we assume that the rhythm of counting and the order which arises out of

[1]   *Space, Time, and Gravitation*, p. 51.

counting answer to a structure of passage itself, apart from the processes which fall into orders through the emergence of events. We never reach the interval itself between events, except in correlations between them and other situations within which we find congruence and replacement, something that can never take place in passage as such. We reach what may be called a functional equality of represented intervals within processes involving balance and rhythm, but on this basis to set up time as a quantity having an essential nature that allows of its being divided into equal portions of itself is an unwarranted use of abstraction. We can hypothetically reconstruct the past processes that are involved in what is going on as a basis for the cognitive construction of the future which is arising. What we are assured of by the experimental data is that we comprehend that which is going on sufficiently to predict what will take place, not that we have attained a correct picture of the past independent of any present, for we expect this picture to change as new events emerge. In this attitude we are relating in our anticipation presents that slip into others, and their pasts belong to them. They have to be reconstructed as they are taken up into a new present and as such they belong to that present, and no longer to the present out of which we have passed into the present present.

A present then, as contrasted with the abstraction of mere passage, is not a piece cut out anywhere from the temporal dimension of uniformly passing reality. Its chief reference is to the emergent event, that is, to the occurrence of something which is more than the processes that have led up to it and which by its change, continuance, or disappearance, adds to later passages a content they would not otherwise have possessed. The mark of passage without emergent events is its formulation in equations in which the so-called instances disappear in an identity, as Meyerson has pointed out.[2]

Given an emergent event, its relations to antecedent processes become conditions or causes. Such a situation is a present. It marks out and in a sense selects what has made its peculiarity possible. It creates with its uniqueness a past and a future. As

[2]   *Identity and Reality, passim.*

soon as we view it, it becomes a history and a prophecy. Its own temporal diameter varies with the extent of the event. There may be a history of the physical universe as an appearance of a galaxy of galaxies. There is a history of every object that is unique. But there would be no such history of the physical universe until the galaxy appeared, and it would continue only so long as the galaxy maintained itself against disruptive and cohesive forces. When we ask what can be the "temporal spread" of the uniqueness which is responsible for a present the answer must be, in Whitehead's terms, that it is a period long enough to enable the object to be what it is. But the question is ambiguous for the term "temporal spread" implies a measure of time. The past as it appears with the present and future, is the relation of the emergent event to the situation out of which it arose, and it is the event that defines that situation. The continuance or disappearance of that which arises is the present passing into the future. Past, present, and future belong to a passage which attains temporal structure through the event, and they may be considered long or short as they are compared with other such passages. But as existing in nature, so far as such a statement has significance, the past and the future are the boundaries of what we term the present, and are determined by the conditioning relationships of the event to its situation.

The pasts and futures to which we refer extend beyond these contiguous relations in passage. We extend them out in memory and history, in anticipation and forecast. They are pre-eminently the field of ideation, and find their locus in what is called mind. While they are in the present, they refer to that which is not in that present, as is indicated by their relation to past and future. They refer beyond themselves, and out of this reference arises their representational nature. They evidently belong to organisms, that is to emergent events whose nature involves the tendency to maintain themselves. In other words, their situation involves adjustment looking toward a past, and selective sensitivity looking toward a future. What may be called the stuff out of which ideas arise are the attitudes of these organisms, habits when we look toward the past, and early adjustments within the act to the results of their responses when we look toward the future. So far these belong to what may be termed the immediate past and future.

This relation of the event to its situation, of the organism to its environment, with their mutual dependence, brings us to relativity and to the perspectives in which this appears in experience. The nature of environment answers to the habits and selective attitudes of organisms, and the qualities that belong to the objects of the environment can only be expressed in terms of sensitivities of these organisms. And the same is true of ideas. The organism, through its habits and anticipatory attitudes, finds itself related to what extends beyond its immediate present. Those characters of things which in the activity of the organism refer to what lies beyond the present take on the value of that to which they refer. The field of mind, then, is the larger environment which the activity of the organism calls for but which transcends the present. What is present in the organism, however, is its own nascent activity, and that in itself and in the environment which sustains it, and there is present also its movement from the past and beyond the present. It belongs to the so-called conscious organism to complete this larger temporal environment by the use of characters found in the present. The mechanism by which the social mind accomplishes this I will discuss later; what I wish to bring out now is that the field of mind is the temporal extension of the environment of the organism, and that an idea resides in the organism because the organism is using that in itself which moves beyond its present to take the place of that toward which its own activity is tending. That in the organism which provides the occasion for mind is the activity which reaches beyond the present within which the organism exists.

*　　*　　*

Durations are a continual sliding of presents into each other.[3] The present is a passage constituted by processes whose earlier

---

[3]　These pages were found among Mr. Mead's papers after his death. They seem to have been written later, possibly as a result of a critical discussion of the above ideas at the University of Chicago Philosophy Club meeting in January 1931.

phases determine in certain respects their later phases. Reality then is always in a present. When the present has passed, it no longer is. The question arises whether the past arising in memory and in the projection of this still further backwards, refers to events which existed as such continuous presents passing into each other, or to that conditioning phase of the passing present which enables us to determine conduct with reference to the future which is also arising in the present. It is this latter thesis which I am maintaining.

The implication of my position is that the past is such a construction that the reference that is found in it is not to events having a reality independent of the present which is the seat of reality, but rather to such an interpretation of the present in its conditioning passage as will enable intelligent conduct to proceed. It is, of course, evident that the materials out of which that past is constructed lie in the present. I refer to the memory images and the evidences by which we build up the past, and to the fact that any reinterpretation of the picture we form of the past will be found in a present, and will be judged by the logical and evidential characters which such data possess in a present. It is also evident that there is no appeal from these in their locus of a present to a real past which lies like a scroll behind us, and to which we may recur to check up on our constructions. We are not deciphering a manuscript whose passages can be made intelligible in themselves and left as secure presentations of that portion of what has gone before, to be supplemented by later final constructions of other passages. We are not contemplating an ultimate unchangeable past that may be spread behind us in its entirety subject to no further change. Our reconstructions of the past vary in their extensiveness, but they never contemplate the finality of their findings. They are always subject to conceivable reformulations, on the discovery of later evidence, and this reformulation may be complete. Even the most vivid of memory images can be in error. In a word our assurances concerning the past are never attained by a congruence between the constructed past and a real past independent of this construction, though we carry this attitude at the back of our heads, because we do bring our immediate hypothetical reconstructions to the test of the accepted past and adjudge them by their agreement with the accepted record; but this accepted past lies in a present and is subject, itself, to possible reconstruction.

Now it is possible to accept all this, with a full admission that no item in the accepted past is final, and yet to maintain that, there remains a reference in our formulation of the past event to a something that happened which we can never expect to resuscitate in the content of reality, something that belonged to the event in the present within which it occurred. This amounts to saying that there is behind us a scroll of elapsed presents, to which our constructions of the past refer, though without the possibility of ever reaching it, and without the anticipation that our continual reconstructions will approach it with increasing exactness. And this brings me to the point at issue. Such a scroll, if attained, is not the account that our pasts desiderate. If we could bring back the present that has elapsed in the reality which belonged to it, it would not serve us. It would be that present and would lack just that character which we demand in the past, that is, that construction of the conditioning nature of now present passage which enables us to interpret what is arising in the future that belongs to this present. When one recalls his boyhood days, he cannot get into them as he then was, without their relationship to what he has become; and if he could, that is if he could reproduce the experience as it then took place, he could not use it, for this would involve his not being in the present within which that use must take place. A string of presents conceivably existing as presents would never constitute a past. If then there is such a reference, it is not to an entity which could fit into any past, and I cannot believe that the reference, in the past as experienced, is to a something which would not have the function or value that in our experience belongs to a past. We are not referring to a real past event which would not be the past event we are seeking. Another way of saying this is that our pasts are always mental in the same manner in which the futures that lie in our imaginations ahead of us are mental. They differ, apart from their successive positions, in that the determining conditions of interpretation and conduct are embodied in the past as that is found in the present, but they are subject to the same test of validity to which our hypothetical futures are subject. And the novelty of every future demands a novel past.

This, however, overlooks one important character of any past, and that is that no past which we can construct can be as adequate as the situation demands. There is always a reference to a past which cannot be reached, and one that is still consonant with the function and import of a past. It is always conceivable that the implications of the present should be carried further than we do actually carry them, and further than we can possibly carry them. There is always more knowledge which would be desirable for the solution of any problem confronting us but which we cannot attain. With the conceivable attainment of this knowledge, we should undoubtedly construct a past truer to the present within which the implications of this past lie. And it is to this past that there is always a reference within every past which imperfectly presents itself to our investigation. If we had every possible document and every possible monument from the period of Julius Caesar, we should unquestionably have a truer picture of the man and of what occurred in his lifetime, but it would be a truth which belongs to this present, and a later present would reconstruct it from the standpoint of its own emergent nature. We can then conceive of a past which in any one present would be irrefragable. So far as that present was concerned it would be a final past, and when we consider the matter, I think that it is this past to which the reference lies in that which goes beyond the statement which the historian can give, and which we are apt to assume to be a past independent of the present.

*   *   *

I have spoken of the present as the seat of reality because its character of a present sheds light upon the nature of reality. The past and the future that appear in the present can be regarded as merely the thresholds of a minute bit of an unbounded extension whose metaphysical reality reduces the present to a negligible element that approaches the world at an instant. This view of reality as an infinite scroll unrolling in snatches before our intermittent vision receives another variant in the picture of reality as a four-dimensional continuum of space-time, of events and intervals, forever determined by its own geometry, and into which we venture with our own subjective frames of reference, receiving momentary impressions whose present character are a function of our minds and not of any section of the ordered events in the universe. I have suggested that such an approach to reality does not answer to the scientific technique and method by which we seek for disclosures of the universe. Scientific procedure fastens upon that necessary conditioning of what takes place by what has taken place which follows from passage itself. In space-time relations, that is, in motion, this conditioning may reach the certainty of deduction, though even here we stand before the possibility that our conclusions may often rest upon statistical results which negate the final determination which we seek. There is evidence that the very effort to refine the technique to absolute precision defeats itself. Then there is the other branch of this determination of passage which we refer to under the caption of probability. Whatever our doctrine of probability, we assume that the happening of earlier events carries with it a probability as to the nature of later events, even if this probability can be reckoned only on a theory of chances. The basis of this determination of the future by the past is found in the fact that something is taking place which has a temporal spread—that reality cannot be reduced to instants—and that earlier stages must be conditions of later phases. It is the undertaking of science to find out what it is that is going on.

Furthermore the study of passage involves the discovery of events. These cannot be simply parts of passage. These events have always characters of uniqueness. Time can only arise through the ordering of passage by these unique events. The scientist finds such events in his observations and experiments. The relation of any event to the conditions under which it occurs is what we term causation. The relation of the event to its preceding conditions at once sets up a history, and the uniqueness of the event makes that history relative to that event. The conditioning passage and the appearance of the unique event then give rise to past and future as they appear in a present. All of the past is in the present as the conditioning nature of passage, and all the future arises out of the present as the unique events that transpire. To unravel this existent past in the present and on the basis of it to previse the future is the task of science. The method is that of ideation.

* * *

The social nature of the present arises out of its emergence. I am referring to the process of readjustment that emergence involves. Nature takes on new characters, for example with the appearance of life, or the stellar system takes on new characters with the loss of mass by the collapse of atoms through the processes that go on within a star. There is an adjustment to this new situation. The new objects enter into relationship with the old. The determining conditions of passage set the conditions under which they survive, and the old objects enter into new relations with what has arisen. I am here using the term "social" with reference not to the new system, but to the process of readjustment. An outstanding illustration is found in ecology. There is an answer in the community in the meadow or the forest to the entrance of any new form, if that form can survive. When the new form has established its citizenship, the botanist can exhibit the mutual adjustments that have taken place. The world has become a different world because of the advent, but to identify sociality with this result is to identify it with system merely. It is rather the stage betwixt and between the old system and the new that I am referring to. If emergence is a feature of reality, this phase of adjustment, which comes between the ordered universe before the emergent has arisen and that after it has come to terms with the newcomer, must be a feature also of reality. It can be illustrated in the appearance of a planet upon the hypothetical approach of the stellar visitor that occasioned the origin of our planetary system. There was a period at which the substance of our own earth was part of the sun's revolving outer sheath. Now it is a body separated from the stellar mass, still revolving, but in its own orbit. The fact that the planet is exhibiting the same momentum in its distant orbit as that which carried it about the star before its advent as a planet, does not do away with the fact that there is now a planetary system where here was formerly only a single stellar body, nor with that stage in which the substance of the planet to be was in both systems. Now what we are accustomed to call social is only a so-called consciousness of such a process, but the process is not identical with the consciousness of it, for that is an awareness of the situation. The social situation must be there if there is to be consciousness of it.

* * *

I wish to make as emphatic as possible the reference of pasts and futures to the activity that is central to the present. Ideation extends spatially and temporally the field within which activity takes place. The presents, then, within which we live are provided with margins, and fitting them into a larger independent chronicle is again a matter of some more extended present which calls for a wider horizon. But the widest horizon belongs to some undertaking, whose past and future refer back to it. For instance, the present history of the sun is relevant to the undertaking of unraveling the atom and, given another analysis of the atom, the sun will have another history and the universe will be launched into a new future. The pasts and the futures are implications of what is being undertaken and carried out in our laboratories.

* * *

It is evident that a statement of the life of each individual in terms of the results of an analysis of that which is immediately experienced would offer a common plane of events, in which the experience of each would differ from the experiences of others only in their extent, and the completeness or incompleteness of their connections. These differences disappear in the generalized formulations of the social sciences. The experiences of the same individuals, insofar as each faces a world in which objects are plans of action, would implicate in each a different succession of events. In the simplest illustration, two persons approach a passing automobile. To one it is a moving object that he will pass before it reaches the portion of the street that is the meeting-place of their two paths. The other sees an object that will pass this meeting-point before he reaches it. Each slices the world from the standpoint of a different time system. Objects which in a thousand ways are identical for the two individuals, are yet fundamentally different through their location in one spatio-temporal plane, involving a certain succession of events, or in another. Eliminate the temporal dimension, and bring all events back to an instant that is timeless, and the individuality of these objects which belongs to them in behavior is lost, except insofar as they can represent the results of past conduct. But taking time seriously, we realize that the seemingly timeless character of our spatial world and its permanent objects is due to the consentient set which each one of us selects. We abstract time from this space for the purposes of our conduct. Certain objects cease to be events, cease to pass as they are in reality passing and in their permanence become the conditions of our action, and events take place with reference to them. Because a whole community selects the same consentient set does not make the selection less the attitude of each one of them. The life-process takes place in individual organisms, so that the psychology which studies that process in its creative determining function becomes a science of the objective world.

14

THE OBJECTIVE REALITY

OF PERSPECTIVES

THE grandiose undertaking of Absolute Idealism to bring the whole of reality within experience failed. It failed because it left the perspective of the finite ego hopelessly infected with subjectivity, and consequently unreal. From its point of view, the theoretical and practical life of the individual had no part in the creative advance of nature. It failed also because scientific method, with its achievements of discovery and invention, could find no adequate statement in its dialectic. It recognized the two dominant forces of modern life, the creative individual and creative science, only to abrogate them as falsifications of the experience of the absolute ego. The task remained unfulfilled, the task of restoring to nature the characters and qualities which a metaphysics of mind and a science of matter and motion had concurred in relegating to consciousness, and of finding such a place for mind in nature that nature could appear in experience. A constructive restatement of the problem was presented by a physiological and experimental psychology that fastened mind

---

Published in the *Philosophy of the Present,* ed. Arthur E. Murphy (LaSalle, Ill.: Open Court Publishing Co., 1932, 1959), pp. 161–75. First published in the Proceedings of the Sixth International Congress of Philosophy.

inextricably in an organic nature which both science and philosophy recognized. The dividend which philosophy declared upon this restatement is indicated in William James's reasoned query, "Does Consciousness exist?" The metaphysical assault upon the dualism of mind and nature, that has been becoming every day more intolerable, has been made in regular formation by Bergson's evolutionary philosophy, by neo-idealism, by neo-realism, and by pragmatism. And no one can say, as yet, that the position has been successfully carried.

I wish to call attention to two unconnected movements which seem to me to be approaching a strategic position of great importance—which may be called the objectivity of perspectives. These two movements are, first, that phase of behavioristic psychology which is planting communication, thinking, and substantive meanings as inextricably within nature as biological psychology has placed general animal and human intelligence; and second, an aspect of the philosophy of relativism which Professor Whitehead has presented.

Professor Whitehead interprets relativity in terms of events passing in a four-dimensional Minkowski world. The order in which they pass, however, is relative to a consentient set. The consentient set is determined by its relation to a percipient event or organism. The percipient event establishes a lasting character of here and there, of now and then, and is itself an enduring pattern. The pattern repeats itself in the passage of events. These recurrent patterns are grasped together or prehended into a unity, which must have as great a temporal spread as the organism requires to be what it is, whether this period is found in the revolutions of the electrons in an iron atom or in the specious present of a human being. Such a percipient event or organism establishes a consentient set of patterns of events that endure in the relations of here and there, of now and then, through such periods or essential epochs, constituting thus slabs of nature, and differentiating space from time. This perspective of the organism is then there in nature. What in the perspective does not preserve the enduring character of here and there, is in motion. From the standpoint of some other organism these moving objects may be at rest, and what is here at rest will be, in the time system of this other perspective, in motion. In Professor Whitehead's phrase, insofar as nature is patient of an organism, it is stratified into perspectives, whose intersections constitute the creative advance of nature. Professor Whitehead has with entire success stated the physical theory of relativity in terms of intersecting time systems.

What I wish to pick out of Professor Whitehead's philosophy of nature is this conception of nature as an organization of perspectives, which are there in nature. The conception of the perspective as there in nature is, in a sense, an unexpected donation by the most abstruse physical science to philosophy. They are not distorted perspectives of some perfect patterns, nor do they lie in consciousnesses as selections among things whose reality is to be found in a noumenal world. They are in their interrelationship the nature that science knows. Biology has dealt with them in terms of forms and their environments, and in ecology deals with the organization of environments, but it has conceded a world of physical particles in absolute space and time that is there independent of any environment of an organism, of any perspective. Professor Whitehead generalizes the conception of organism to include any unitary structure whose nature demands a period within which to be itself, which is therefore not only a spatial but also a temporal structure, or a process. Any such structure stratifies nature by its intersection into its perspective and differentiates its own permanent space and time from the general passage of events. Thus the world of the physical sciences is swept into the domain of organic environments, and there is no world of independent physical entities out of which the perspectives are merely selections. In the place of such a world appear all of the perspectives in their interrelationship to each other.

I do not wish to consider Professor Whitehead's Bergsonian edition of Spinoza's underlying substance that individualizes itself in the structure of the events nor his Platonic heaven of eternal objects where lie the hierarchies of patterns that are there envisaged as possibilities and have ingression into events, but rather his Leibnizian filiation, as it appears in his conception of the perspective as the mirroring in the event of all other events.

Leibniz made a psychological process central in his philosophy of nature. The contents of his monads were psychical states, perceptions, and *petites perceptions,* which were inevitably representative of the rest of the reality of the universe of which they were but partially developed expressions. The represented content of all monads was identical, insofar as it was clear and distinct, so that the organization of these perspectives was a harmony preestablished in an identity of rational content. Professor Whitehead's principle of organization of perspectives is not the representation of an identical content, but the intersection by different time systems of the same body of events. It is, of course, the abandonment of simple location as the principle of physical existence, that is, the existence of a physical object is found in its occupancy of a certain volume of absolute space in an instant of absolute time; and the taking of time seriously, that is, the recognition that there are an indefinite number of possible simultaneities of any event with other events, and consequently an indefinite number of possible temporal orders of the same events that make it possible to conceive of the same body of events as organized into an indefinite number of different perspectives.

Without undertaking to discuss Professor Whitehead's doctrine of the prehension into the unity of the event of the aspects of other events, which I am unable to work out satisfactorily, from the summary statements I have found in his writings, I wish to consider the conception of a body of events as the organization of different perspectives of these events from the standpoint of the field of social science, and that of behavioristic psychology.

In the first place, this seems to be exactly the subject matter of any social science. The human experience with which social science occupies itself is primarily that of individuals. It is only so far as the happenings, the environmental conditions, the values, their uniformities and laws enter into the experience of individuals as individuals that they become the subject of consideration by these sciences. Environmental conditions, for example, exist only insofar as they affect actual individuals, and only as they affect these individuals. The laws of these happenings are but the statistical uniformities of the happenings to and in the experiences of A, B, C, and D. Furthermore the import of these happenings and these values must be found in the experiences of these individuals if they are to exist for these sciences at all.

In the second place, it is only insofar as the individual acts not only in his own perspective but also in the perspective of others, especially in the common perspective of a group, that a society arises and its affairs become the object of scientific inquiry. The limitation of social organization is found in the inability of individuals to place themselves in the perspectives of others, to take their points of view. I do not wish to belabor the point, which is commonplace enough, but to suggest that we find here an actual organization of perspectives, and that the principle of it is fairly evident. This principle is that the individual enters into the perspectives of others, insofar as he is able to take their attitudes, or occupy their points of view.

But while the principle is a commonplace for social conduct, its implications are very serious if one accepts the objectivity of perspectives and recognizes that these perspectives are made up of other selves with minds; that here is no nature that can be closed to mind. The social perspective exists in the experience of the individual insofar as it is intelligible, and it is its intelligibility that is the condition of the individual entering into the perspectives of others, especially of the group. In the field of any social science the objective data are those experiences of the individuals in which they take the attitude of the community, that is, in which they enter into the perspectives of the other members of the community. Of course, the social scientist can generalize from the standpoint of his universe of discourse what remains hopelessly subjective in the experiences of another community, as the psychologist can interpret what for the individual is an unintelligible feeling. I am speaking not from the standpoint of the epistemologist, nor that of the metaphysician. I am asking simply what is objective for the social scientist, what is the subject matter of his science, and I wish to point out that the critical scientist is only replacing the narrower social perspectives of other communities by that of a more highly organized and hence more universal community.

It is instructive to note that never has the character of that common perspective changed more rapidly than since we have gained further control over the technique by which the individual perspective becomes the perspective of the most universal community, that of thinking men, that is, the technique of the experimental method. We are deluded, by the ease with which we can, by what may be fairly called transformation formulae, translate the experience of other communities into that of our own, into giving finality to the perspective of our own thought; but a glance at the bewildering rapidity with which different histories, that is, different pasts have succeeded each other, and new physical universes have arisen, is sufficient to assure us that no generation has been so uncertain as to what will be the common perspective of the next. We have never been so uncertain as to what are the values which economics undertakes to define, what are the political rights and obligations of citizens, what are the community values of friendship, of passion, of parenthood, of amusement, of beauty, of social solidarity in its unnumbered forms or of those values which have been gathered under the relations of man to the highest community or to God. On the other hand, there has never been a time at which men could determine so readily the conditions under which values, whatever they are, can be secured. In terms of common conditions, by transformation formulae, we can pass from one value field to another, and thus come nearer finding out which is more valuable, or rather how to conserve each. The common perspective is comprehensibility, and comprehensibility is the statement in terms of common social conditions.

It is the relation of the individual perspective to the common perspective that is of importance. To the biologist, there is a common environment of an anthill or of a beehive, which is rendered possible by the intricate social relationships of the ants and the bees. It is entirely improbable that this perspective exists in the perspectives of individual ants or bees, for there is no evidence of communication. Communication is a social process whose natural history shows that it arises out of co-operative activities, such as those involved in sex, parenthood, fighting, herding, and the like, in which some phase of the act of one form, which can be called a gesture, acts as a stimulus to others to carry on their parts of the social act. It does not become communication in the full sense, that is, the stimulus does not become a significant symbol, until the gesture tends to arouse the same response in the individual who makes it that it arouses in the others. The history of the growth of language shows that in its earlier stages, the vocal gesture addressed to another awakens in the individual who makes the gesture not simply the tendency to the response which it calls forth in the other, such as the seizing of a weapon or the avoiding of a danger, but primarily the social role which the other plays in the co-operative act. This is indicated in the early play period in the development of the child, and in the richness in social implication of language structures in the speech of primitive peoples.

In the process of communication, the individual is an other before he is a self. It is in addressing himself in the role of an other that his self arises in experience. The growth of the organized game out of simple play in the experience of the child and of organized group activities in human society, placed the individual then in a variety of roles insofar as these were parts of the social act, and the very organization of these in the whole act gave them a common character in indicating what he had to do. The individual is able then to become a generalized other in addressing himself in the attitude of the group or the community. In this situation, he has become a definite self over against the social whole to which he belongs. This is the common perspective. It exists in the organisms of all the members of the community, because the physiological differentiation of human forms belongs largely to the consummatory phase of the act.

The overt phase within which social organization takes place is occupied with things, physical things or implements. In the societies of the invertebrates, which have indeed a complexity comparable with human societies, the organization is largely dependent upon physiological differentiation. In such a society, evidently, there is no phase of the act of the individual in which he can find himself taking the attitude of the other. Physiological differentiation, apart from the direct relations of sex and parenthood, plays no part in the organization of human society. The mechanism of human society is that of bodily selves who assist or hinder each other in their co-operative acts by the manipulation of physical things. In the earliest forms of society these physical things are treated as selves, that is, those social responses, which we can all detect in ourselves to inanimate things which aid or hinder us, are dominant among primitive peoples in the social organization that depends on the use of physical means. The primitive man keeps *en rapport* with implements and weapons by conversation in the form of magic rites and ceremonies. On the other hand, the bodily selves of members of the social group are as clearly implemental as the implements are social. Social beings are things as definitely as physical things are social.

The key to the genetic development of human intelligence is found in the recognition of these two aspects. It arises in those early stages of communication in which the organism arouses in itself the attitude of the other and so addresses itself and thus becomes an object to itself, becomes in other words a self, while the same sort of content in the act constitutes the other that constitutes the self. Out of this process thought arises, that is, conversation with one's self, in the role of the specific other and then in the role of the generalized other, in the fashion I indicated above. It is important to recognize that the self does not project itself into the other. The others and the self arise in the social act together. The content of the act may be said to lie within the organism, but it is projected into the other only in the sense in which it is projected into the self, a fact upon which the whole of psychoanalysis rests. We pinch ourselves to be sure that we are awake as we grasp an object to be sure that it is there. The other phase of human intelligence is that it is occupied with physical things. Physical things are perceptual things. They also arise within the act. This is initiated by a distant stimulus and leads through approximation or withdrawal to contact or the avoidance of contact. The outcome of the act is in consummation, for example, as in eating, but in the behavior of the human animal a mediate stage of manipulation intervenes. The hand fashions the physical or perceptual thing. The perceptual thing is fully there in the manipulatory area, where it is both seen and felt, where is found both the promise of the contact and its fulfilment, for it is characteristic of the distant stimulation and the act that it initiates that there are already aroused the attitudes of manipulation—what I will call terminal attitudes of the perceptual act, that readiness to grasp, to come into effective contact, which in some sense control the approach to the distant stimulation. It is in the operation with these perceptual or physical things which lie within the physiological act short of consummation that the peculiar human intelligence is found. Man is an implemental animal. It is mediate to consummation. The hand carries the food to the mouth, or the child to the breast, but in the social act this mediation becomes indefinitely complicated, and the task arises of stating the consummation, or the end, in terms of means. There are two conditions for this: one is the inhibition, which takes place when conflicting ways of completing the act check the expression of any one way, and the other is the operation of the social mechanism, which I have described, by which the individual can indicate to others and to himself the perceptual things that can be seized and manipulated and combined. It is within this field of implemental things picked out by the significant symbols of gesture, not in that of physiological differentiation, that the complexities of human society have developed. And, to recur to my former statement, in this field selves are implemental physical things just as among primitive peoples physical things are selves.

My suggestion was that we find in society and social experience, interpreted in terms of a behavioristic psychology, an instance of that organization of perspectives, which is for me at least the most obscure phase of Professor Whitehead's philosophy. In his objective statement of relativity the existence of motion in the passage of events depends not upon what is taking place in an absolute space and time, but upon the relation of a consentient set to a percipient event. Such a relation stratifies nature. These stratifications are not only there in nature but they are the only forms of nature that are there. This dependence of nature upon the percipient event is not a reflection of nature into consciousness. Permanent spaces and times, which are successions of these strata, rest and motion, are there, but they are there only in their relationship to percipient events or organisms. We can then go further and say that the sensuous qualities of nature are there in nature, but there in their relationship to animal organisms. We can advance to the other values which have been regarded as dependent upon appetence, appreciation, and affection, and thus restore to nature all that a dualistic doctrine has relegated to consciousness, since the spatio-temporal structure of the world and the motion with which exact physical science is occupied is found to exist in nature only in its relationship to percipient events or organisms.

But rest and motion no more imply each other than do objectivity and subjectivity. There are perspectives which cease to be objective, such as the Ptolemaic order, since it does not select those consentient sets with the proper dynamical axes, and there are those behind the mirror and those of an alcoholic brain. What has happened in all of these instances, from the most universal to the most particular, is that the rejected perspective fails to agree with that common perspective which the individual finds himself occupying as a member of the community of minds, which is constitutive of his self. This is not a case of the surrender to a vote of the majority, but the development of another self through its intercourse with others and hence with himself.

What I am suggesting is that this process, in which a perspective ceases to be objective, becomes if you like, subjective, and in which new common minds and new common perspectives arise, and is an instance of the organization of perspectives in nature, of the creative advance of nature. This amounts to the affirmation that mind as it appears in the mechanism of social conduct is the organization of perspectives in nature and at least a phase of the creative advance of nature. Nature in its relationship to the organism, and including the organism, is a perspective that is there. A state of mind of the organism is the establishment of simultaneity between the organism and a group of events through the arrest of action under inhibition as above described. This arrest of action means the tendencies within the organism to act in conflicting ways in the completion of the whole act. The attitude of the organism calls out or tends to call out responses in other organisms, which responses, in the case of human gesture, the organism calls out in itself, and thus excites itself to respond to these responses. It is the identification of these responses with the distant stimuli that establishes simultaneity, that gives insides to these distant stimuli, and a self to the organism. Without such an establishment of simultaneity, these stimuli are spatio-temporally distant from the organism and their reality lies in the future of passage. The establishment of simultaneity wrenches this future reality into a possible present, for all our presents beyond the manipulatory area are only possibilities, as respects their perceptual reality. We are acting toward the future realization of the act, as though it were present, because the organism is taking the role of the other. In the perceptual inanimate object, the organic content that survives is the resistance that the organism both feels and exerts in the manipulatory area. The actual spatio-temporal structure of passing events with those characters which answer to the susceptibilities of the organism are there in nature, but they are temporally as well as spatially away from the organism. The reality awaits upon the success of the act. Present reality is a possibility. It is what would be if we were there instead of here. Through the social mechanism of significant symbols, the organism places itself there as a possibility, which acquires increasing probability as it fits into the spatio-temporal structure and the demands of the whole complex act of which its conduct is a part. But the possibility is there in nature, for it is made up of actual structures of events and their contents and the possible realizations of the acts in the form of adjustments and readjustments of the processes involved. When we view them as possibilities, we call them mental or working hypotheses.

I submit that the only instance we have of prehension in experience is this holding together of future and past as possibilities —for all pasts are as essentially subject to revision as the futures, and are, therefore, only possibilities—and the common content which endures is that which is common to the organism and environment in the perspective. This in the organism is identified with the spatio-temporally distant stimuli as a possibly real present, past, and future. The unity lies in the act or process, the prehension is the exercise of this unity, when the process has been checked through conflicting tendencies, and the conditions and results of these tendencies are held as possibilities in a specious present.

Thus the social and psychological process is but an instance of what takes place in nature, if nature is an evolution, that is, if it proceeds by reconstruction in the presence of conflicts, and if, therefore, possibilities of different reconstructions are present, reconstructing its pasts as well as its futures. It is the relativity of time, that is, an indefinite number of possible orders of events, that introduces possibility in nature. When there was but one recognized order of nature, possibility had no other place than in the mental constructions of the future or the incompletely known past. But the reality of a spatio-temporally distant situation lies ahead and any present existence of it beyond the manipulatory area can be only a possibility. Certain characters are there, but what *things* they are can only be realized when the acts these distant stimulations arouse are completed. What they are now is represented by a set of possible spatio-temporal structures. That these future realizations appear as present possibilities is due to the arrest of the act of the organism and its ability to indicate these possibilities.

That these possibilities have varying degrees of probability is due to the relation of the various inhibited tendencies in the organism to the whole act. The organization of this whole act, the human social organism can indicate to others and to itself. It has the pattern which determines other selves and physical things, and the organism as a self and a thing, and the meanings which are indicated have the universality of the whole community to which the organism belongs. They constitute a universe of discourse. It is the fitting in of the particular tendencies into this larger pattern of the whole process that constitutes the probability of the present existence of the things which any one act implies. Its full reality is still dependent upon the accomplishment of the act, upon experimental evidence. It is then such a coincidence of the perspective of the individual organism with the pattern of the whole act in which it is so involved that the organism can act within it that constitutes the objectivity of the perspective.

The pattern of the whole social act can lie in the individual organism because it is carried out through implemental things to which any organism can react and because indications of these reactions to others and the organism itself can be made by significant symbols. The reconstruction of the pattern can take place in the organism, and does take place in the so-called conscious process of mind. The psychological process is an instance of the creative advance of nature.

In living forms lower than man, the distant perspective may through sensitivity exist in the experience of the form and the grasping of this in the adjustments of conduct answer to the formation of the stratification of nature, but the reconstruction of the pattern within which the life of the organism lies does not fall within the experience of the organism. In inanimate organisms, the maintenance of a temporal structure, that is, of a process, still stratifies nature, and gives rise to spaces and times, but neither they, nor the entities that occupy them, enter as experiential facts into the processes of the organisms. The distinction of objectivity and subjectivity can only arise where the pattern of the larger process, within which lies the process of the individual organism, falls in some degree within the experience of the individual organism, that is, it belongs only to the experience of the social organism.

BIBLIOGRAPHY
The Writings of George H. Mead

Chronologically Arranged

Review of K. Lasswitz, *Die moderne Energetik in ihrer Bedeutung für Erkenntniskritik,* in *Psychological Review,* I (1894), 210–13.

Abstract. "Herr Lasswitz on Energy and Epistemology," *ibid.,* pp. 172–75.

Review of C. L. Morgan, *An Introduction to Comparative Psychology,* in *Psychological Review,* II (1895), 399–402.

Abstract. "A Theory of Emotions from the Physiological Standpoint," *ibid.,* pp. 162–64.

Abstract. "Some Aspects of Greek Philosophy," *University of Chicago Record,* I (1896–97), 42.

"The Relation of Play to Education," *ibid.,* pp. 140–45.

Review of Le Bon, *Psychology of Socialism,* in *American Journal of Sociology,* V (1899), 404–12.

"The Working Hypothesis in Social Reform," *ibid.,* pp. 367–71.

"Suggestions toward a Theory of the Philosophical Disciplines," *Philosophical Review,* IX (1900), 1–17.

"The Definition of the Psychical," *Decennial Publications, University of Chicago,* III (1903), 77–112.

"The Basis for a Parents' Association," *Elementary School Teacher,* IV (1903–4), 337–46.

"Image or Sensation," *Journal of Philosophy,* I (1904), 604–7.

"The Relations of Psychology and Philology," *Psychological Bulletin,* I (1904), 375–91.

Reviews of D. Draghicesco, *Du rôle de l'individu dans le déterminisme social,* and *Le problème du déterminisme, déterminisme biologique et déterminisme social,* in *Psychological Bulletin,* II (1905), 399–405.

"The Teaching of Science in College," *Science,* XXIV (1906), 390–97.

"The Imagination in Wundt's Treatment of Myth and Religion," *Psychological Bulletin,* III (1906), 393–99.

"Science in the High School," *School Review,* XIV (1906), 237–49.

"Editorial Notes," *ibid.,* XV (1907), 160, 164.

Review of Jane Addams, *The Newer Ideal of Peace,* in *American Journal of Sociology,* XIII (1907), 121–28.

"Concerning Animal Perception," *Psychological Review,* XIV (1907), 383–90.

Abstract. "The Relation of Imitation to the Theory of Animal Perception," *Psychological Bulletin,* IV (1907), 210–11.

"On the Educational Situation in the Chicago Public Schools," *City Club Bulletin,* I (1907–8), 131–38.

"Industrial Education and Trade Schools," *Elementary School Teacher,* VIII (1907–8), 402–6.

"Policy of the *Elementary School Teacher," ibid.,* pp. 281–84.

"The Philosophical Basis of Ethics," *International Journal of Ethics,* XVIII (1908), 311–23.

"The Social Settlement: Its Basis and Function," *University of Chicago Record,* XII (1908), 108–10.

"Educational Aspects of Trade Schools," *Union Labor Advocate,* VIII, No. 7 (1908), 19–20.

"Industrial Education and the Working Man and the School," *Elementary School Teacher,* IX (1908–9), 369–83.

"On the Problem of History in the Elementary School," *ibid.,* p. 433.

"Moral Training in the Schools," *ibid.,* pp. 327–28.

"Social Psychology as Counterpart to Physiological Psychology," *Psychological Bulletin,* VI (1909), 401–8.

"What Social Objects Must Psychology Presuppose?" *Journal of Philosophy,* VII (1910), 174–80.

"Social Consciousness and the Consciousness of Meaning," *Psychological Bulletin,* VII (1910), 397–405.

"Psychology of Social Consciousness Implied in Instruction," *Science,* XXXI (1910), 688–93.

Review of B. M. Anderson, Jr., *Social Value, a Study in Economic Theory,* in *Psychological Bulletin,* VIII (1911), 432–36.

Review of Warner Fite, *Individualism: Four Lectures on the Significance of Consciousness for Social Relations,* in *Psychological Bulletin,* VIII (1911), 323–28.

"Remarks on Labor Night," *City Club Bulletin,* V (1912), 214–15.

"Exhibit of City Club Committee on Public Education," *ibid.*, p. 9.

"The Mechanism of Social Consciousness," *Journal of Philosophy*, IX (1912), 401–6.

A Report on Vocational Training in Chicago and in Other Cities, by a committee of the City Club, George H. Mead, Chairman. (Chicago: City Club of Chicago, 1912), pp. 315. Reviewed by Judd, *Elementary School Teacher*, XIII (1912–13), 248–49.

"The Social Self," *Journal of Philosophy*, X (1913), 374–80.

"A Heckling School Board and an Educational Stateswoman," *Survey*, XXXI (1913–14), 443–44.

"The Psychological Bases of Internationalism," *ibid.*, XXXIII (1914–15), 604–7.

"Natural Rights and the Theory of the Political Institution," *Journal of Philosophy*, XII (1915), 141–55.

"Madison—The Passage of the University through the State Political Agitation of 1914; the Survey by Wm. H. Allen and His Staff and the Legislative Fight of 1915, with Indications these offer of the Place the State University Holds in the Community," *Survey*, XXXV (1915–16), 349–51, 354–61.

"Smashing the Looking Glass, Rejoinder," *ibid.*, pp. 607, 610.

"Professor Hoxie and the Community," *University of Chicago Magazine*, IX (1916–17), 114–17.

The Conscientious Objector, Pamphlet No. 33, "Patriotism through Education Series," issued by National Security League, New York City, 1917.

"Josiah Royce—a Personal Impression," *International Journal of Ethics*, XXVII (1917), 168–70.

"Scientific Method and Individual Thinker," *Creative Intelligence* (New York: Henry Holt & Co., 1917), pp. 176–227.

Review of Edith Abbott and Sophonisba P. Breckinridge, *Truancy and Non-Attendance in the Chicago Public Schools*, in *Survey*, XXXVIII (1917), 369–70.

"The Psychology of Punitive Justice," *American Journal of Sociology*, XXIII (1917–18), 577–602.

"Retiring President's Address," *City Club Bulletin*, XIII (1920), 94.

"A Behavioristic Account of the Significant Symbol," *Journal of Philosophy*, XIX (1922), 157–63.

"Scientific Method and the Moral Sciences," *International Journal of Ethics*, XXXIII (1923), 229–47.

"The Genesis of the Self and Social Control," *ibid.*, XXXV (1924–25), 251–77.

"The Objective Reality of Perspectives," *Proceedings of the Sixth International Congress of Philosophy* (1926), pp. 75–85. Reprinted in *The Philosophy of the Present* (Chicago, 1932); *see* No. 67.

"The Nature of Aesthetic Experience," *International Journal of Ethics*, XXXVI (1926), 382–92.

"A Pragmatic Theory of Truth," *Studies in the Nature of Truth, University of California Publications in Philosophy*, XI (1929), 65–88.

"The Nature of the Past," *Essays in Honor of John Dewey* (New York: Henry Holt & Co., 1929), pp. 235–42.

"National-Mindedness and International-Mindedness," *International Journal of Ethics*, XXXIX (1929), 385–407.

"Bishop Berkeley and His Message," *Journal of Philosophy*, XXVI (1929), 421–30.

"Cooley's Contribution to American Social Thought," *American Journal of Sociology*, XXXV (1929–30), 693–706.

"The Philosophies of Royce, James, and Dewey, in Their American Setting," *International Journal of Ethics*, XL (1930), 211–31. Also in the co-operative volume, *John Dewey: The Man and His Philosophy* (Cambridge, Massachusetts: Harvard University Press, 1930), pp. 75–105.

"Philanthropy from the Point of View of Ethics," *Intelligent Philanthropy*, edited by Faris, Lane, and Dodd (Chicago: University of Chicago Press, 1930), pp. 133–48.

"Dr. A. W. Moore's Philosophy," *University of Chicago Record*, N.S., XVII (1931), 47–49.

The Philosophy of the Present, The Paul Carus Foundation Lectures, III (Chicago: Open Court Publ. Co., 1932), with an Introduction by Arthur E. Murphy and Prefatory Remarks by John Dewey. Pp. xl+195.

"The Philosophy of John Dewey," *International Journal of Ethics*, XLVI (1936).